HISTORY COMICS

THE
AMERICAN BISON
THE BUFFALO'S SURVIVAL TALE

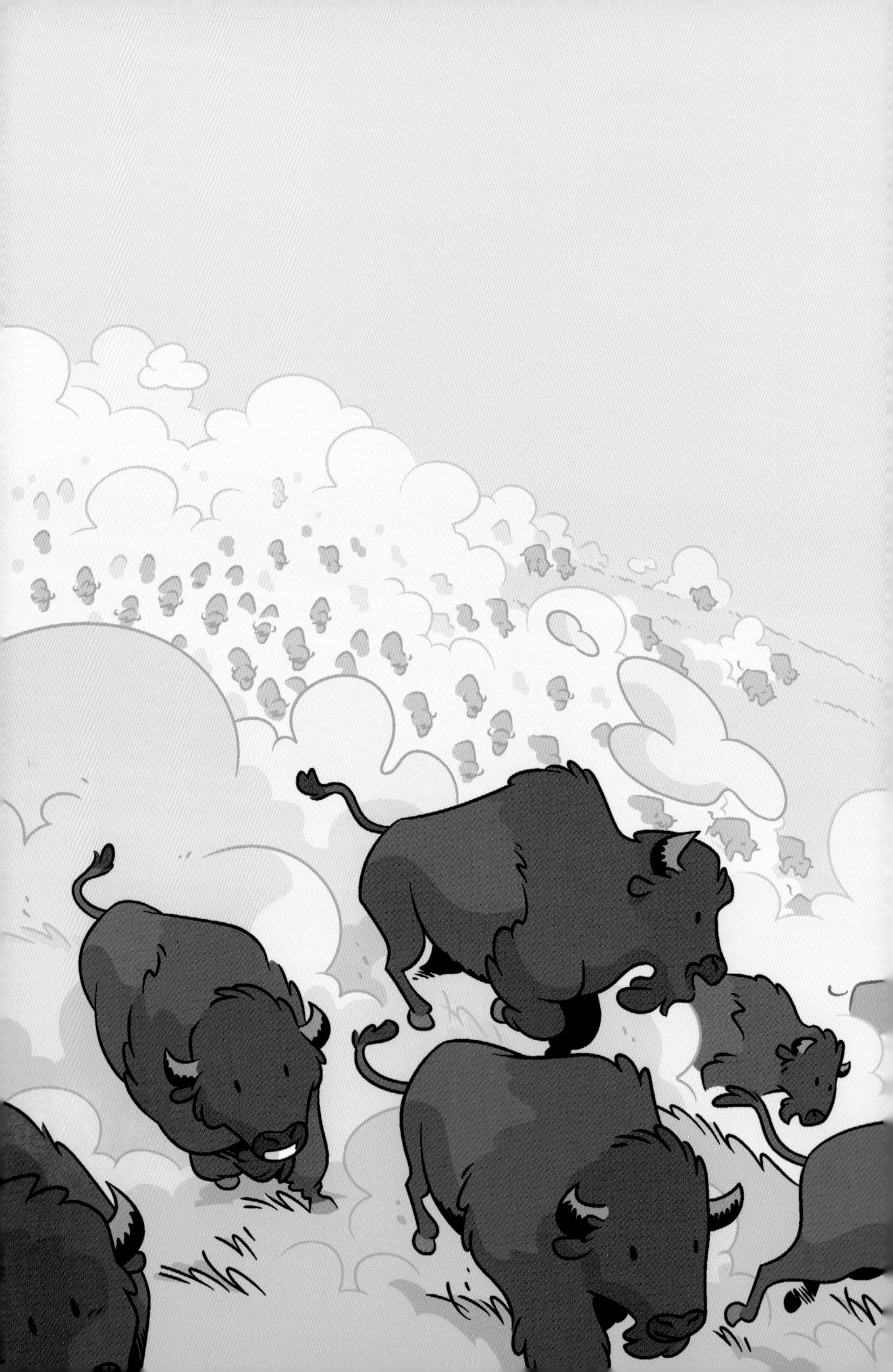

First Second

Published by First Second
First Second is an imprint of Roaring Brook Press, a division of Holtzbrinck Publishing Holdings Limited
Partnership
120 Broadway, New York, NY 10271
firstsecondbooks.com
mackids.com

Library of Congress Control Number: 2020919361

Our books may be purchased in bulk for promotional, educational, or business use. Please contact your local
bookseller or the Macmillan Corporate and Premium Sales Department at (800) 221-7945 ext. 5442 or by
email at MacmillanSpecialMarkets@macmillan.com.

FIRST
EDITION

First edition, 2021
Edited by Dave Roman
Cover and interior book design by Sunny Lee
Map on page 120 by William T. Hornaday
With special thanks to Elise McMullen-Ciotti
Printed in China by Toppan Leefung Printing Ltd., Dongguan City,
Guangdong Province

Drawn in Clip Studio Paint. Colored in Adobe Photoshop CC. Lettered with Soliloquous font from
Comicraft.

ISBN 978-1-250-26582-1 (paperback)
10 9 8 7 6 5 4 3

ISBN 978-1-250-26583-8 (hardcover)
10 9 8 7 6 5 4 3 2 1

Don't miss your next favorite book from First Second! For the latest updates go to firstsecondnewsletter.com
and sign up for our enewsletter.

I grew up along the Rocky Mountain front in Montana, an area known for its natural beauty and wide-open spaces. It was a place where the bison once roamed free and native grasses grew abundantly. It is also a place where Native Americans like my family continue to live.

And while there are definitely fewer of us—less Native Americans, less bison, and less native grasses than in the 19th century—the news is good. We are all still here, the three sides to North America's most interesting ecological triangle.

As a kid, I learned about native plants and their uses from my Blackfeet grandmother. She lived to be 97 years old. She learned about plants from her grandmother, who learned from her grandmother. As an adult, I am now an ethnobotanist, which is a scientist who studies the relationship between people and plants. And I am also an environmental historian, which is someone who is interested in the history of our natural world.

Bison are amazing to me, not only because my ancestors used to hunt and eat them, but because of their ecological relationship with native grasses and interconnection with humans. Bison historically formed one side of a "perfect ecological triangle" scientists say, between bison, grass, and Native Americans. Bison ate prairie grasses, Native Americans ate bison, and grass grew healthy due to strategic fire manipulation and grazing by bison. These interdependent ecological relationships existed for thousands of years before the near demise of bison in the 19th century. But as our story *Bison* will demonstrate, all is not lost.

Scientists are lucky because they get to study some pretty cool stuff. One of those things is bison mucus, also called bison boogers or snot. Bison mucus is central to understanding how the bison-grass-people ecological triangle functions.

Bison need microbes, such as bacteria, fungi, and protozoa, in their digestive tract to break down the cellulose (or hard coating) in grasses to digest the edible parts of grass. Scientists tell us that bison eat grass by swinging their heads back and forth. With their noses near the ground, they inhale the microbes found in the soil. As the bison stop to clean off their noses with their tongues, they stick their tongues up their noses and ingest their own mucus. The microbes from the soil then relocate to the bison digestive tract to help the bison digest their food—the native grasses. Without these microbes, the bison would not be able to digest grass. Bison also helped in the reseeding of grass in new areas on the prairie, both when grass seeds attached to their woolly head fur and was redeposited elsewhere, and when grass seeds were digested and later deposited in the bison's poop, ready for germination.

But why is grass so hard to digest? Grass has a strong outer coating called cellulose, which scientists think probably evolved as a protective device against being easily devoured by animals. Grasses also have another unique feature for survival. They grow from the bottom up, unlike trees, which grow from their tips. This means that when grass is eaten by a bison, cut by a lawnmower, or even burned in a prairie fire, it will continue to survive and grow. But ancient Native Americans knew this, too.

Native Americans knew that bison loved to eat grass. They also knew which species of grasses during spring, summer, or fall bison loved the best. My grandmother used to tell me about the kinds of grasses bison liked to eat.

Over time, Native people learned how to create healthy landscapes for bison to enjoy. One way they did that was through man-made fire, or anthropogenic fire. They burned certain areas, which then grew back with fresh and more nutritious grasses for the bison to eat. In this way, Native Americans could also create places where they could hunt bison. They did not have to "follow" bison but could "bring" the bison right to an area that was easy for hunting.

Today, scientists and Native Americans are working to reestablish this ancient ecological triangle of healthy landscapes with healthy grass, created by fire and grazing; healthy bison eating native grasses; and healthy Native people eating bison and managing the landscape.

Native American grandmothers with traditional ecological knowledge are also working to revitalize and share their knowledge and the important relationship between bison, plants, and people.

It is a win-win-win, which is what restoring healthy ecosystems is all about.

—**Rosalyn LaPier** (Blackfeet/Métis), PhD
Associate Professor, Environmental Studies Program, University of Montana
Research Associate, National Museum of Natural History, Smithsonian Institution

The University of Montana is located in the heart of traditional Seliš-Qlispé (Salish) territory.

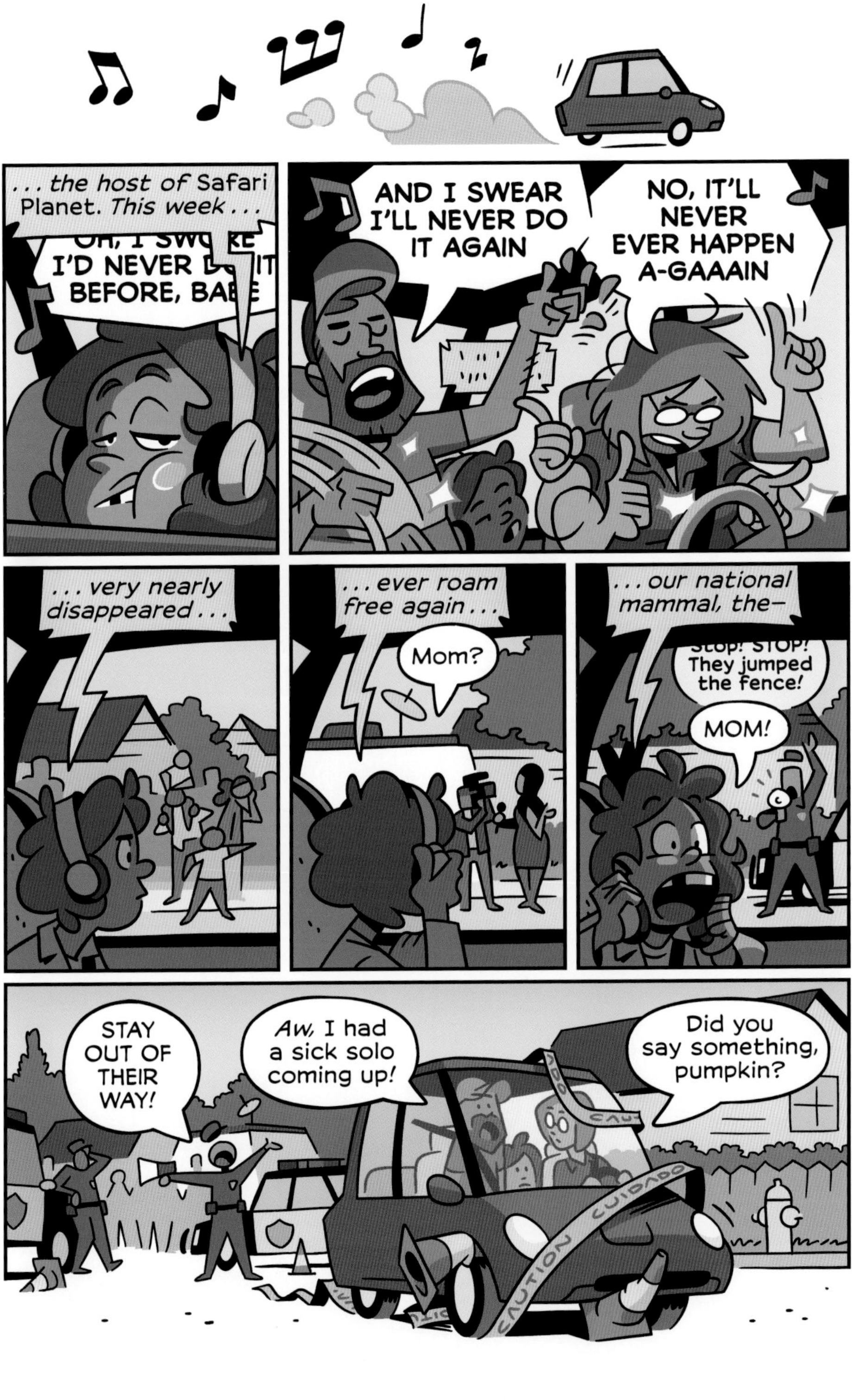

. . . the host of Safari Planet. This week . . .
AND I SWEAR I'LL NEVER DO IT AGAIN
NO, IT'LL NEVER EVER HAPPEN A-GAAAIN
. . . very nearly disappeared . . .
. . . ever roam free again . . .
Mom?
. . . our national mammal, the–
They jumped the fence!
MOM!
STAY OUT OF THEIR WAY!
Aw, I had a sick solo coming up!
Did you say something, pumpkin?

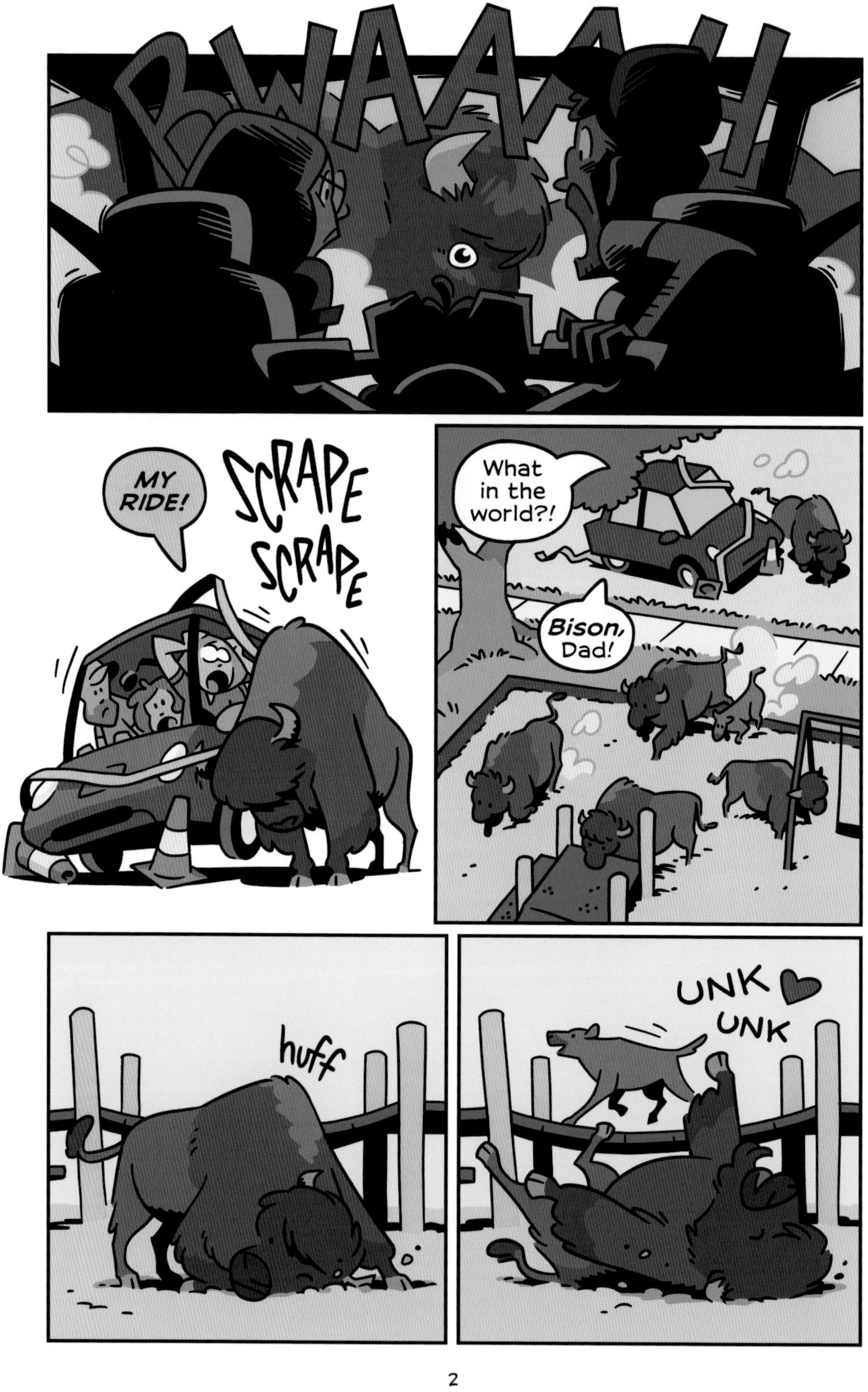
BWAAAAH
MY RIDE!
SCRAPE
SCRAPE
What in the world?!
Bison, Dad!
huff
UNK
UNK

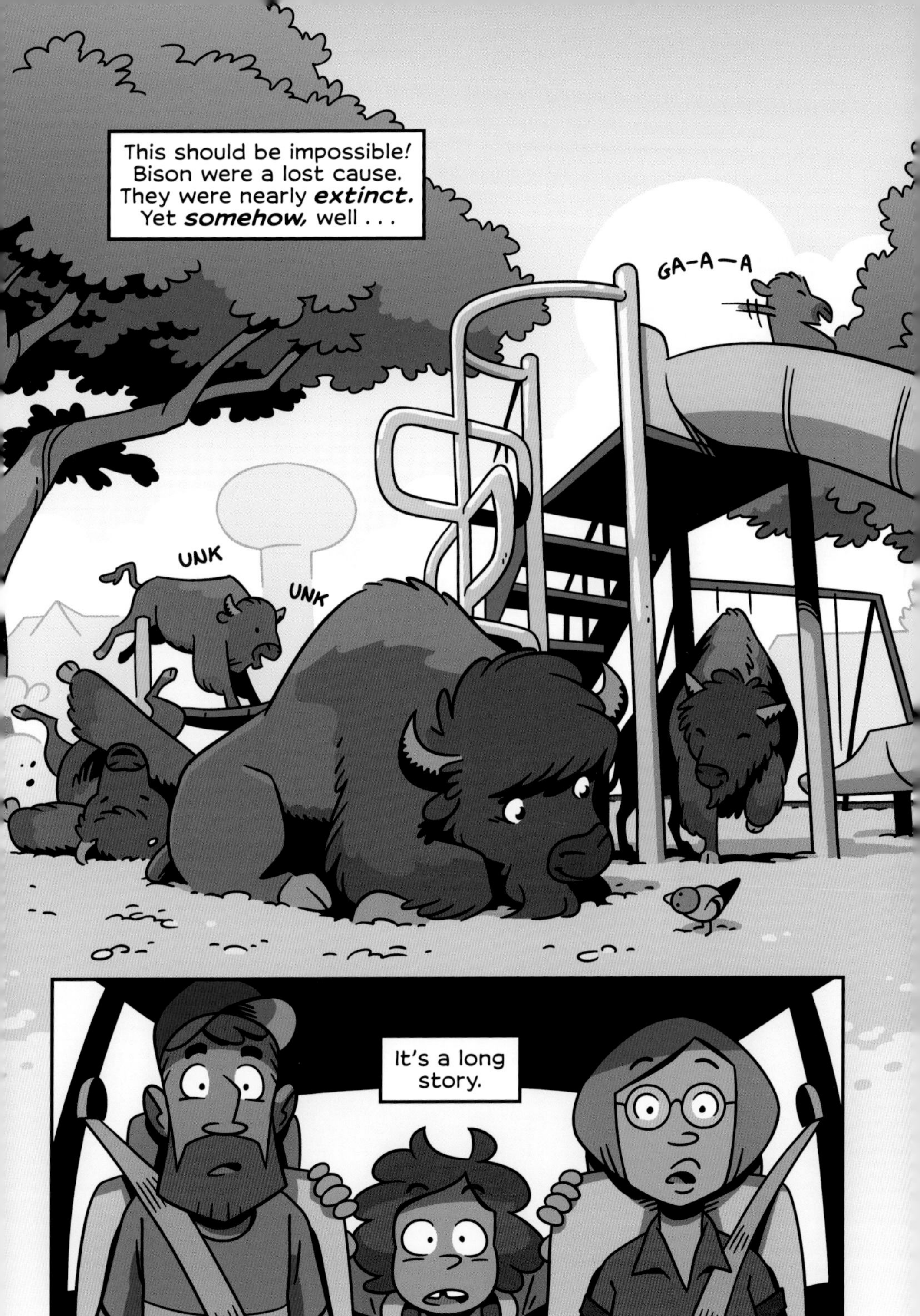
This should be impossible! Bison were a lost cause. They were nearly *extinct.* Yet *somehow,* well . . .
GA-A-A
UNK
UNK
It's a long story.

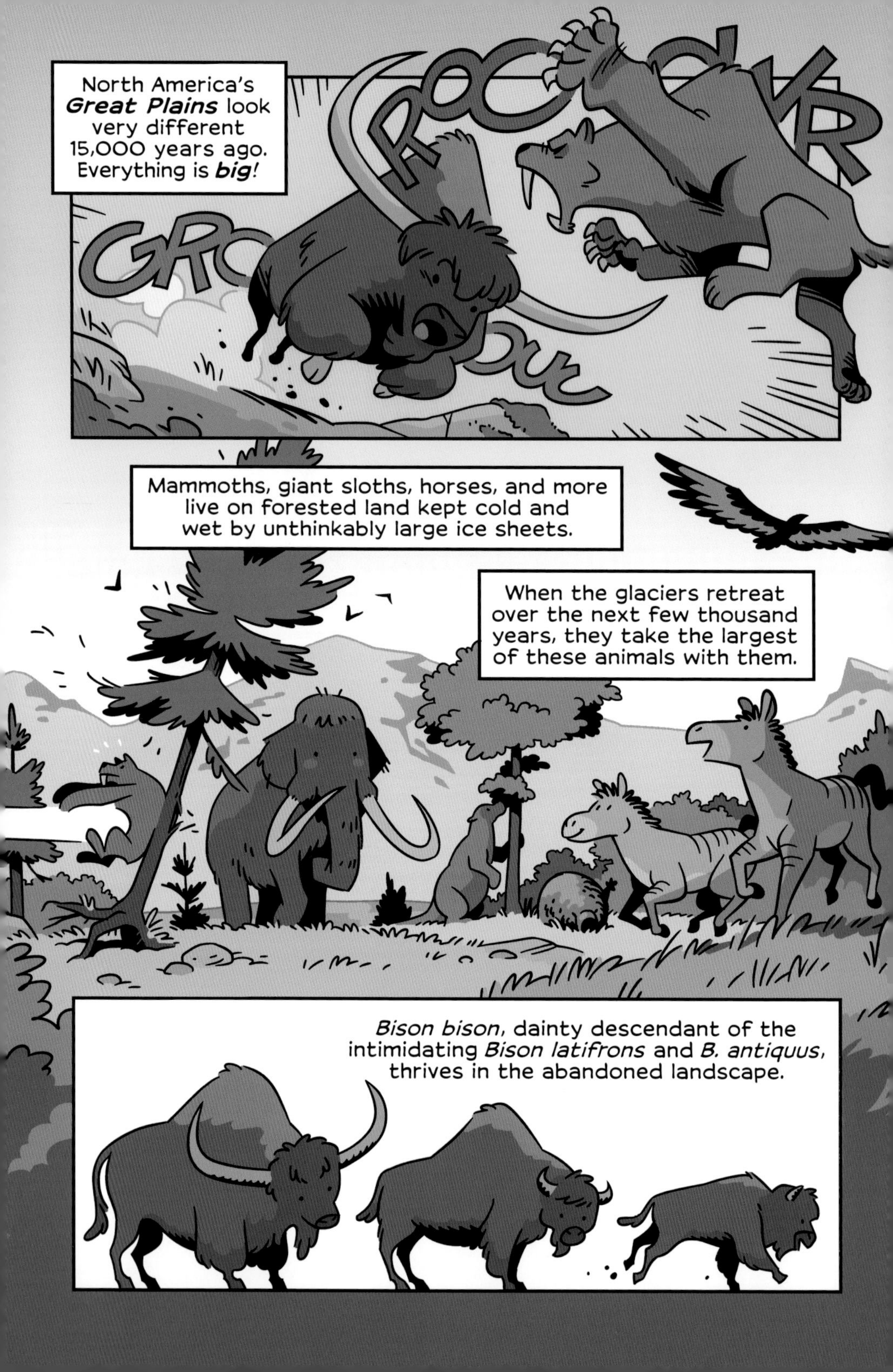
North America's *Great Plains* look very different 15,000 years ago. Everything is *big*!
Mammoths, giant sloths, horses, and more live on forested land kept cold and wet by unthinkably large ice sheets.
When the glaciers retreat over the next few thousand years, they take the largest of these animals with them.
Bison bison, dainty descendant of the intimidating *Bison latifrons* and *B. antiquus*, thrives in the abandoned landscape.

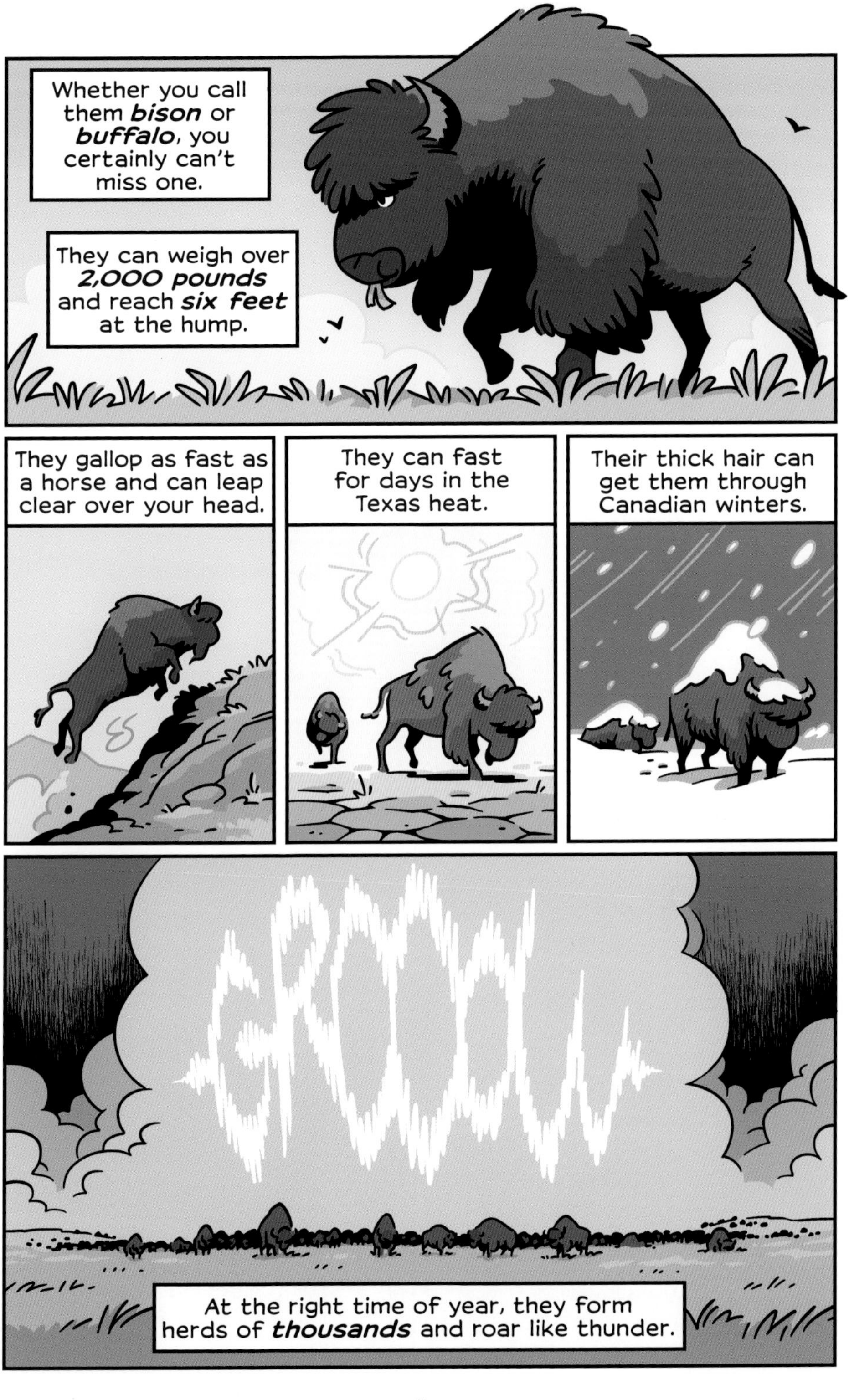
Whether you call them **bison** or **buffalo**, you certainly can't miss one.
They can weigh over **2,000 pounds** and reach **six feet** at the hump.
They gallop as fast as a horse and can leap clear over your head.
They can fast for days in the Texas heat.
Their thick hair can get them through Canadian winters.
At the right time of year, they form herds of **thousands** and roar like thunder.

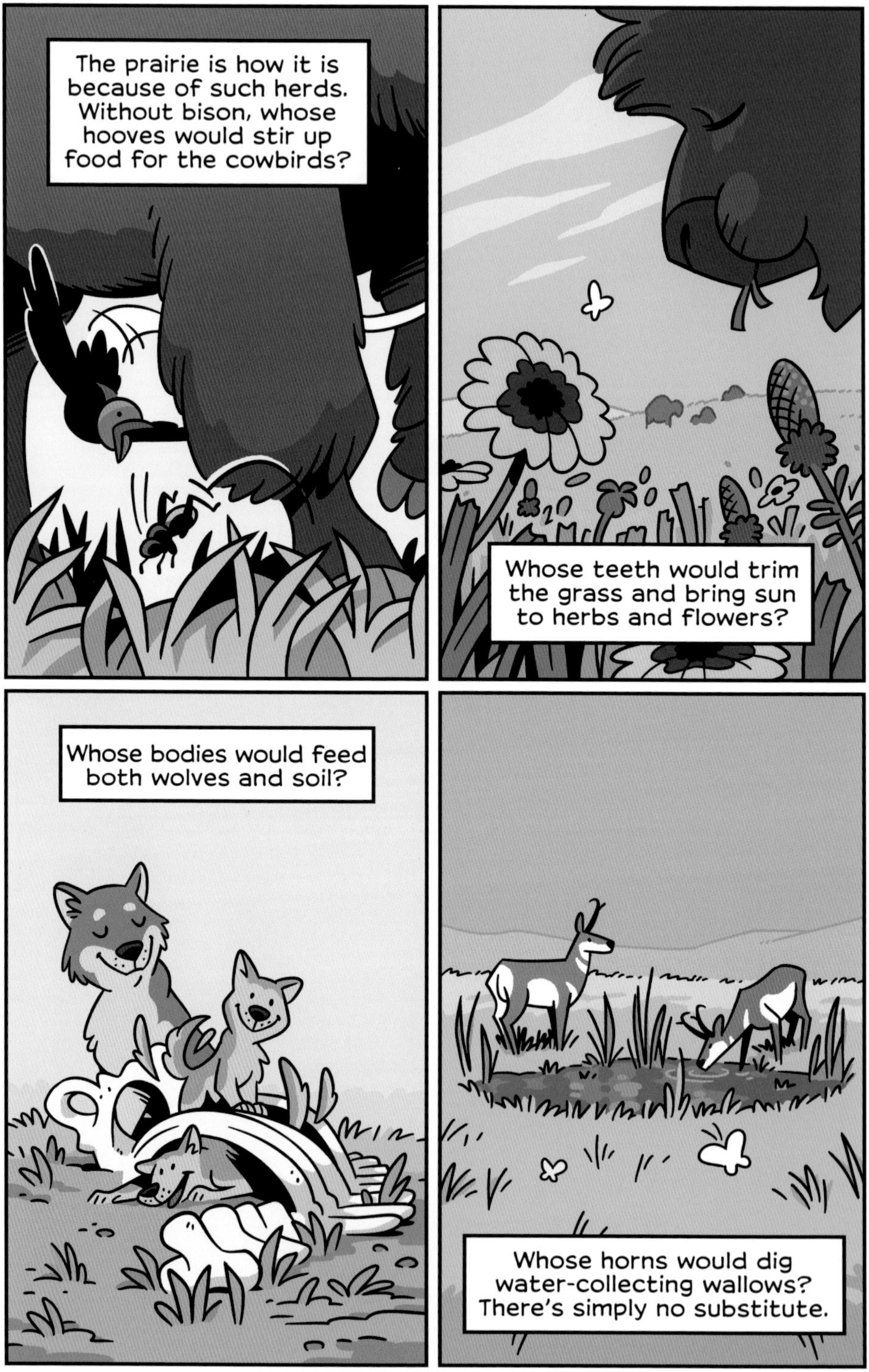
The prairie is how it is because of such herds. Without bison, whose hooves would stir up food for the cowbirds?
Whose teeth would trim the grass and bring sun to herbs and flowers?
Whose bodies would feed both wolves and soil?
Whose horns would dig water-collecting wallows? There's simply no substitute.

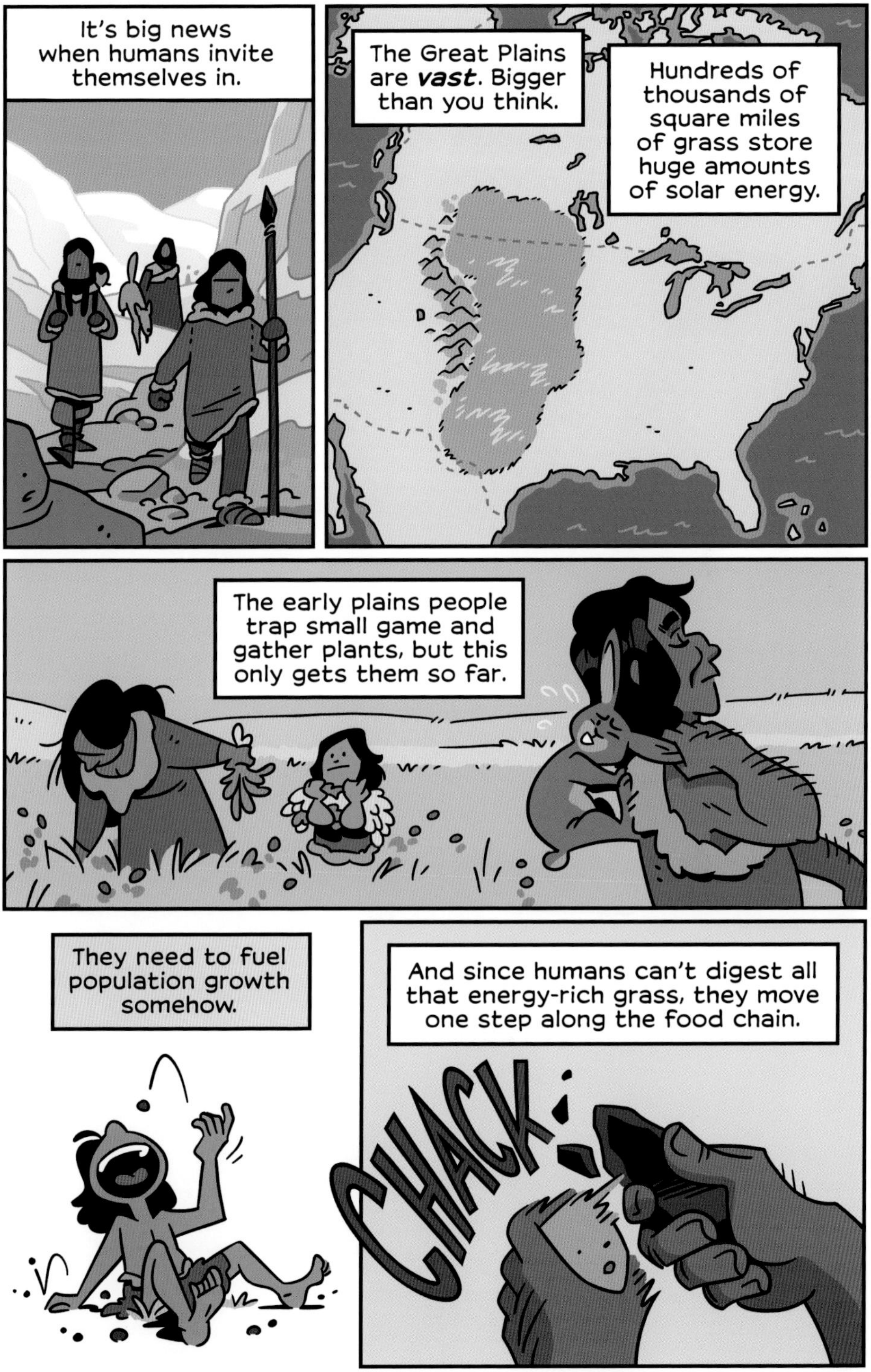
It's big news when humans invite themselves in.
The Great Plains are ***vast***. Bigger than you think.
Hundreds of thousands of square miles of grass store huge amounts of solar energy.
The early plains people trap small game and gather plants, but this only gets them so far.
They need to fuel population growth somehow.
And since humans can't digest all that energy-rich grass, they move one step along the food chain.
CHACK

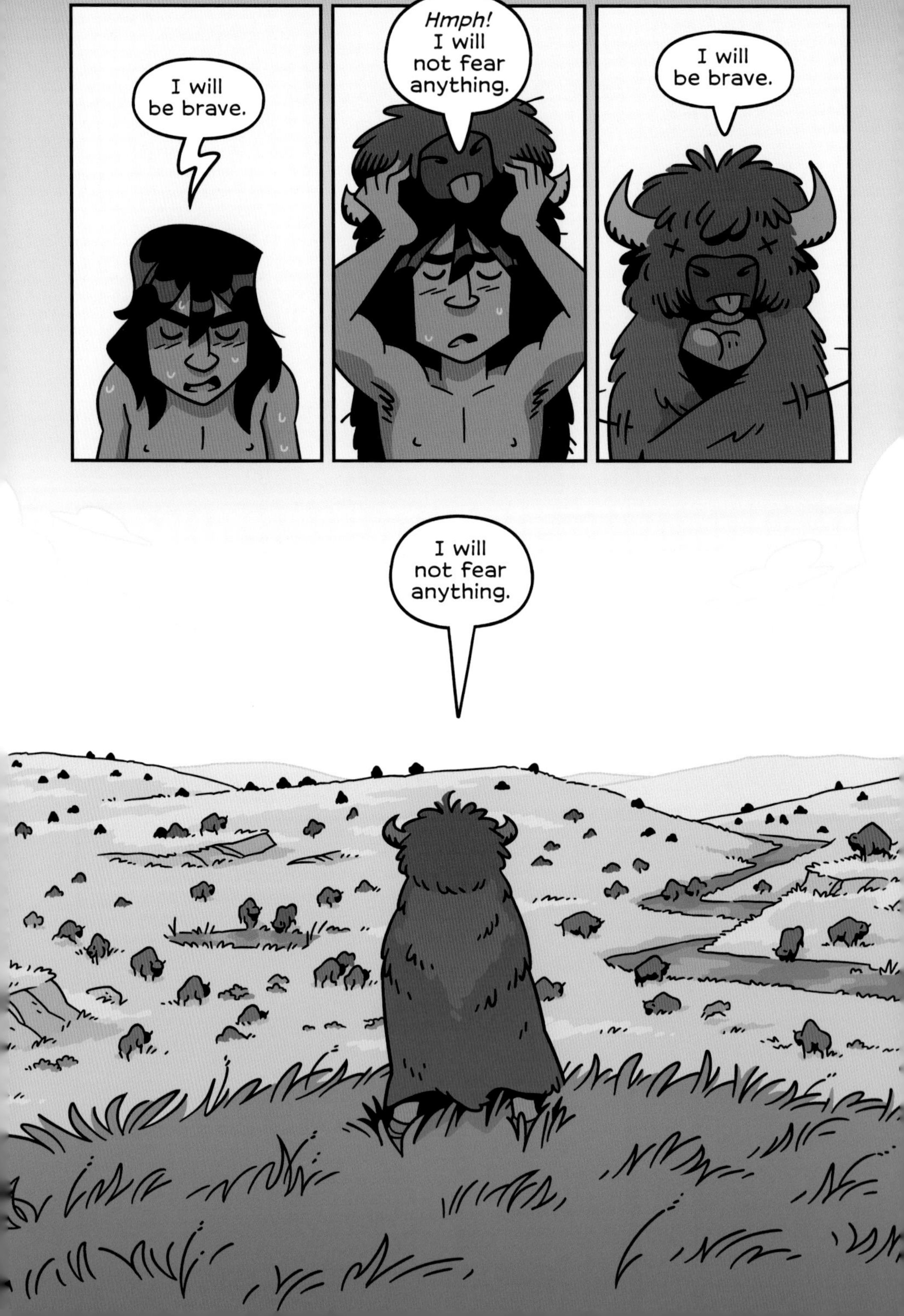
I will be brave.
Hmph! I will not fear anything.
I will be brave.
I will not fear anything.

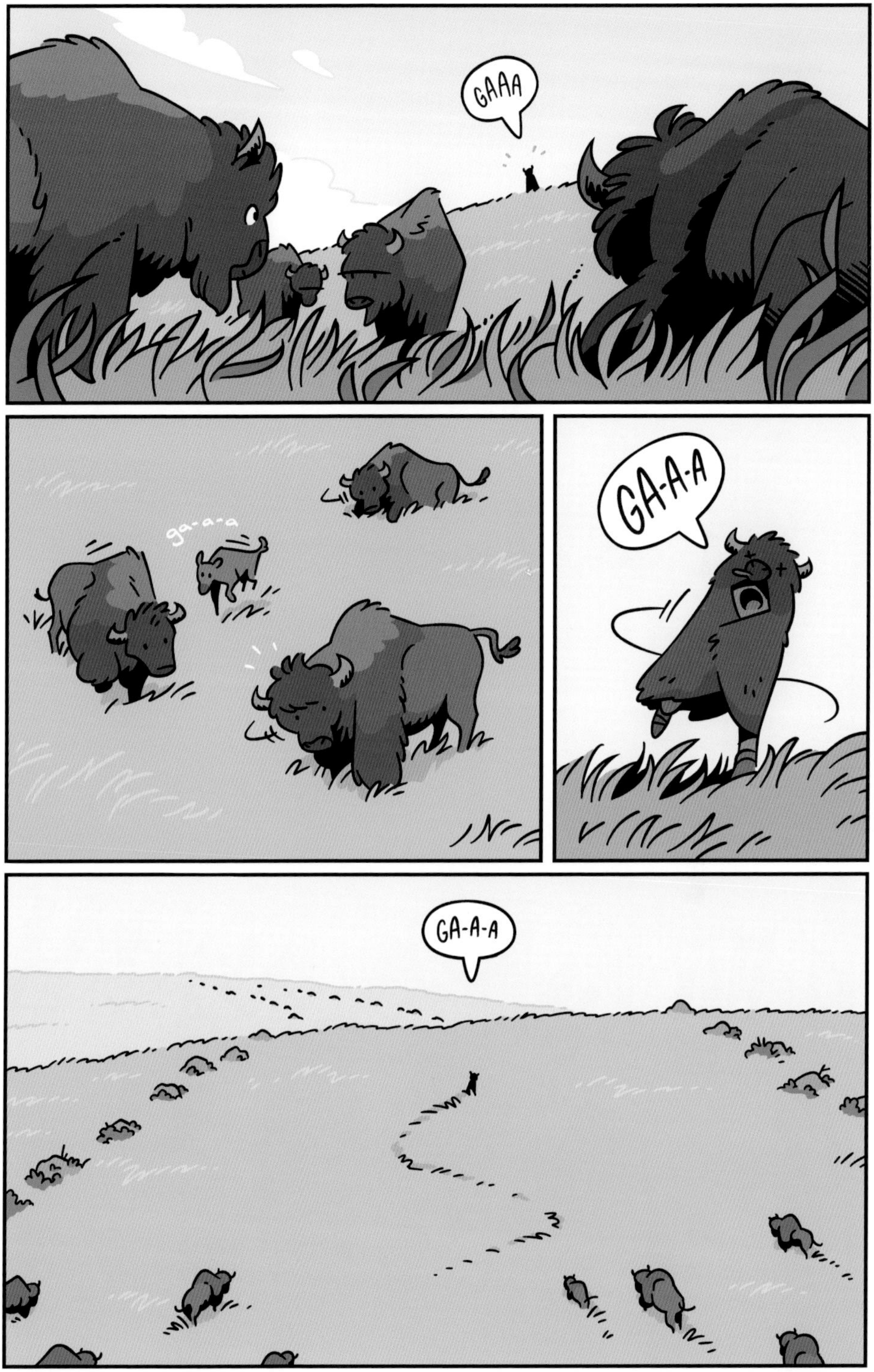
GAAA
ga-a-a
GA-A-A
GA-A-A

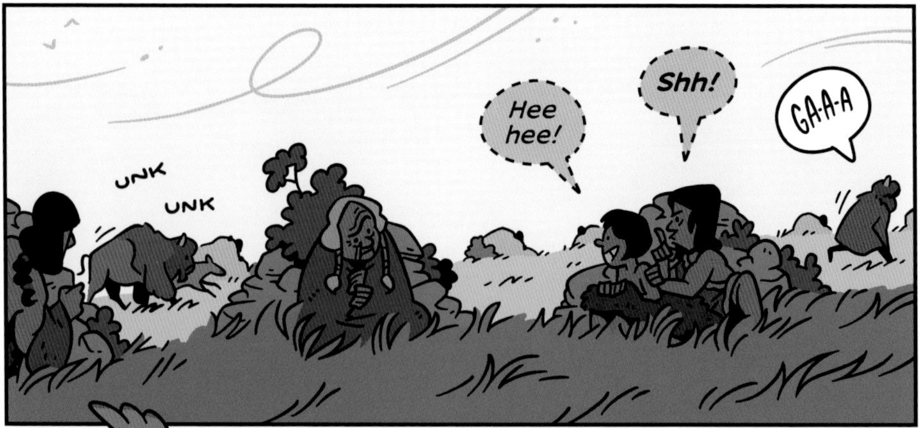
UNK
UNK
Hee hee!
Shh!
GA-A-A

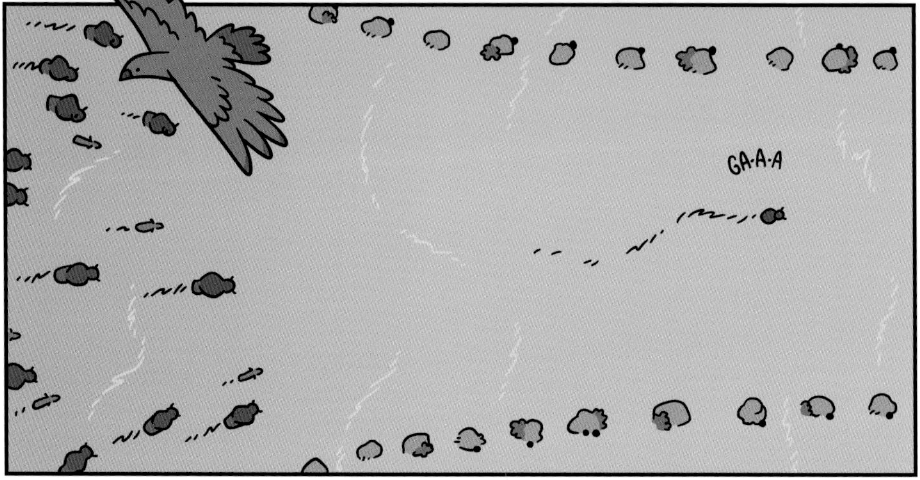
GA-A-A

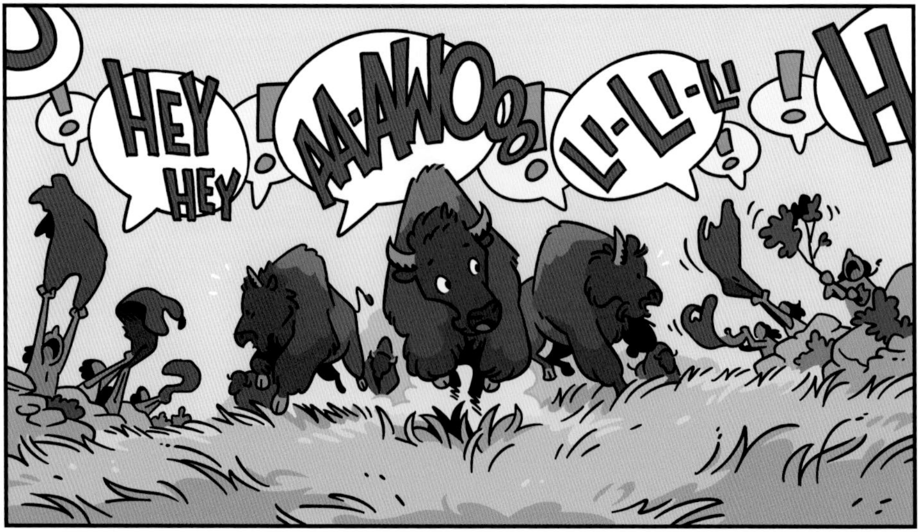
HEY HEY
AA-AWOOO
LI-LI-LI

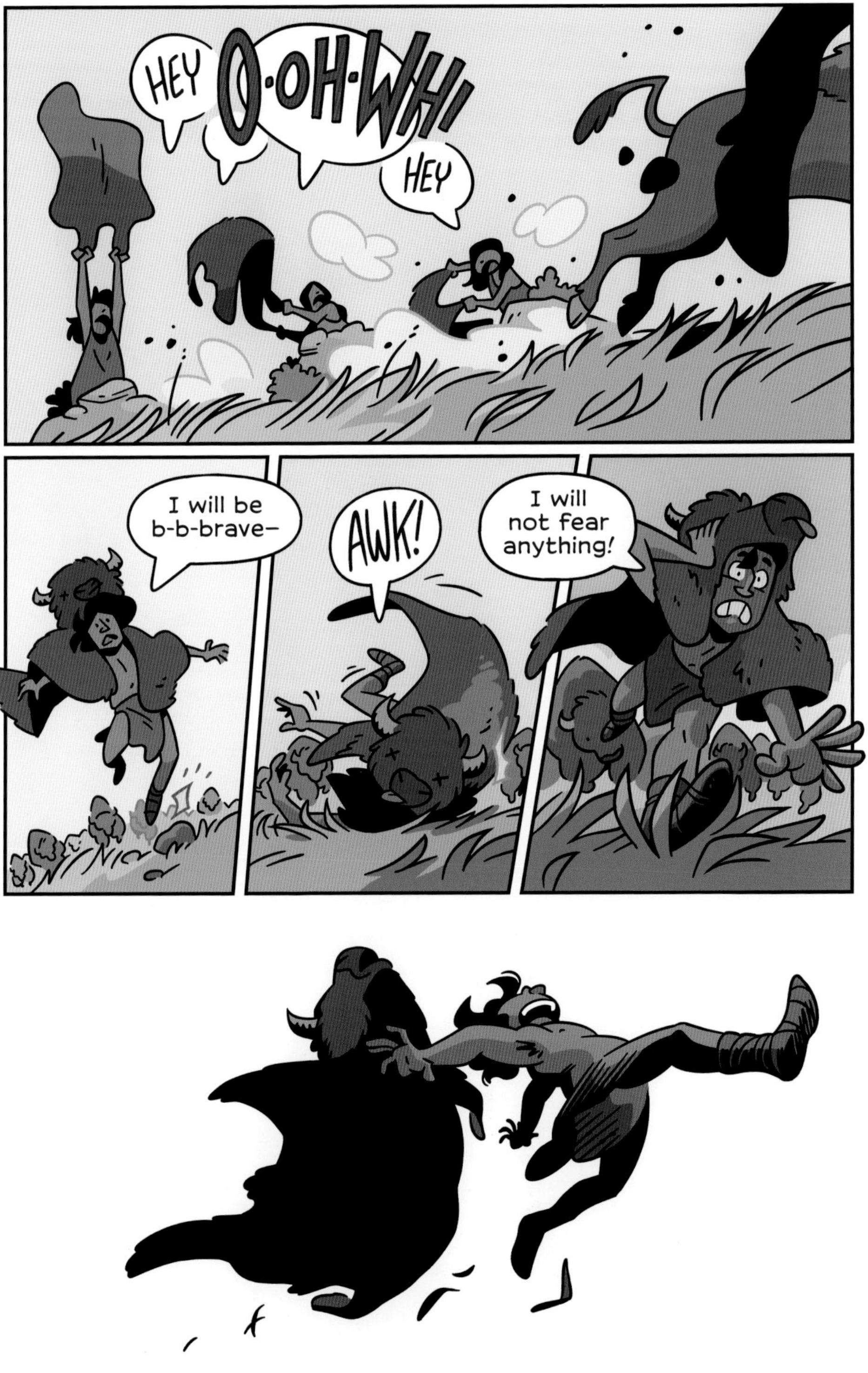
HEY
O-OH-WHI
HEY
I will be b-b-brave–
AWK!
I will not fear anything!

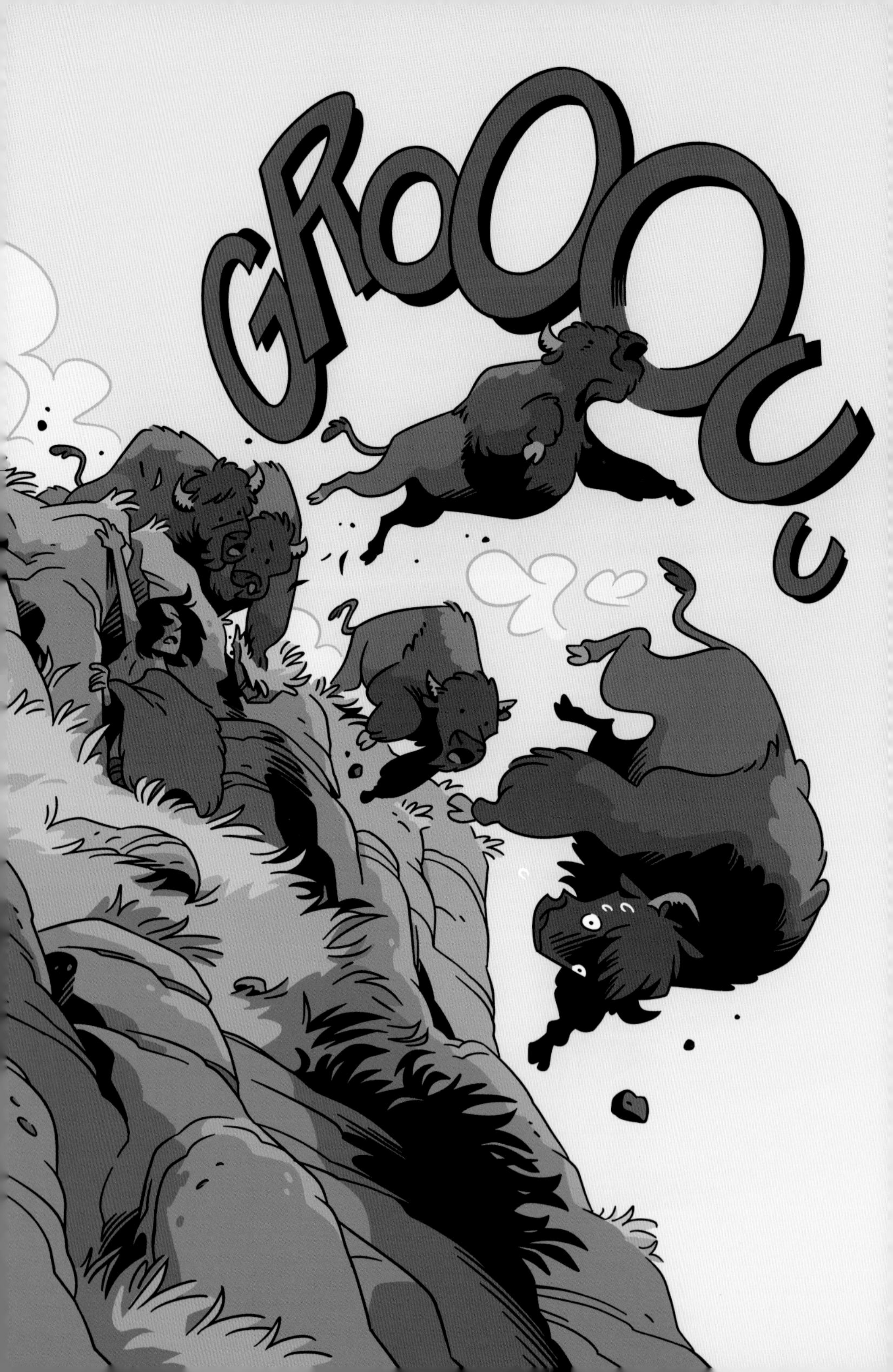
GROOOOUu

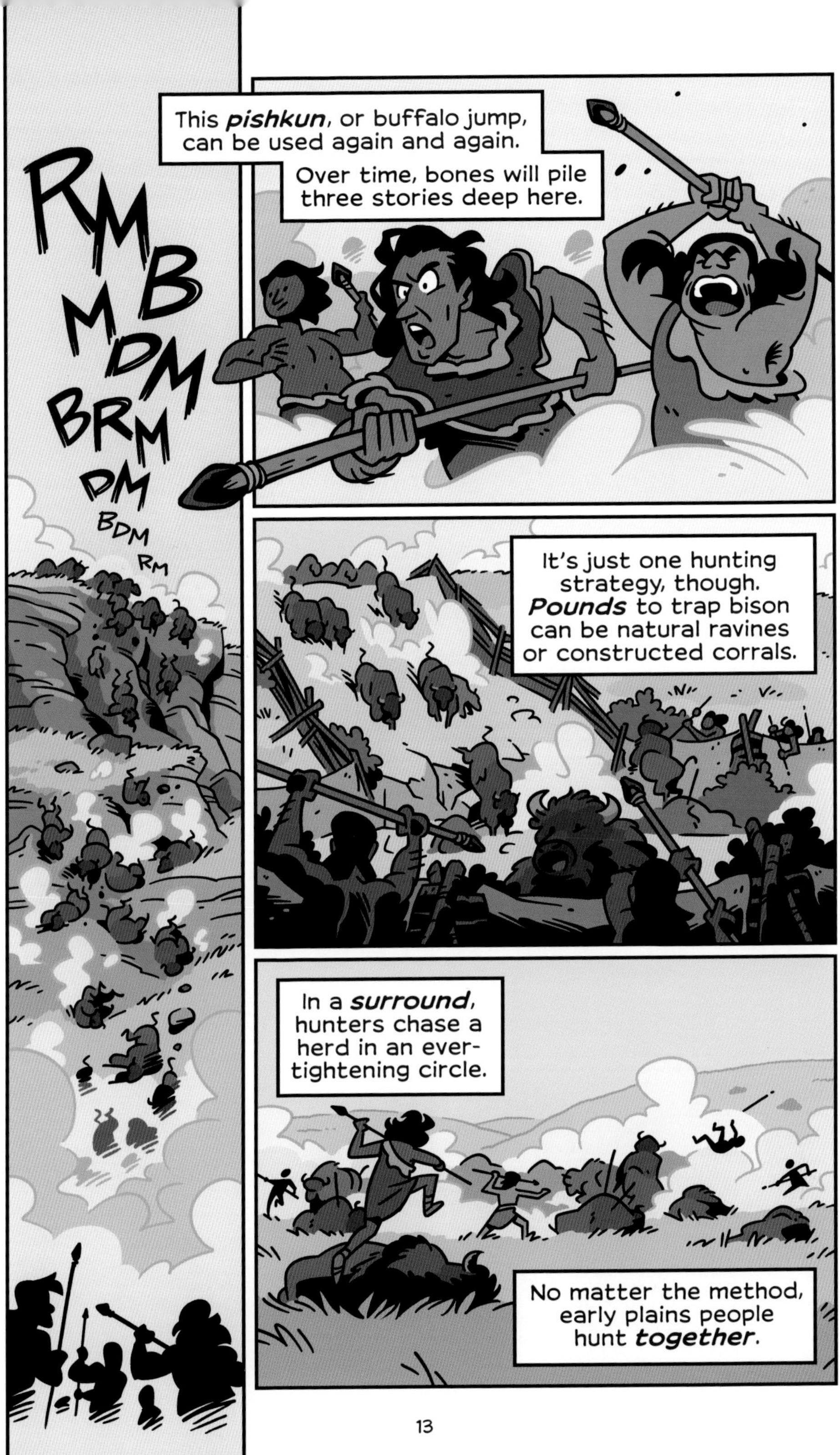
RMB
MDM
BRM
DM
BDM
RM
This *pishkun*, or buffalo jump, can be used again and again.
Over time, bones will pile three stories deep here.
It's just one hunting strategy, though. *Pounds* to trap bison can be natural ravines or constructed corrals.
In a *surround*, hunters chase a herd in an ever-tightening circle.
No matter the method, early plains people hunt *together*.

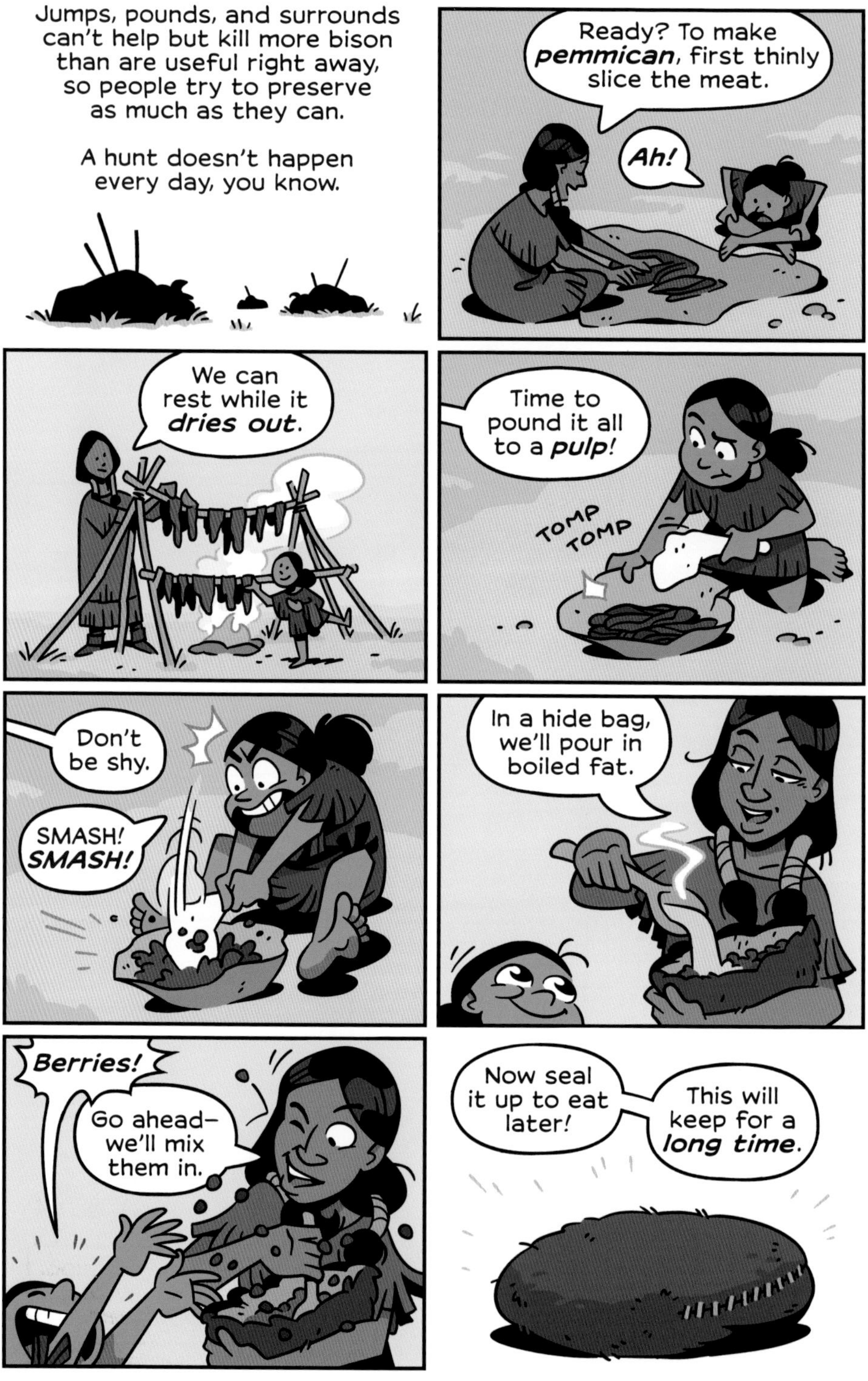
Jumps, pounds, and surrounds can't help but kill more bison than are useful right away, so people try to preserve as much as they can.
A hunt doesn't happen every day, you know.
Ready? To make *pemmican*, first thinly slice the meat.
Ah!
We can rest while it *dries out*.
Time to pound it all to a *pulp*!
TOMP TOMP
Don't be shy.
SMASH! *SMASH!*
In a hide bag, we'll pour in boiled fat.
Berries!
Go ahead— we'll mix them in.
Now seal it up to eat later!
This will keep for a *long time*.

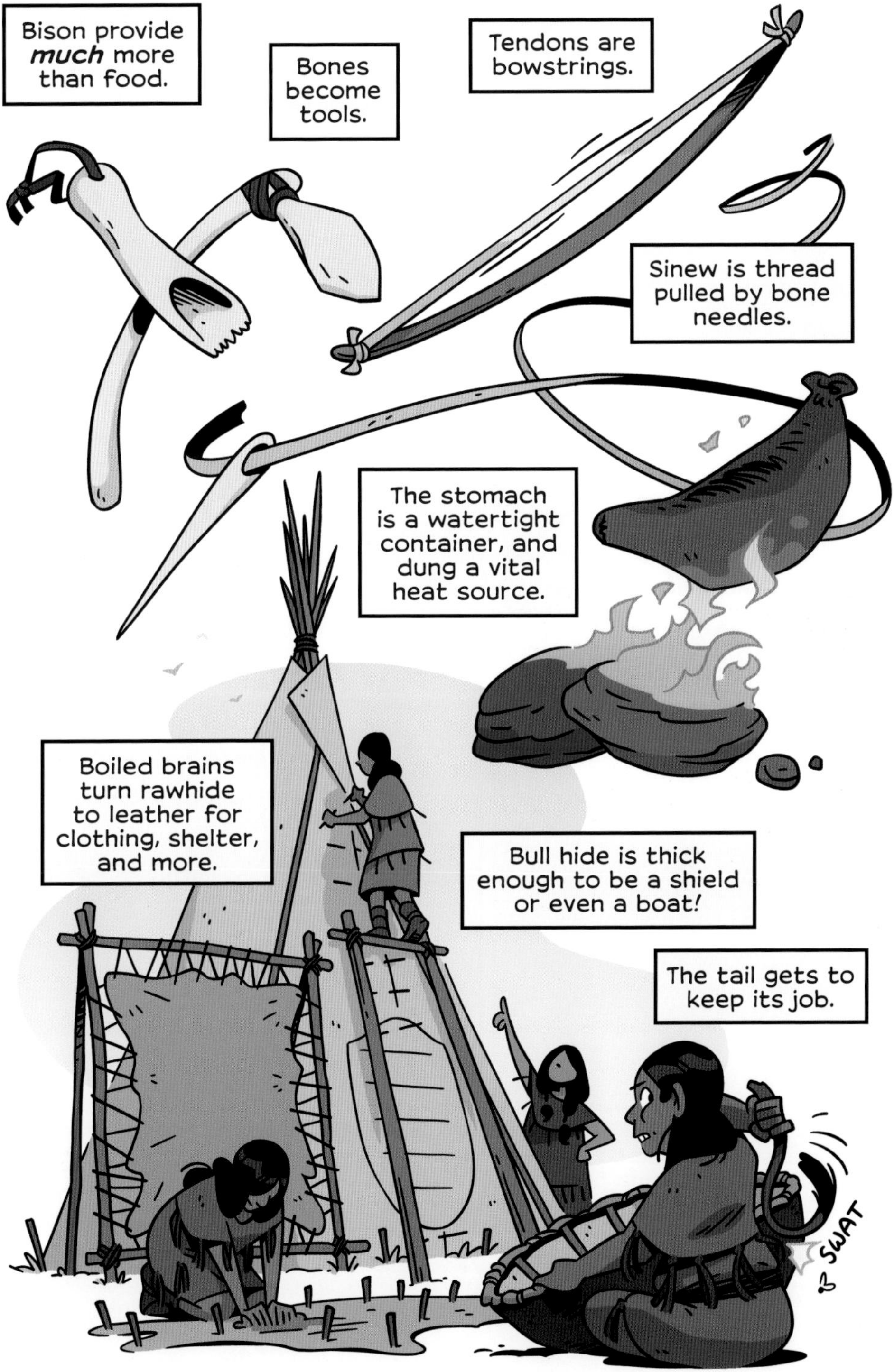
Bison provide *much* more than food.
Bones become tools.
Tendons are bowstrings.
Sinew is thread pulled by bone needles.
The stomach is a watertight container, and dung a vital heat source.
Boiled brains turn rawhide to leather for clothing, shelter, and more.
Bull hide is thick enough to be a shield or even a boat!
The tail gets to keep its job.
SWAT

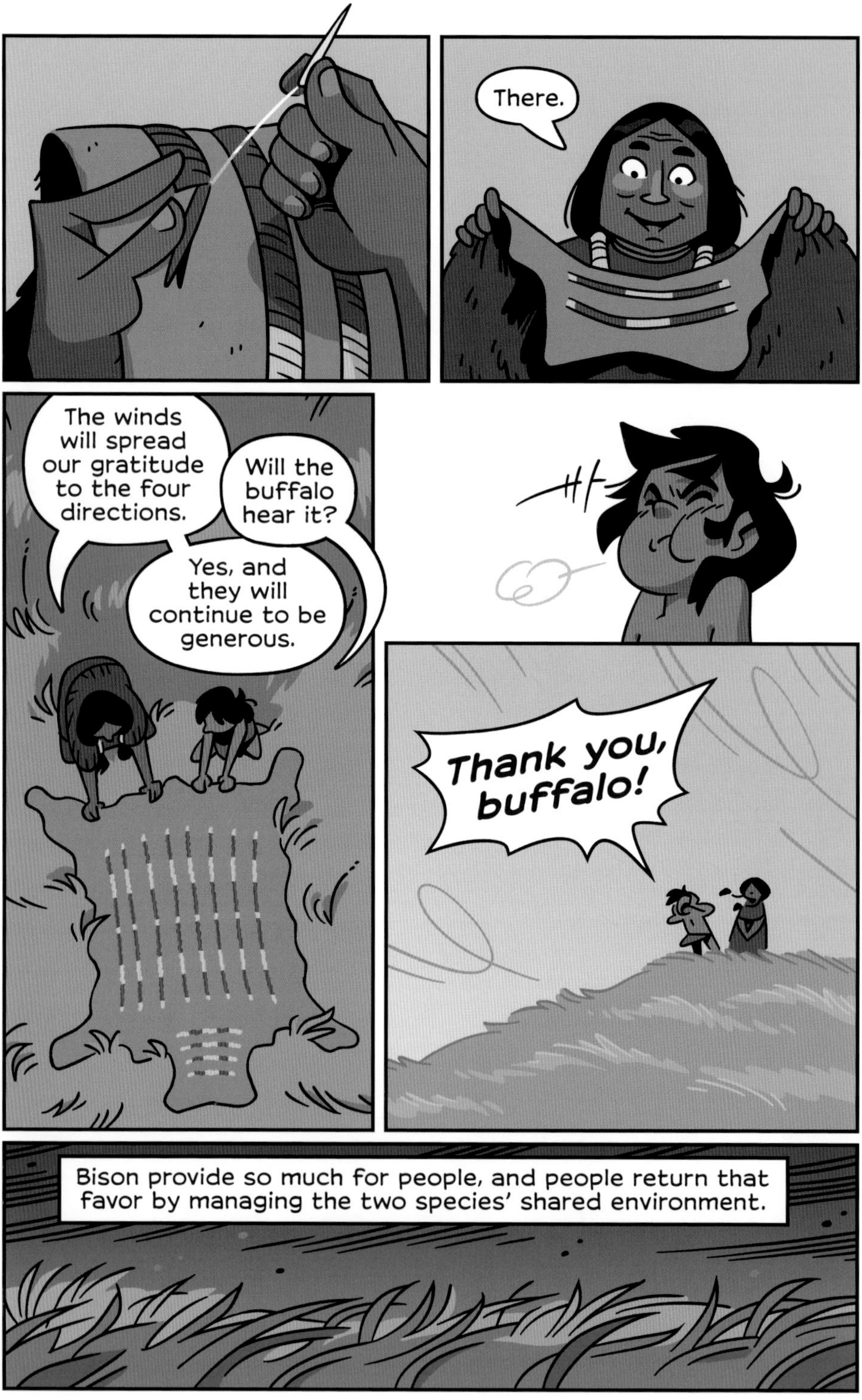
There.
The winds will spread our gratitude to the four directions.
Will the buffalo hear it?
Yes, and they will continue to be generous.
Thank you, buffalo!
Bison provide so much for people, and people return that favor by managing the two species' shared environment.

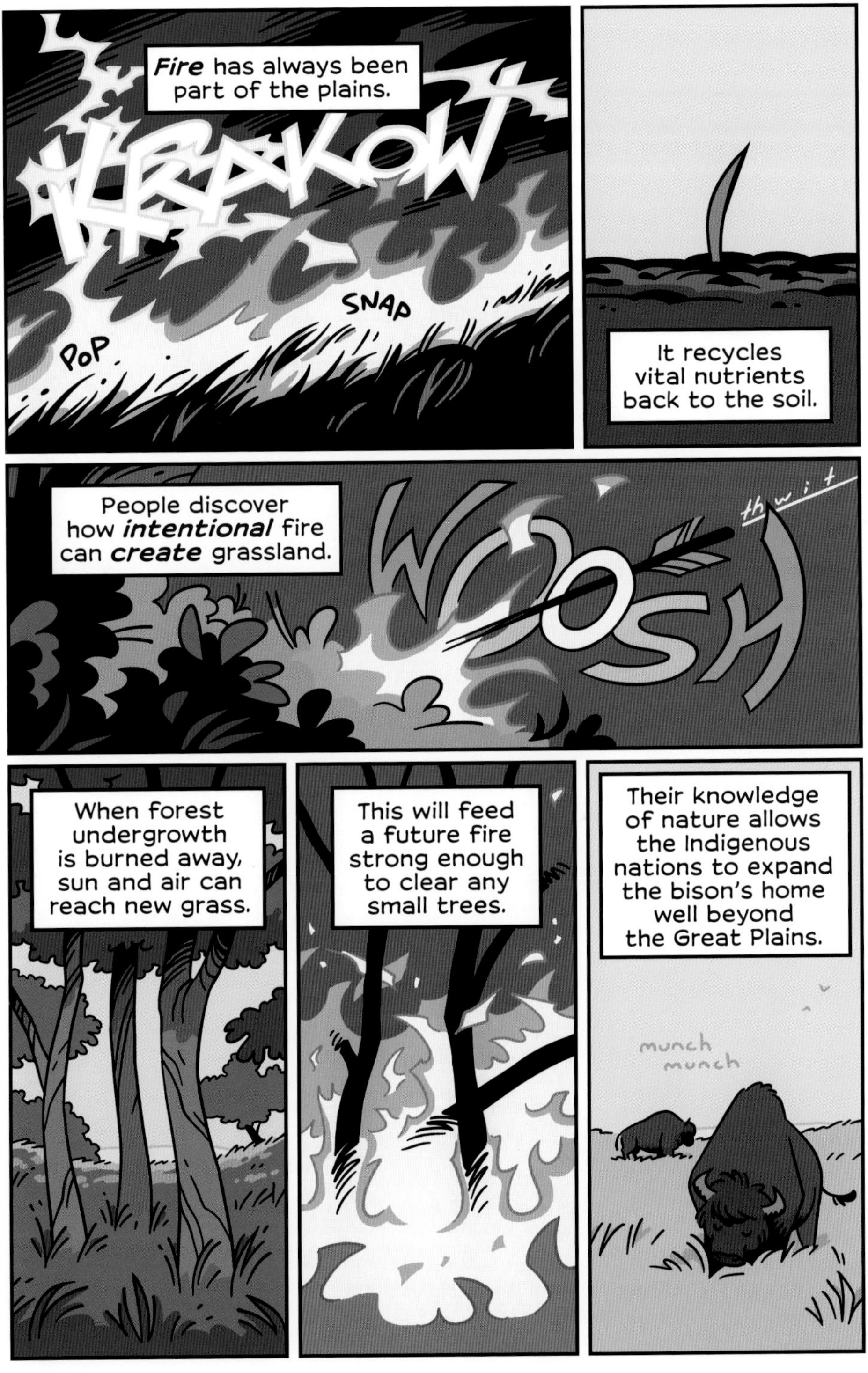
Fire has always been part of the plains.
KRAKOW
SNAP
POP
It recycles vital nutrients back to the soil.
People discover how intentional fire can create grassland.
WOOSH
thwit
When forest undergrowth is burned away, sun and air can reach new grass.
This will feed a future fire strong enough to clear any small trees.
Their knowledge of nature allows the Indigenous nations to expand the bison's home well beyond the Great Plains.
munch munch

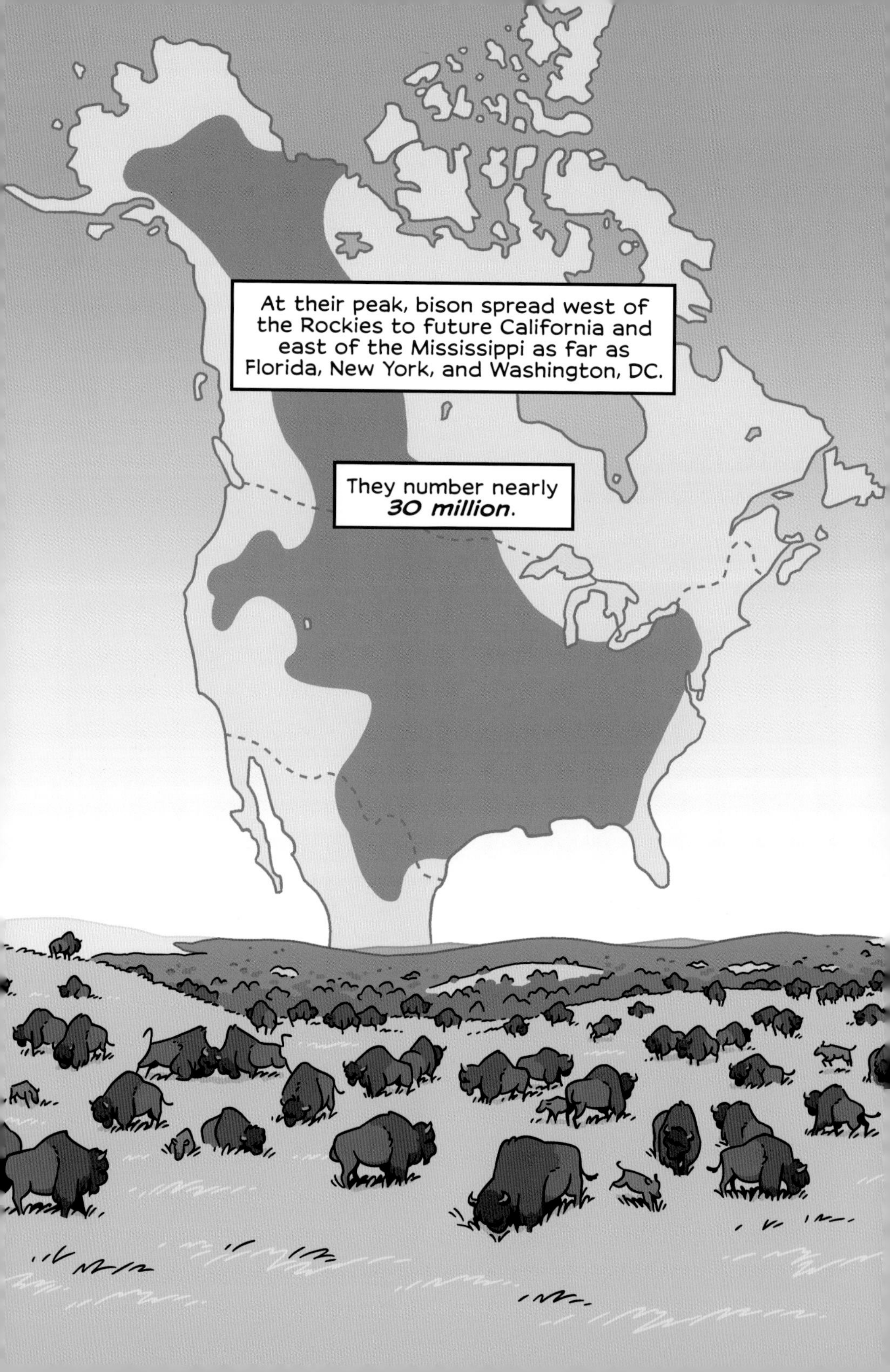
At their peak, bison spread west of the Rockies to future California and east of the Mississippi as far as Florida, New York, and Washington, DC.
They number nearly ***30 million***.

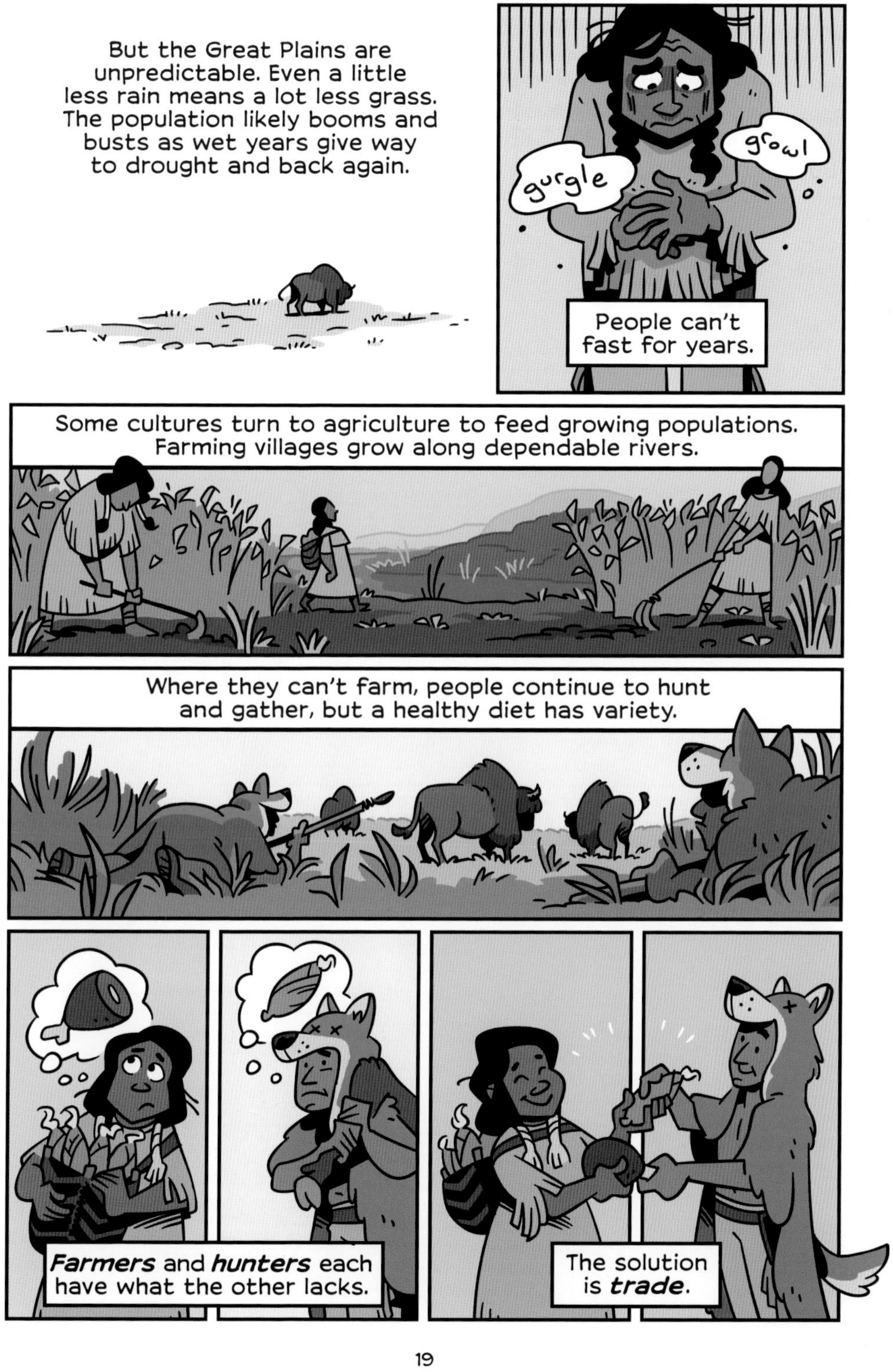

But the Great Plains are unpredictable. Even a little less rain means a lot less grass. The population likely booms and busts as wet years give way to drought and back again.
gurgle
growl
People can't fast for years.
Some cultures turn to agriculture to feed growing populations. Farming villages grow along dependable rivers.
Where they can't farm, people continue to hunt and gather, but a healthy diet has variety.
Farmers and ***hunters*** each have what the other lacks.
The solution is ***trade***.

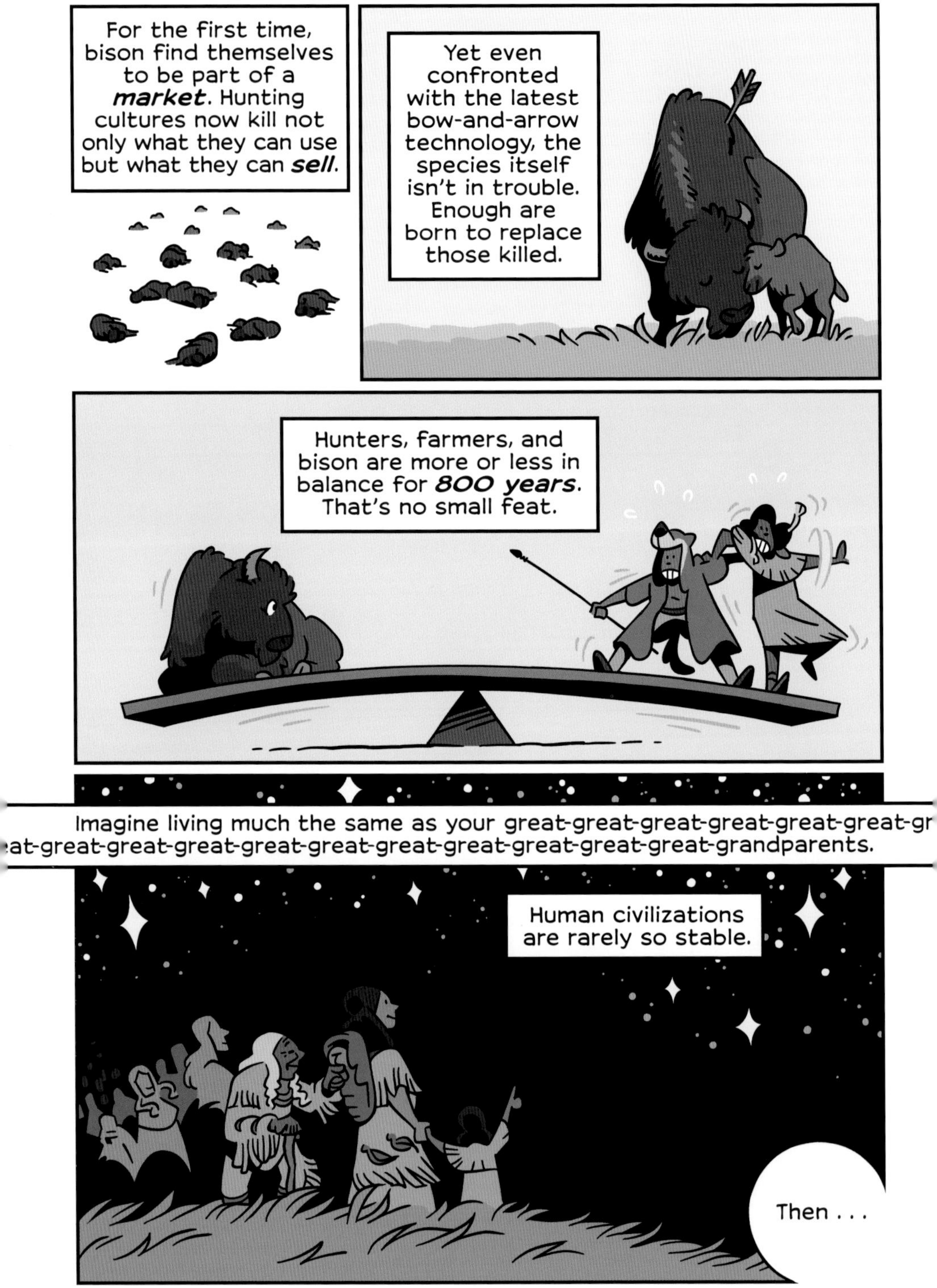
For the first time, bison find themselves to be part of a ***market***. Hunting cultures now kill not only what they can use but what they can ***sell***.
Yet even confronted with the latest bow-and-arrow technology, the species itself isn't in trouble. Enough are born to replace those killed.
Hunters, farmers, and bison are more or less in balance for ***800 years***. That's no small feat.
Imagine living much the same as your great-great-great-great-great-great-gr
eat-great-great-great-great-great-great-great-great-great-great-grandparents.
Human civilizations are rarely so stable.
Then . . .

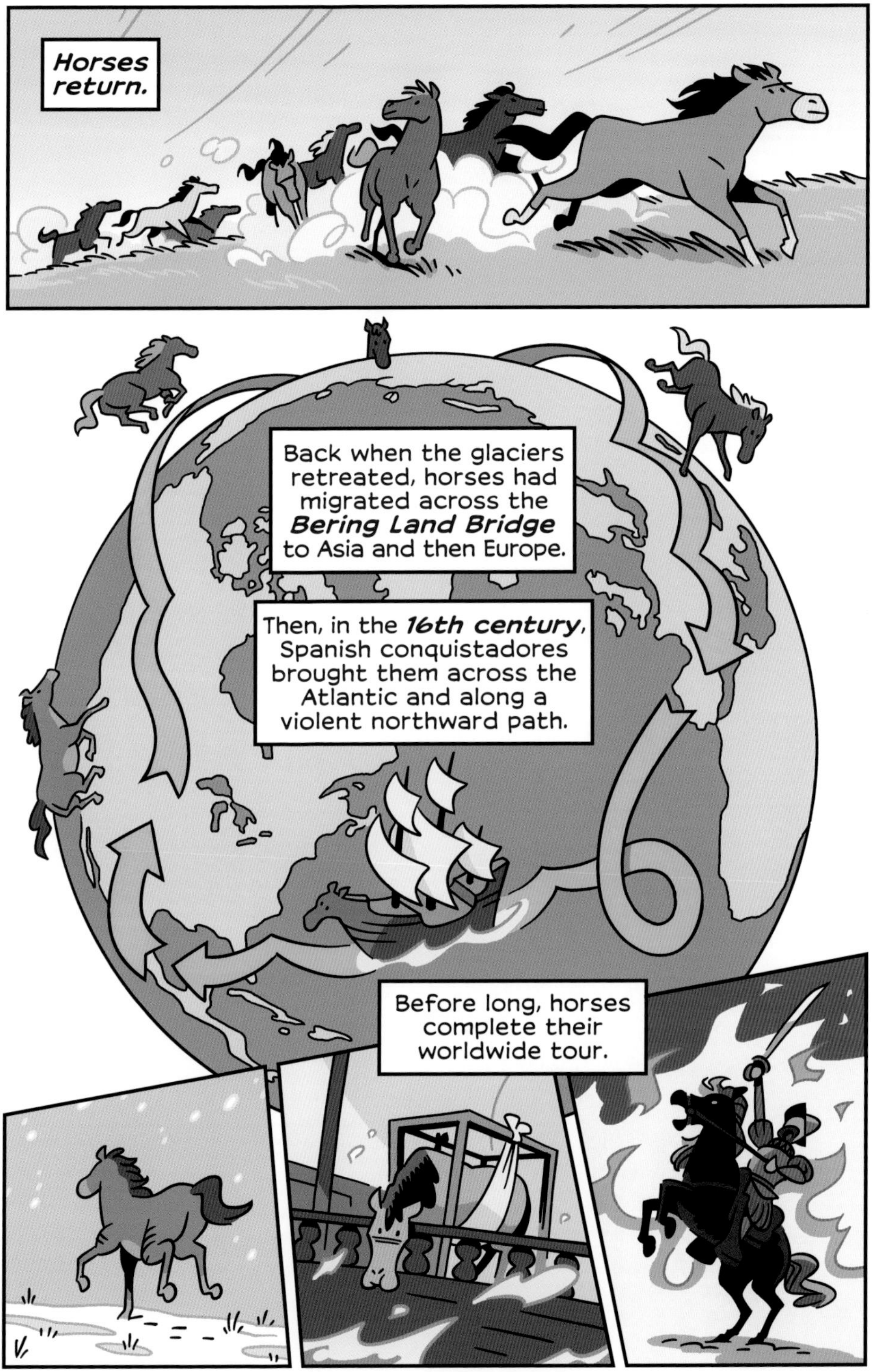

Horses return.
Back when the glaciers retreated, horses had migrated across the ***Bering Land Bridge*** to Asia and then Europe.
Then, in the ***16th century***, Spanish conquistadores brought them across the Atlantic and along a violent northward path.
Before long, horses complete their worldwide tour.

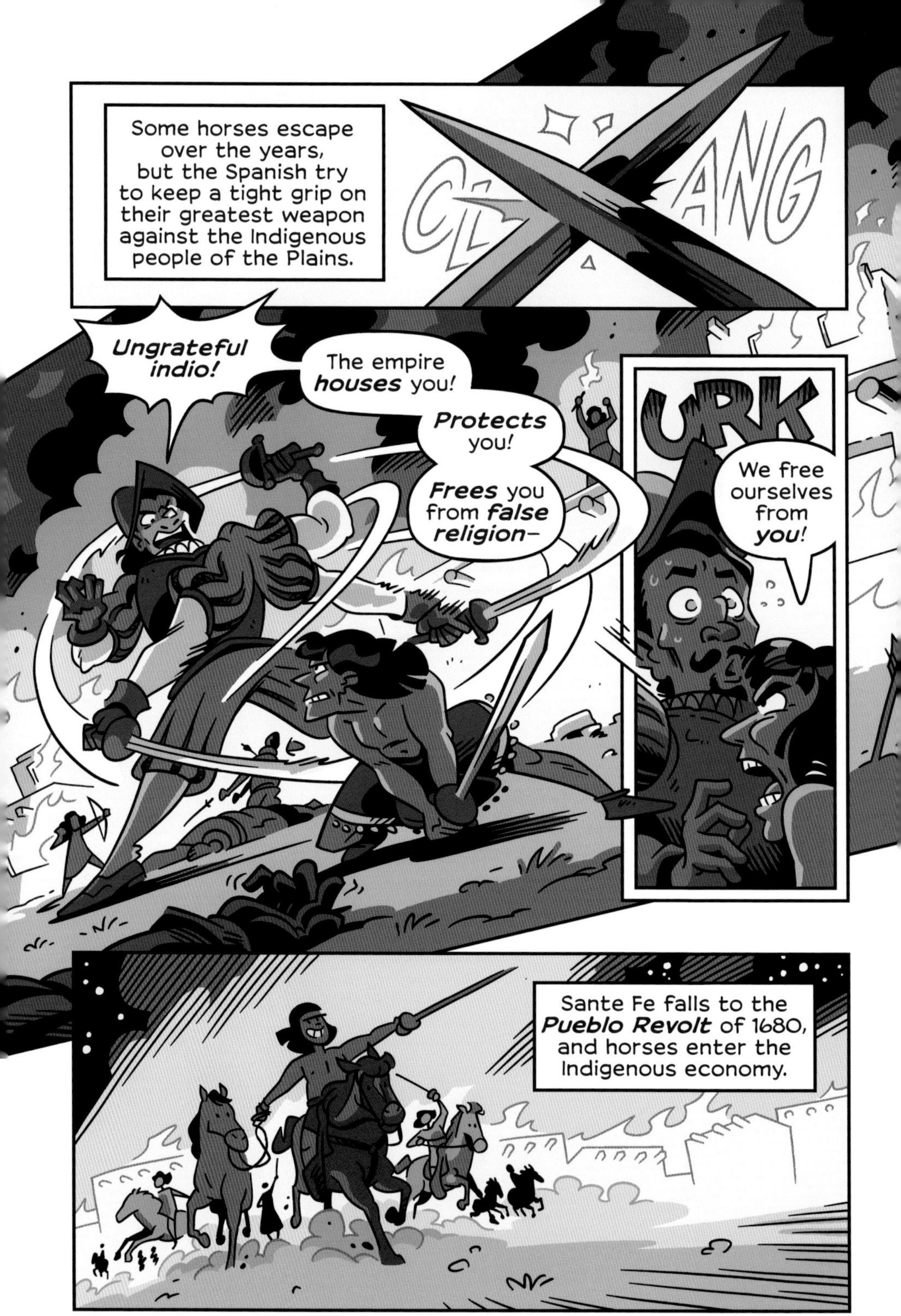

Some horses escape over the years, but the Spanish try to keep a tight grip on their greatest weapon against the Indigenous people of the Plains.
CLANG
Ungrateful indio!
The empire houses you!
Protects you!
Frees you from false religion–
URK
We free ourselves from you!
Sante Fe falls to the Pueblo Revolt of 1680, and horses enter the Indigenous economy.

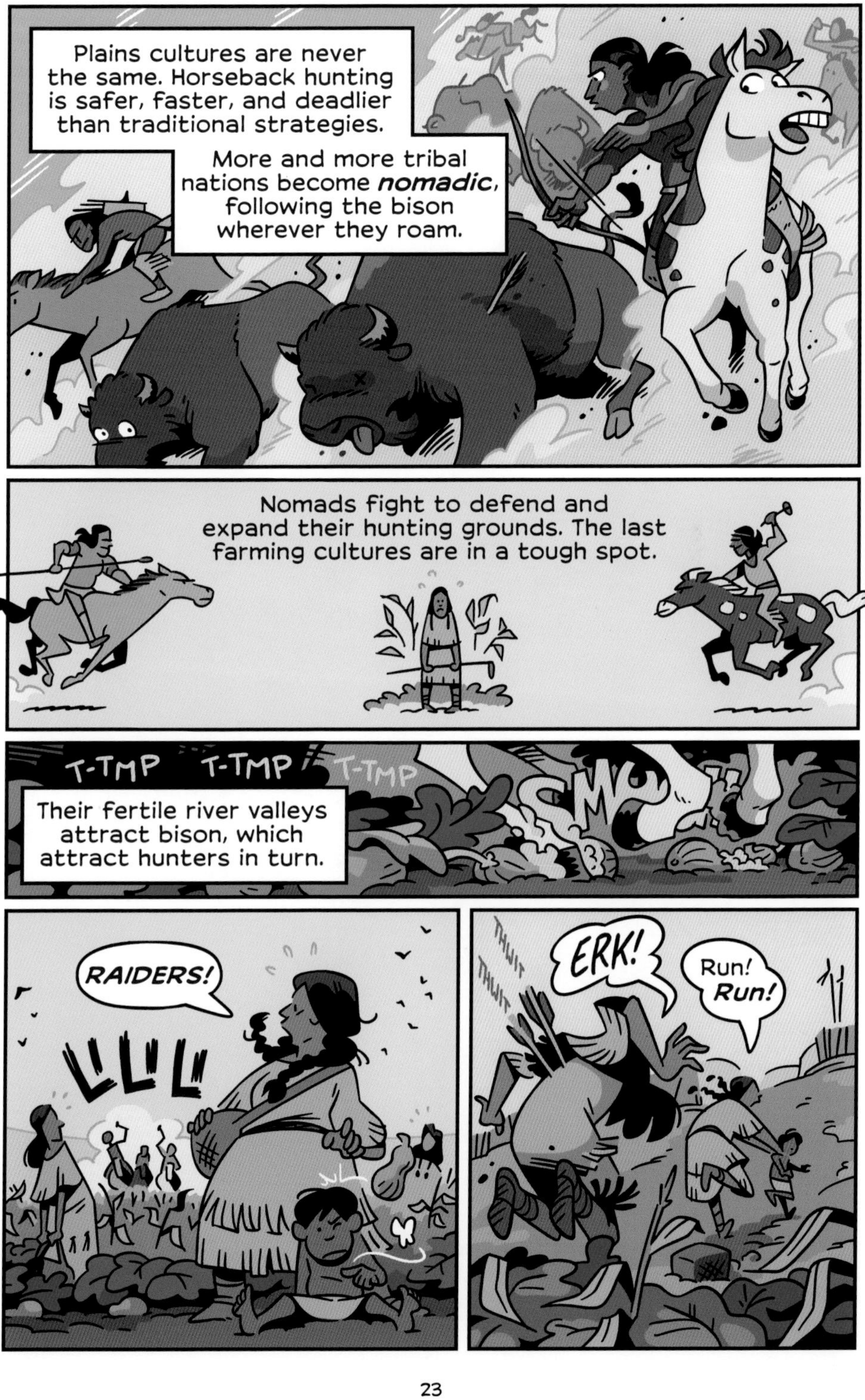
Plains cultures are never the same. Horseback hunting is safer, faster, and deadlier than traditional strategies.
More and more tribal nations become ***nomadic***, following the bison wherever they roam.
Nomads fight to defend and expand their hunting grounds. The last farming cultures are in a tough spot.
T-TMP T-TMP T-TMP
Their fertile river valleys attract bison, which attract hunters in turn.
RAIDERS!
LILILI
ERK!
THWIT
THWIT
Run! ***Run!***

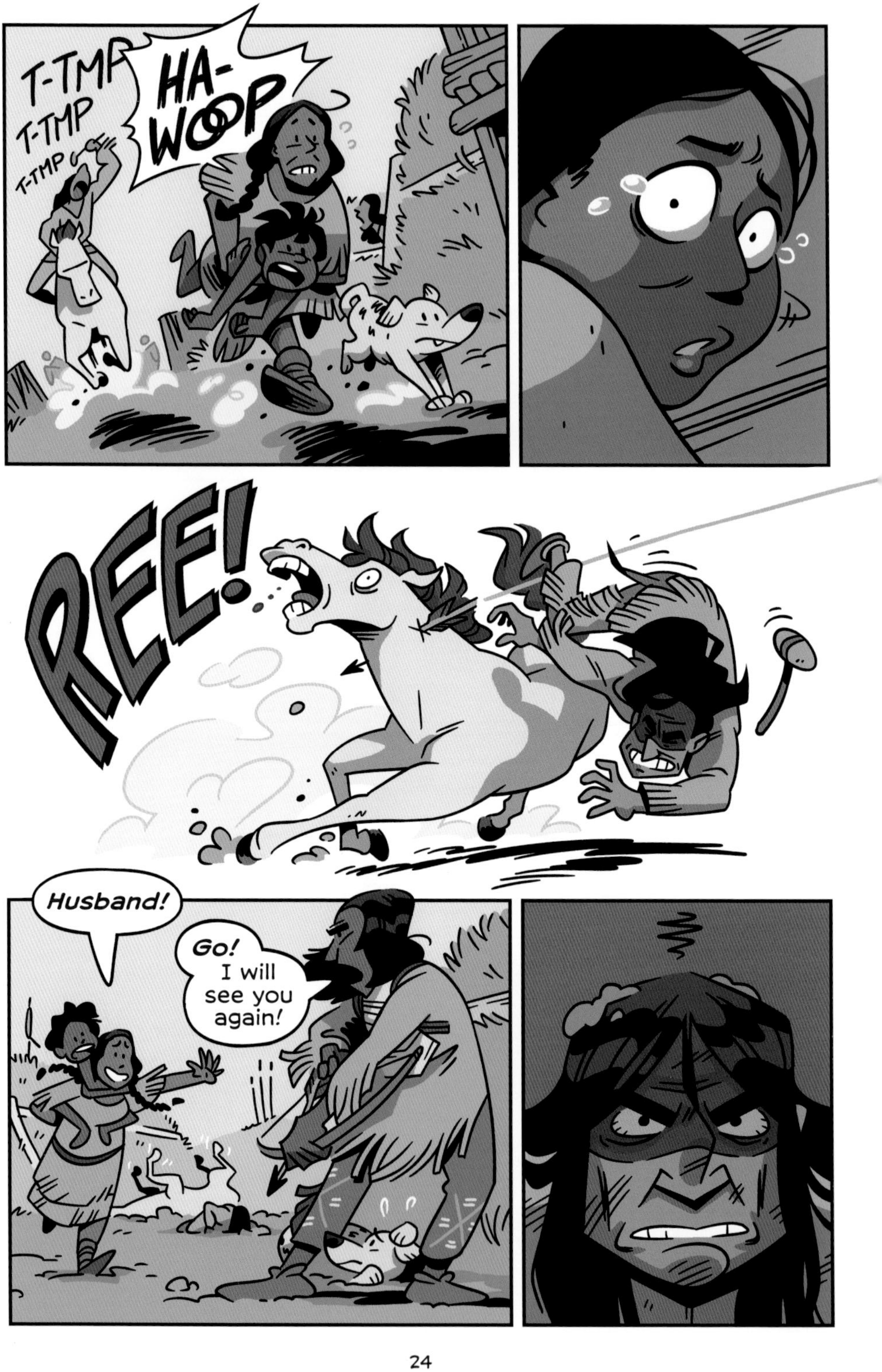
T-TMP
T-TMP
T-TMP
HA-WOOP
REE!
Husband!
Go! I will see you again!

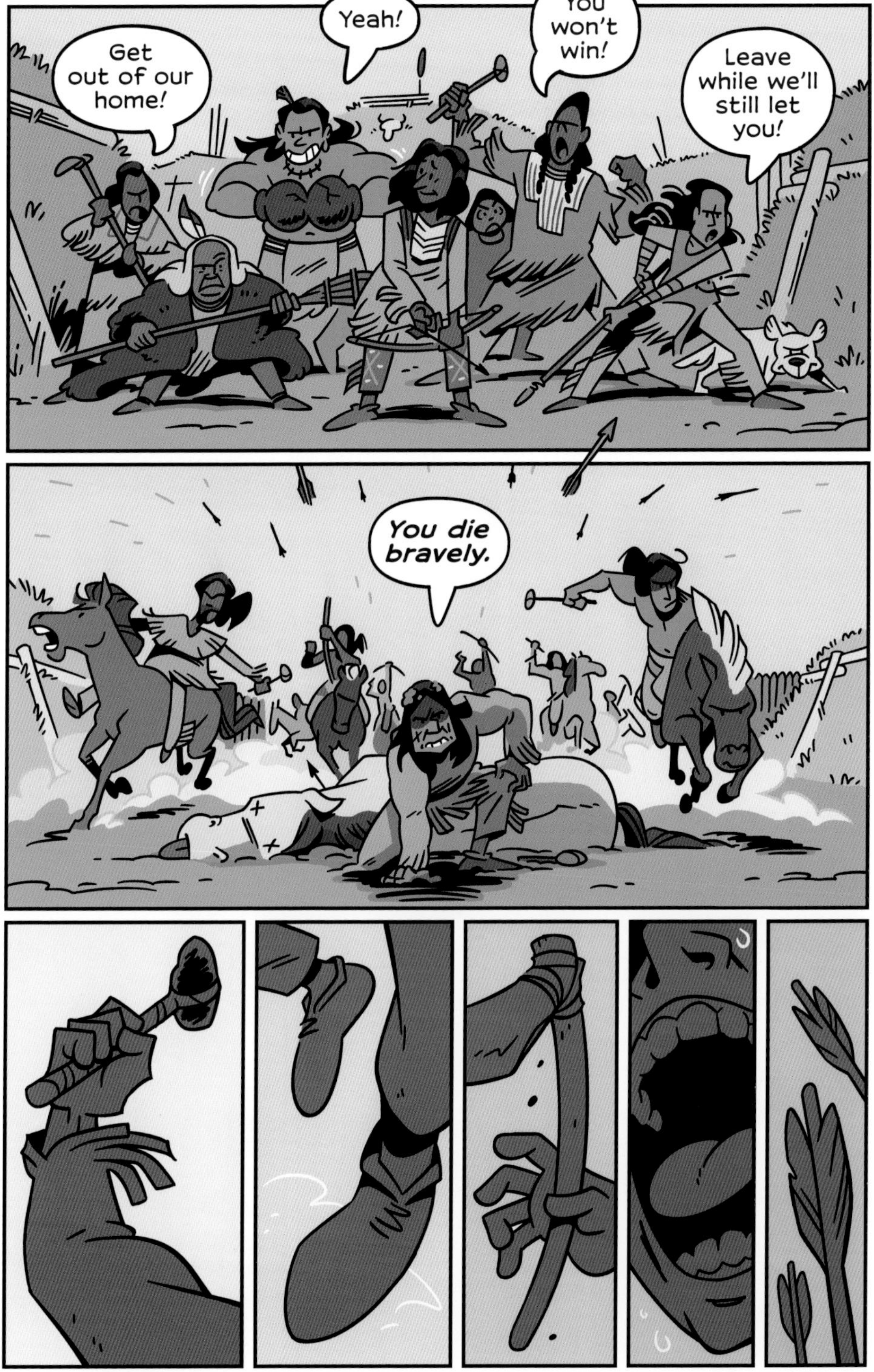

Get out of our home!
Yeah!
You won't win!
Leave while we'll still let you!
You die bravely.

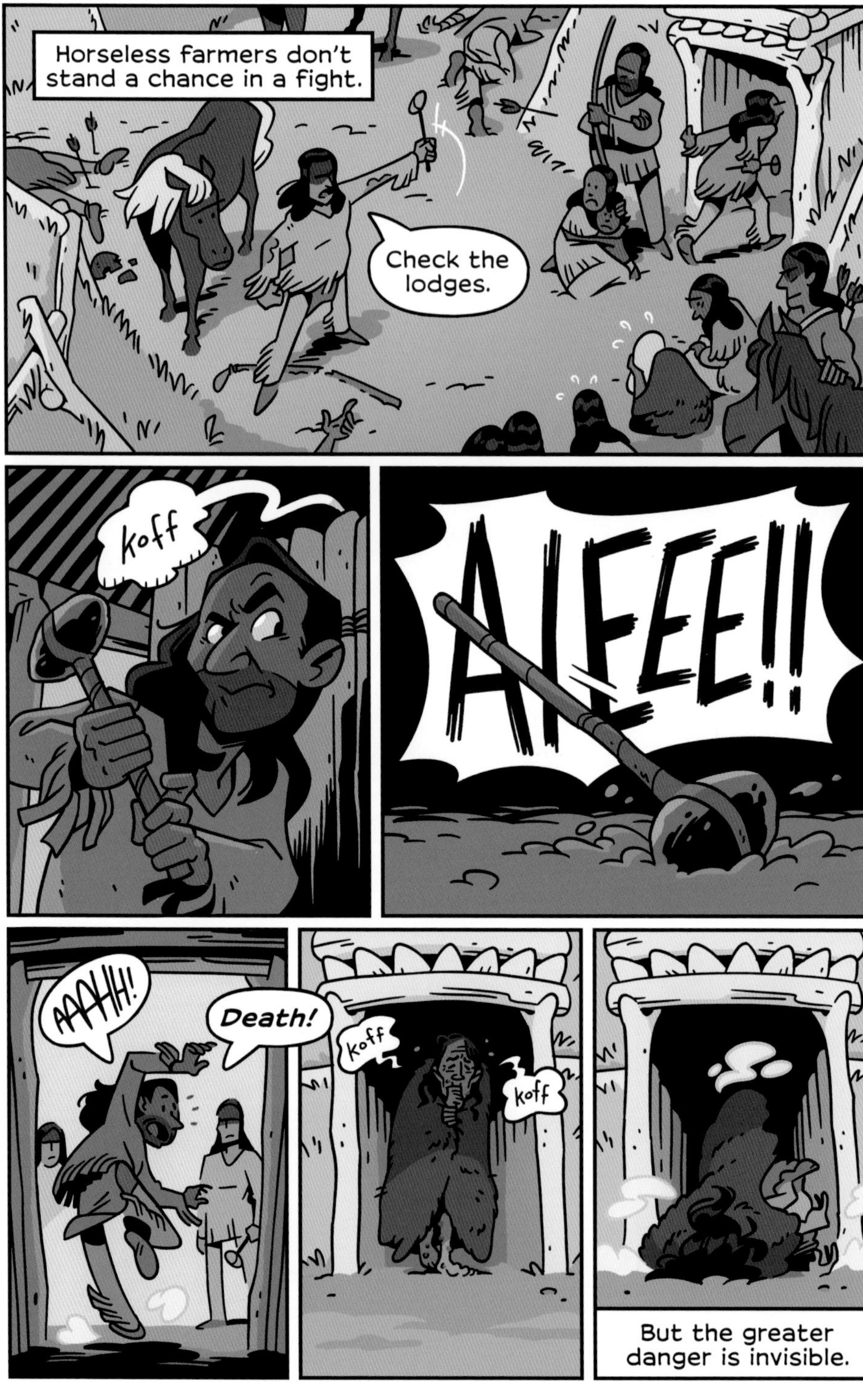
Horseless farmers don't stand a chance in a fight.
Check the lodges.
koff
AIEEE!!
AAAHH!
Death!
koff
koff
But the greater danger is invisible.

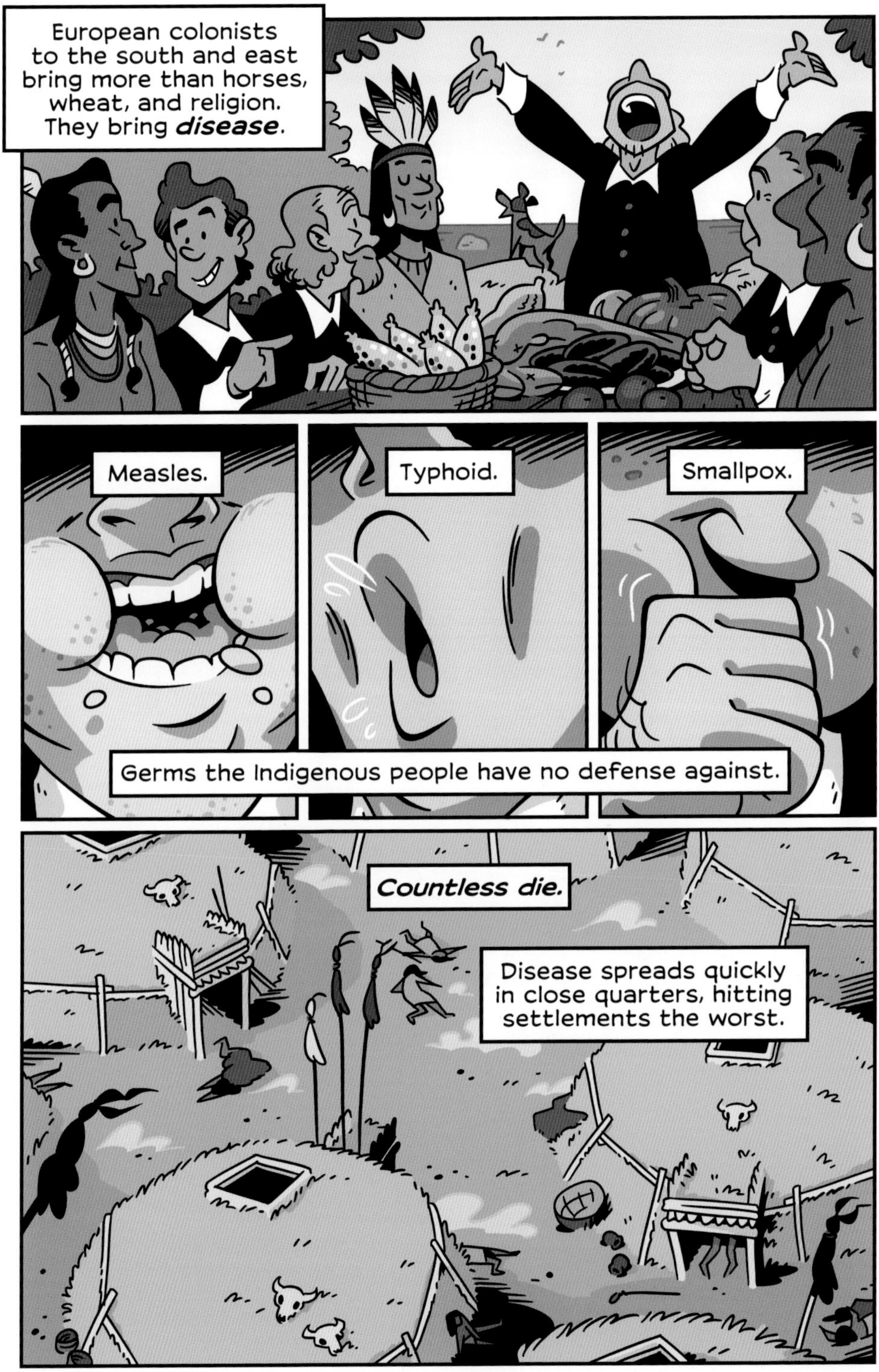
European colonists to the south and east bring more than horses, wheat, and religion. They bring *disease*.
Measles.
Typhoid.
Smallpox.
Germs the Indigenous people have no defense against.
Countless die.
Disease spreads quickly in close quarters, hitting settlements the worst.

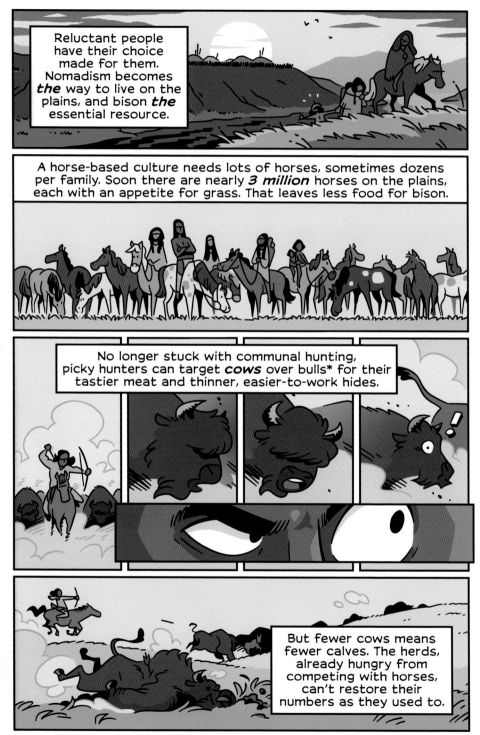

Reluctant people have their choice made for them. Nomadism becomes *the* way to live on the plains, and bison *the* essential resource.

A horse-based culture needs lots of horses, sometimes dozens per family. Soon there are nearly *3 million* horses on the plains, each with an appetite for grass. That leaves less food for bison.

No longer stuck with communal hunting, picky hunters can target *cows* over bulls* for their tastier meat and thinner, easier-to-work hides.

But fewer cows means fewer calves. The herds, already hungry from competing with horses, can't restore their numbers as they used to.

*cows = females and bulls = males

28

Millions of bison are already lost.

It's a terrible time for demand to increase.

TRADING CO.

Oh *ho!* You know, this pemmican is the only way my boys make it through winter.

BEAVER FASHI

HIM & HER

With this, your credit's quite good, *quite* good.

New items are in, by the by. Quality *iron*.

CLANG
ping
CLANG

Did I mention seeing more of your *new neighbors* lately?

This will do.

Mmm... A *fine* choice.
The other fellow couldn't afford *that* one.

War and a growing desire for *trade goods* tie Indigenous people to the white economy. Beaver pelts are in high demand, and trappers depend on pemmican to do their long, lonely work. When prices fall, it takes more bison to maintain modern life.

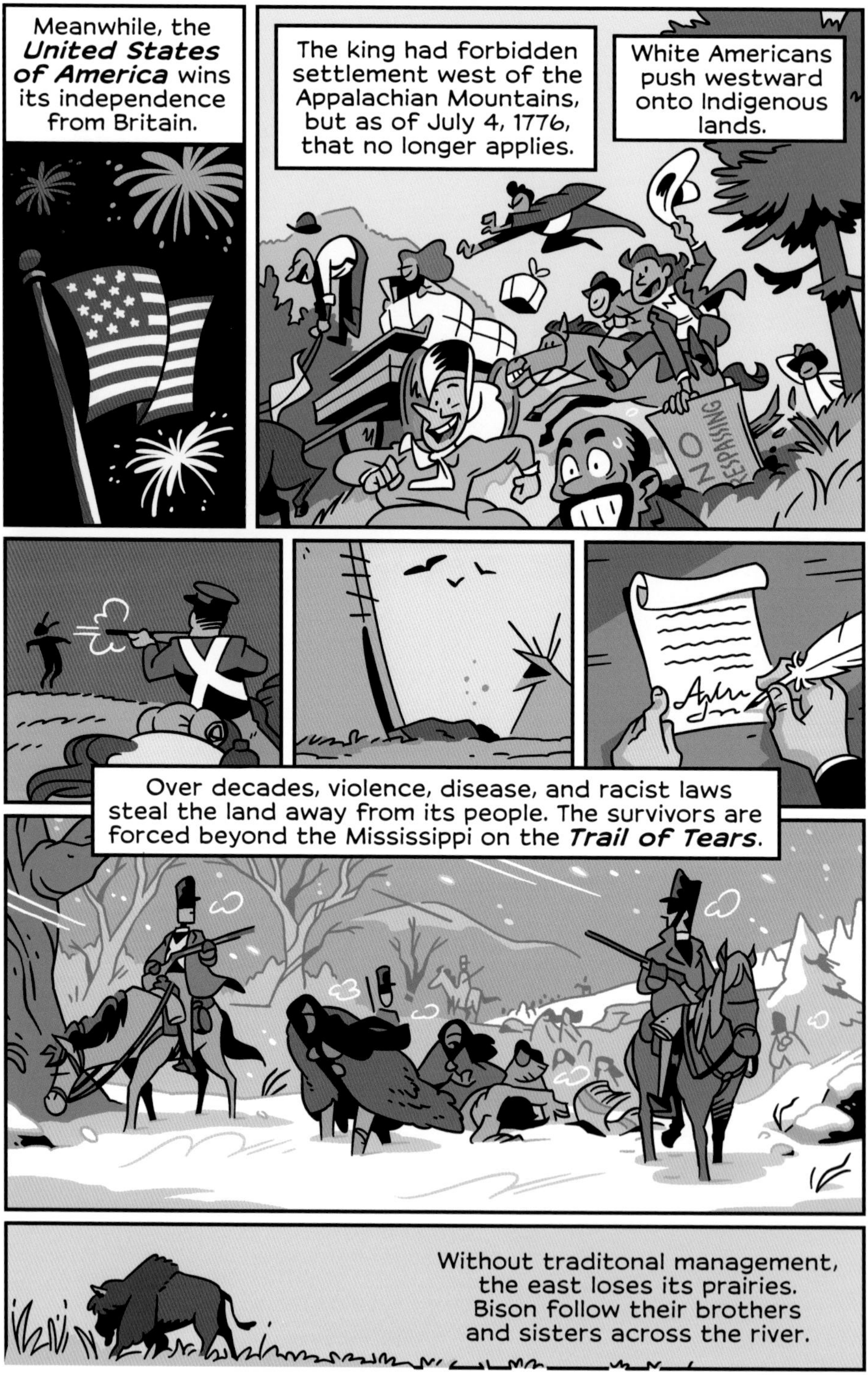
Meanwhile, the ***United States of America*** wins its independence from Britain.
The king had forbidden settlement west of the Appalachian Mountains, but as of July 4, 1776, that no longer applies.
White Americans push westward onto Indigenous lands.
NO RESPASSING
Over decades, violence, disease, and racist laws steal the land away from its people. The survivors are forced beyond the Mississippi on the ***Trail of Tears***.
Without traditonal management, the east loses its prairies. Bison follow their brothers and sisters across the river.

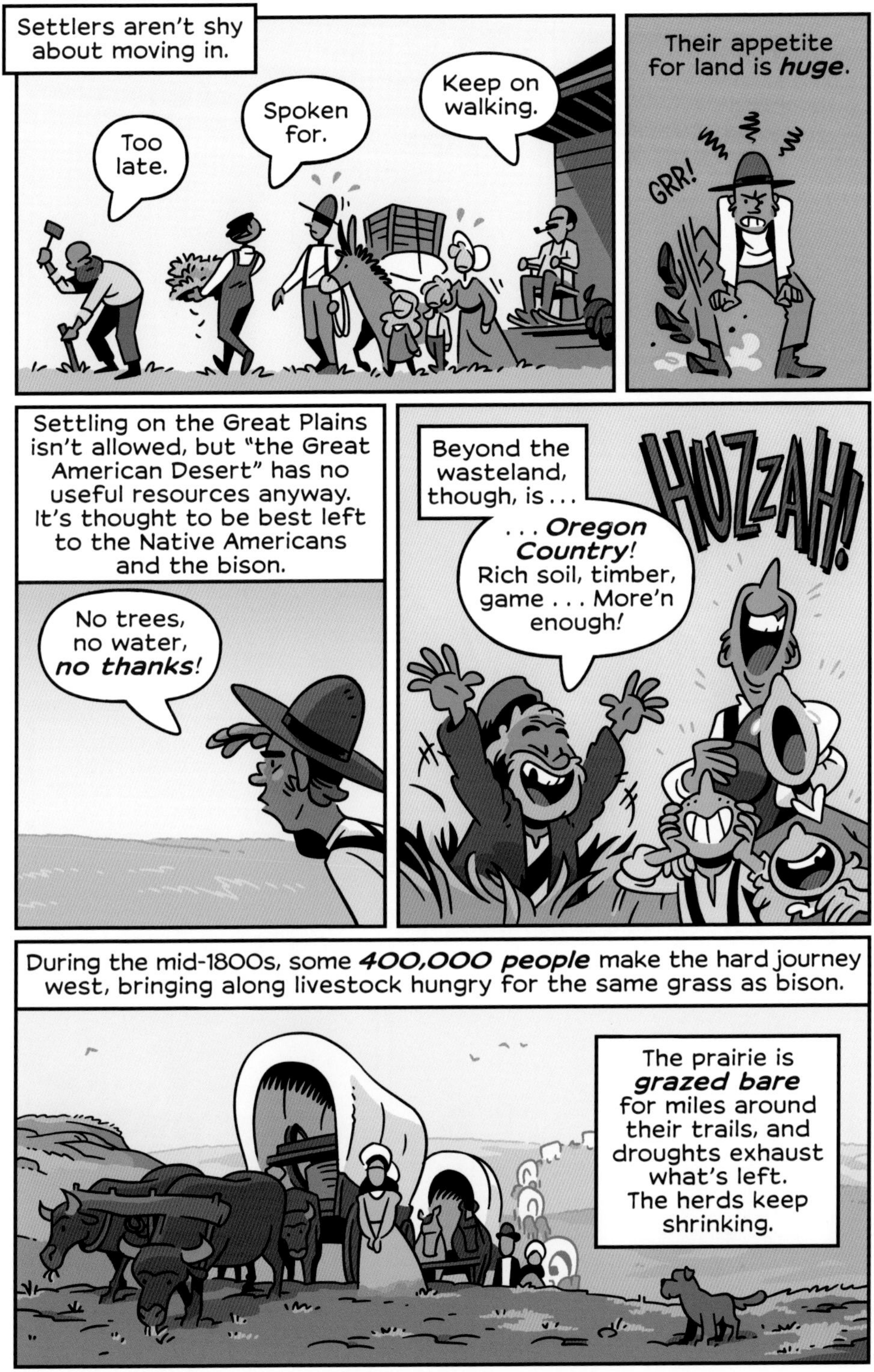

Settlers aren't shy about moving in.
Too late.
Spoken for.
Keep on walking.
Their appetite for land is *huge*.
GRR!
Settling on the Great Plains isn't allowed, but "the Great American Desert" has no useful resources anyway. It's thought to be best left to the Native Americans and the bison.
No trees, no water, ***no thanks***!
Beyond the wasteland, though, is . . .
. . . ***Oregon Country***! Rich soil, timber, game . . . More'n enough!
HUZZAH!
During the mid-1800s, some ***400,000 people*** make the hard journey west, bringing along livestock hungry for the same grass as bison.
The prairie is ***grazed bare*** for miles around their trails, and droughts exhaust what's left. The herds keep shrinking.

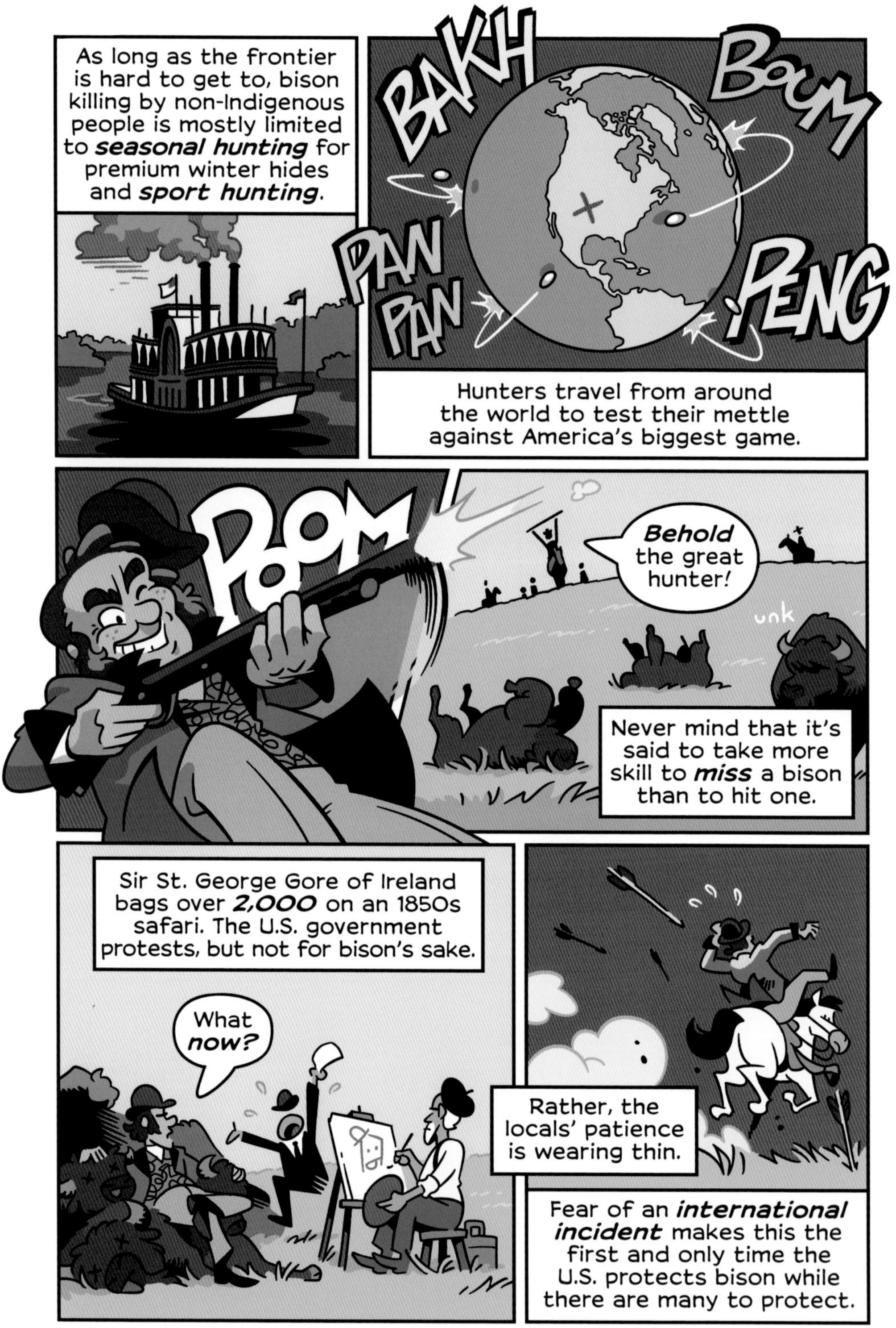

As long as the frontier is hard to get to, bison killing by non-Indigenous people is mostly limited to ***seasonal hunting*** for premium winter hides and ***sport hunting***.
BAKH
BOUM
PAN PAN
PENG
Hunters travel from around the world to test their mettle against America's biggest game.
POOM
Behold the great hunter!
unk
Never mind that it's said to take more skill to ***miss*** a bison than to hit one.
Sir St. George Gore of Ireland bags over ***2,000*** on an 1850s safari. The U.S. government protests, but not for bison's sake.
What *now?*
Rather, the locals' patience is wearing thin.
Fear of an ***international incident*** makes this the first and only time the U.S. protects bison while there are many to protect.

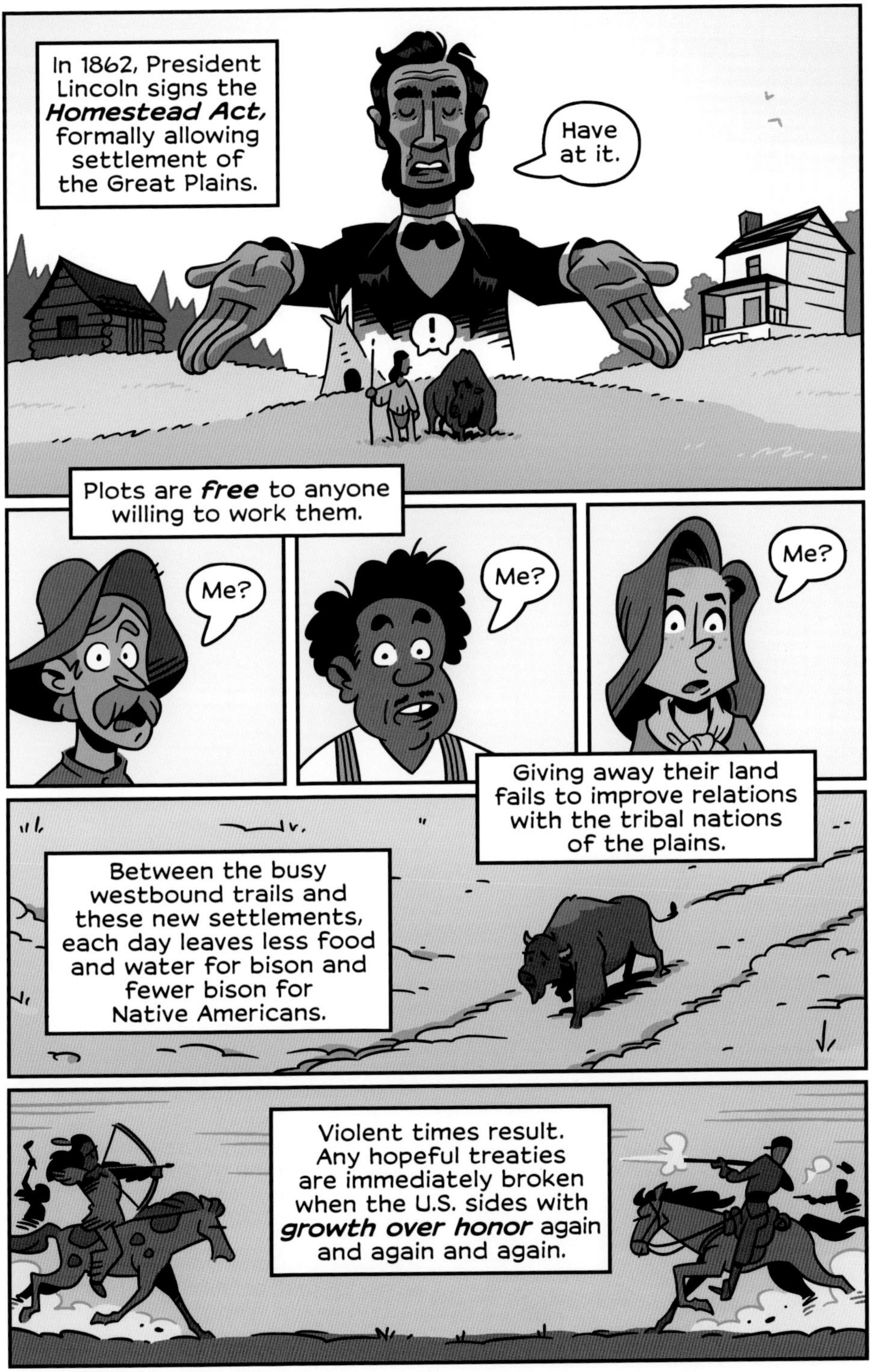
In 1862, President Lincoln signs the ***Homestead Act,*** formally allowing settlement of the Great Plains.
Have at it.
!
Plots are ***free*** to anyone willing to work them.
Me?
Me?
Me?
Giving away their land fails to improve relations with the tribal nations of the plains.
Between the busy westbound trails and these new settlements, each day leaves less food and water for bison and fewer bison for Native Americans.
Violent times result. Any hopeful treaties are immediately broken when the U.S. sides with ***growth over honor*** again and again and again.

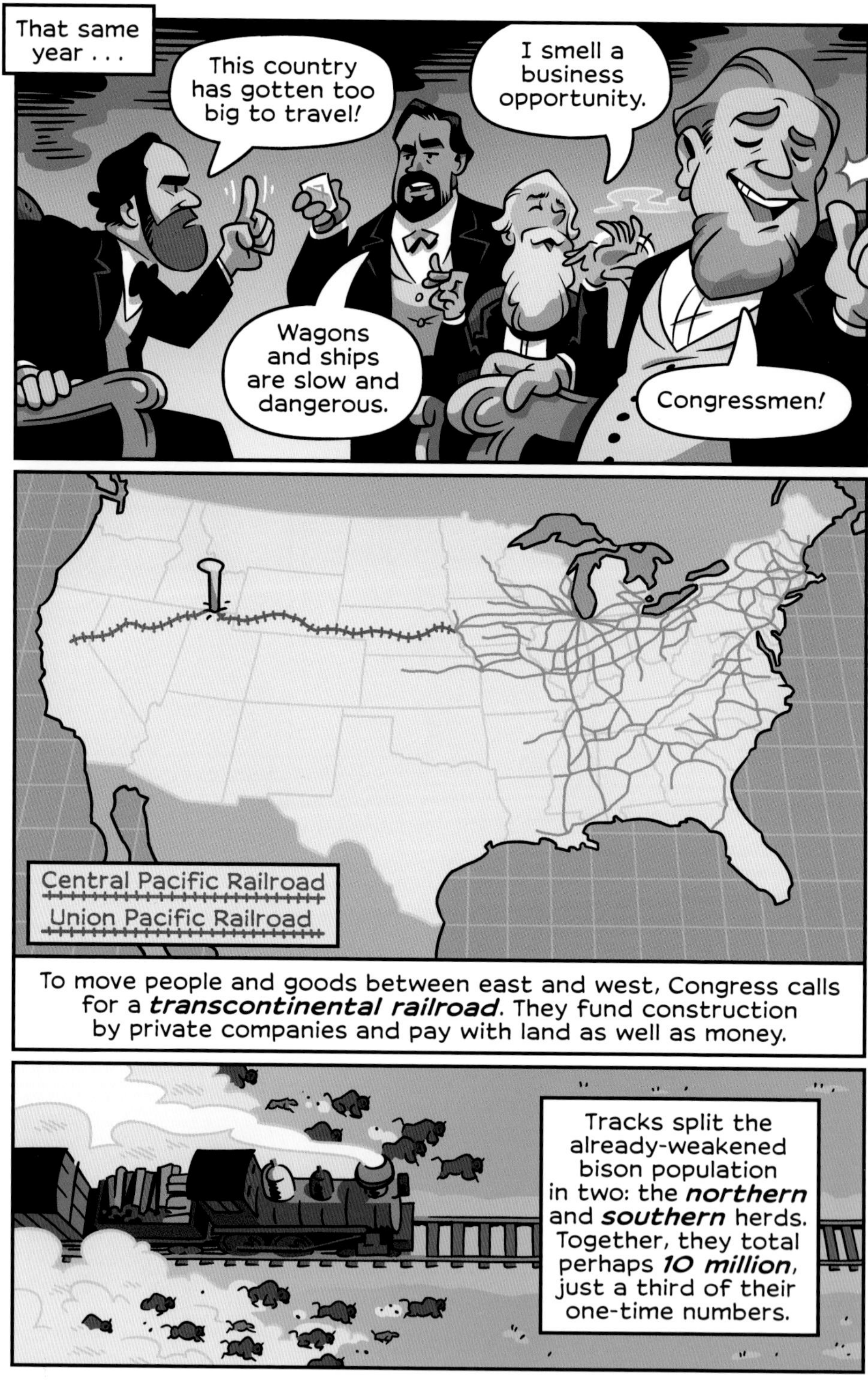
That same year . . .
This country has gotten too big to travel!
I smell a business opportunity.
Wagons and ships are slow and dangerous.
Congressmen!
Central Pacific Railroad
Union Pacific Railroad
To move people and goods between east and west, Congress calls for a ***transcontinental railroad***. They fund construction by private companies and pay with land as well as money.
Tracks split the already-weakened bison population in two: the ***northern*** and ***southern*** herds. Together, they total perhaps ***10 million***, just a third of their one-time numbers.

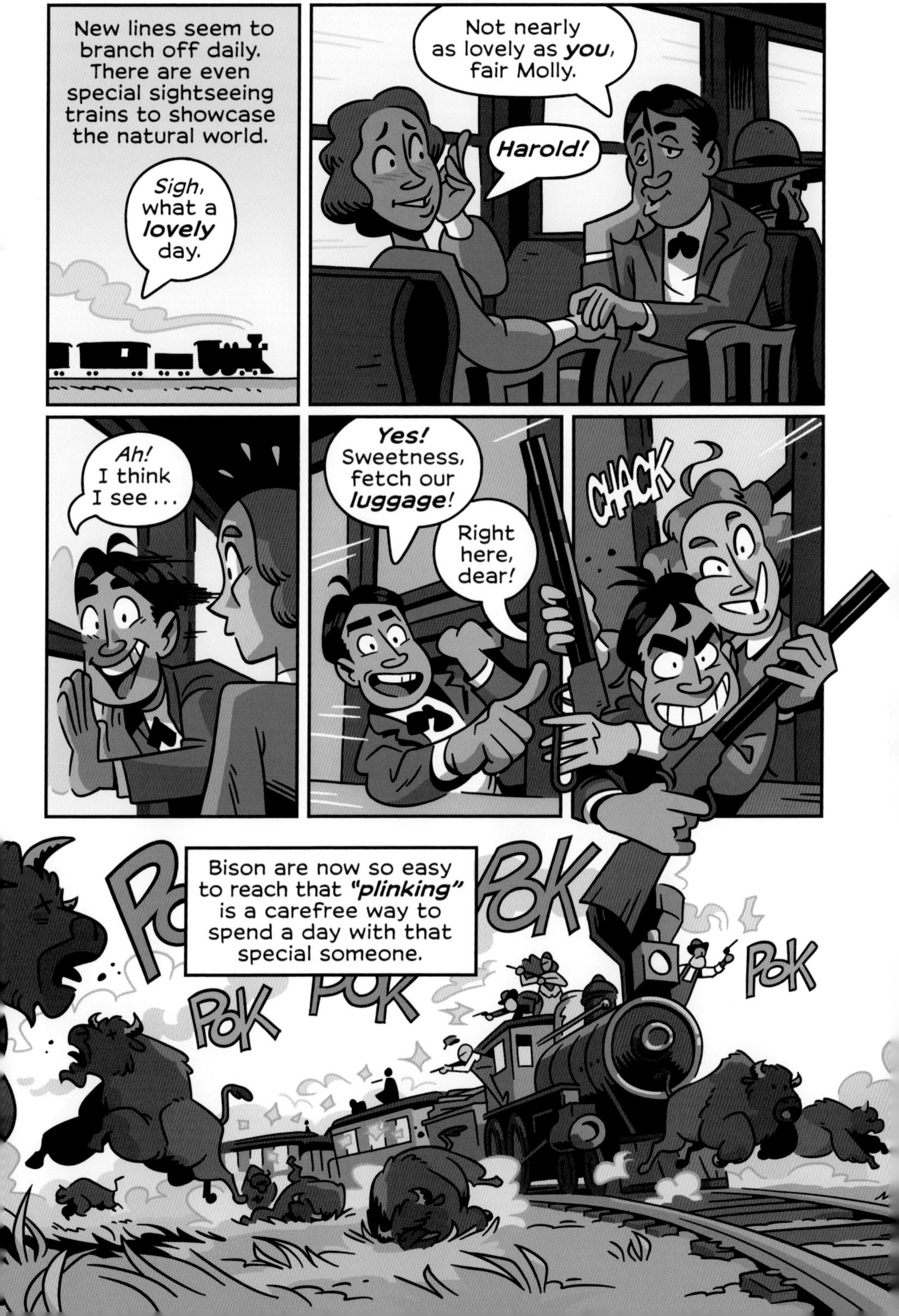
New lines seem to branch off daily. There are even special sightseeing trains to showcase the natural world.
Sigh, what a ***lovely*** day.
Not nearly as lovely as ***you***, fair Molly.
Harold!
Ah! I think I see . . .
Yes! Sweetness, fetch our ***luggage***!
Right here, dear!
CHACK
Bison are now so easy to reach that ***"plinking"*** is a carefree way to spend a day with that special someone.
POK
POK
POK
POK
POK
POK

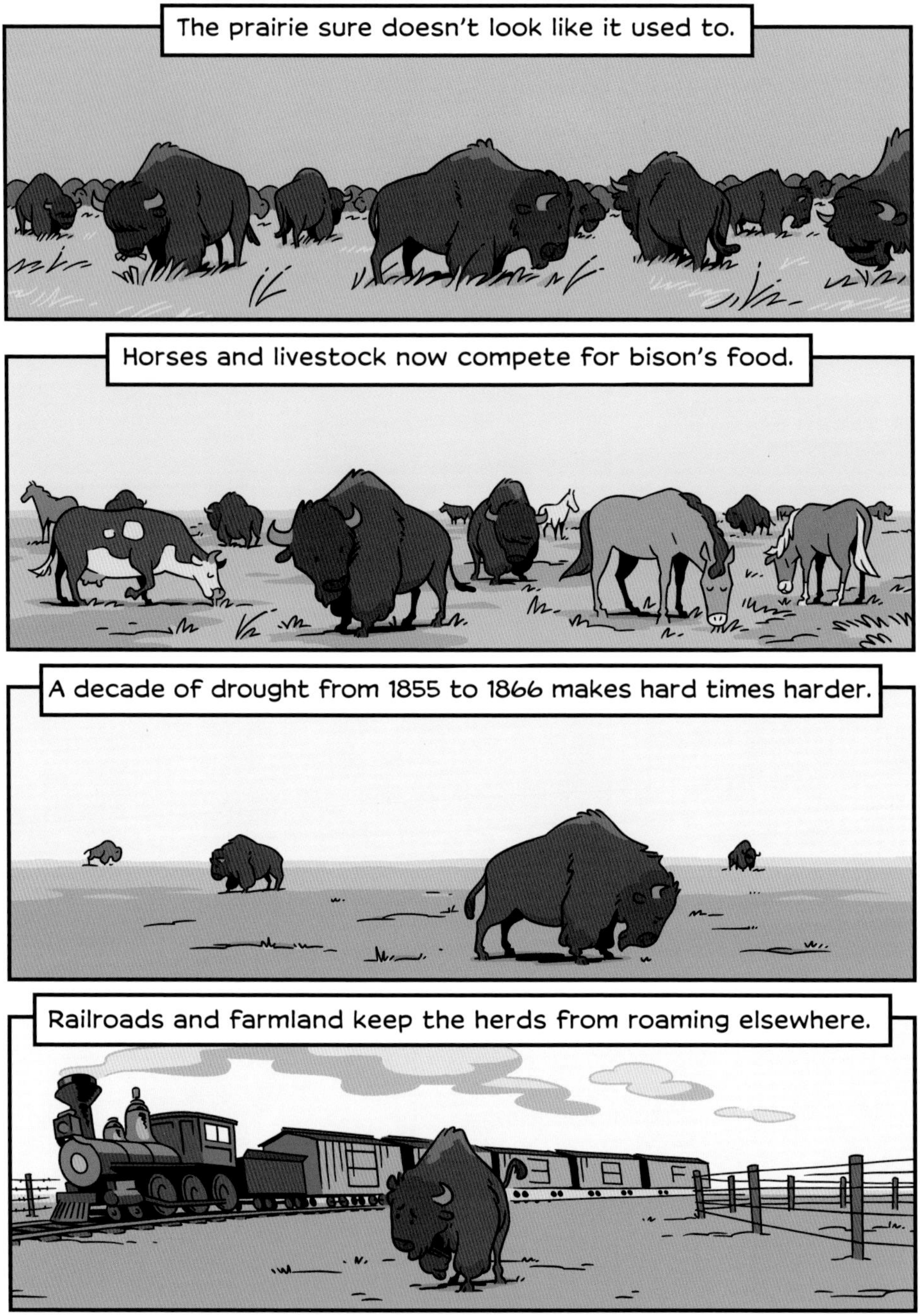
The prairie sure doesn't look like it used to.
Horses and livestock now compete for bison's food.
A decade of drought from 1855 to 1866 makes hard times harder.
Railroads and farmland keep the herds from roaming elsewhere.

Their habitat is under attack,
and that's not even the end of it . . .

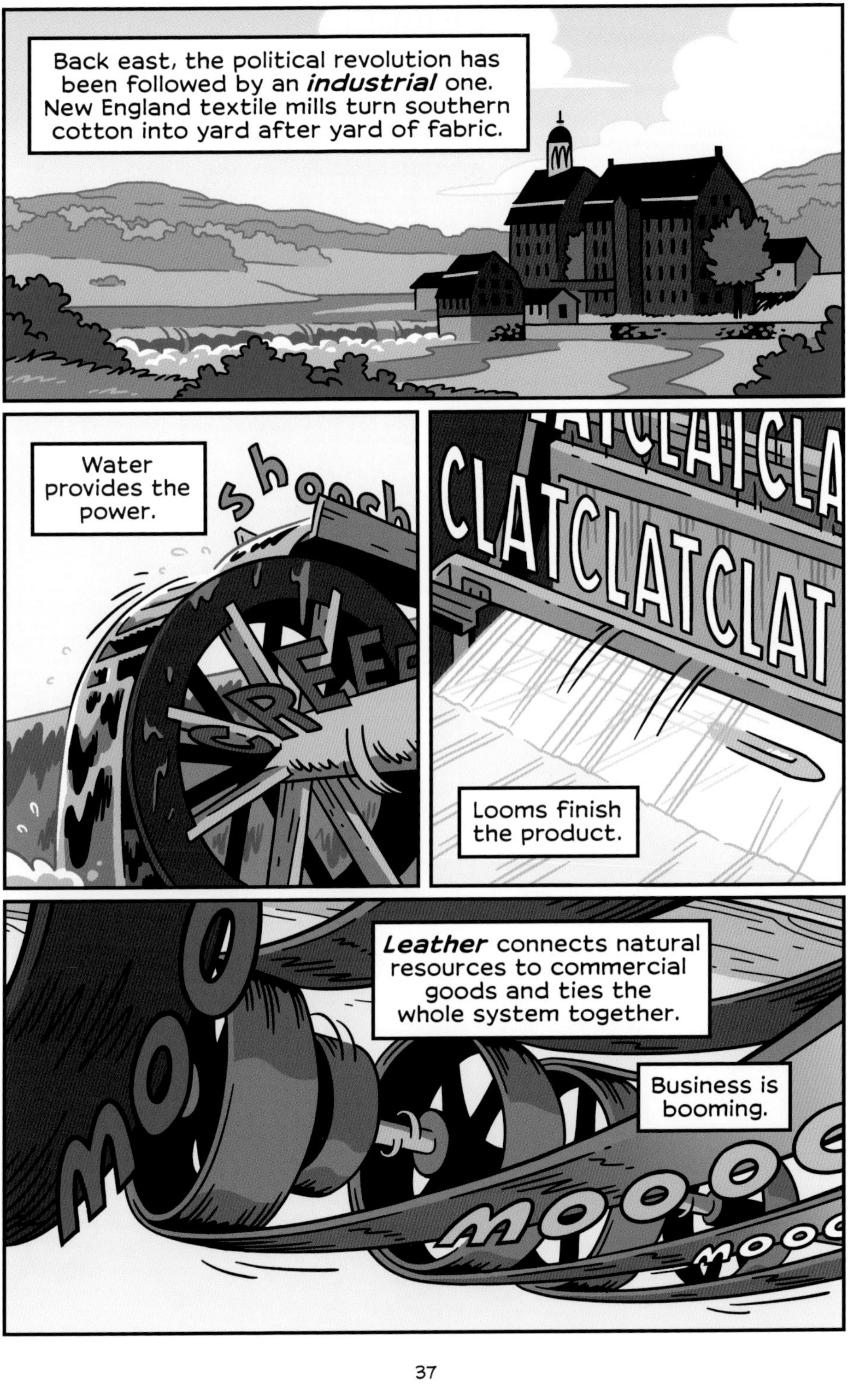
Back east, the political revolution has been followed by an *industrial* one. New England textile mills turn southern cotton into yard after yard of fabric.
Water provides the power.
CLATCLATCLAT
Looms finish the product.
Leather connects natural resources to commercial goods and ties the whole system together.
Business is booming.
MOO

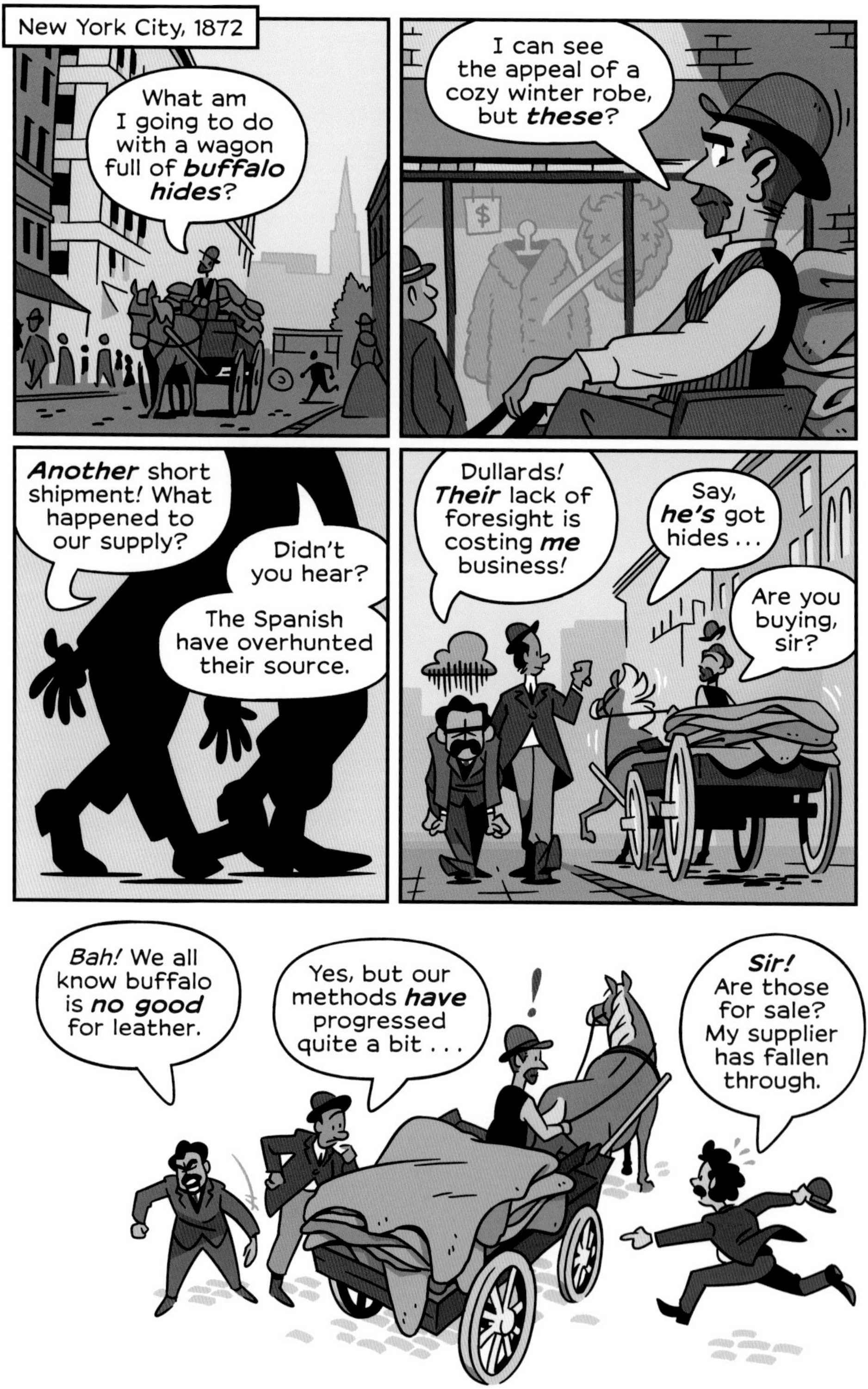
New York City, 1872
What am I going to do with a wagon full of *buffalo hides*?
I can see the appeal of a cozy winter robe, but *these*?
Another short shipment! What happened to our supply?
Didn't you hear?
The Spanish have overhunted their source.
Dullards! *Their* lack of foresight is costing *me* business!
Say, *he's* got hides . . .
Are you buying, sir?
Bah! We all know buffalo is *no good* for leather.
Yes, but our methods *have* progressed quite a bit . . .
!
Sir! Are those for sale? My supplier has fallen through.
$

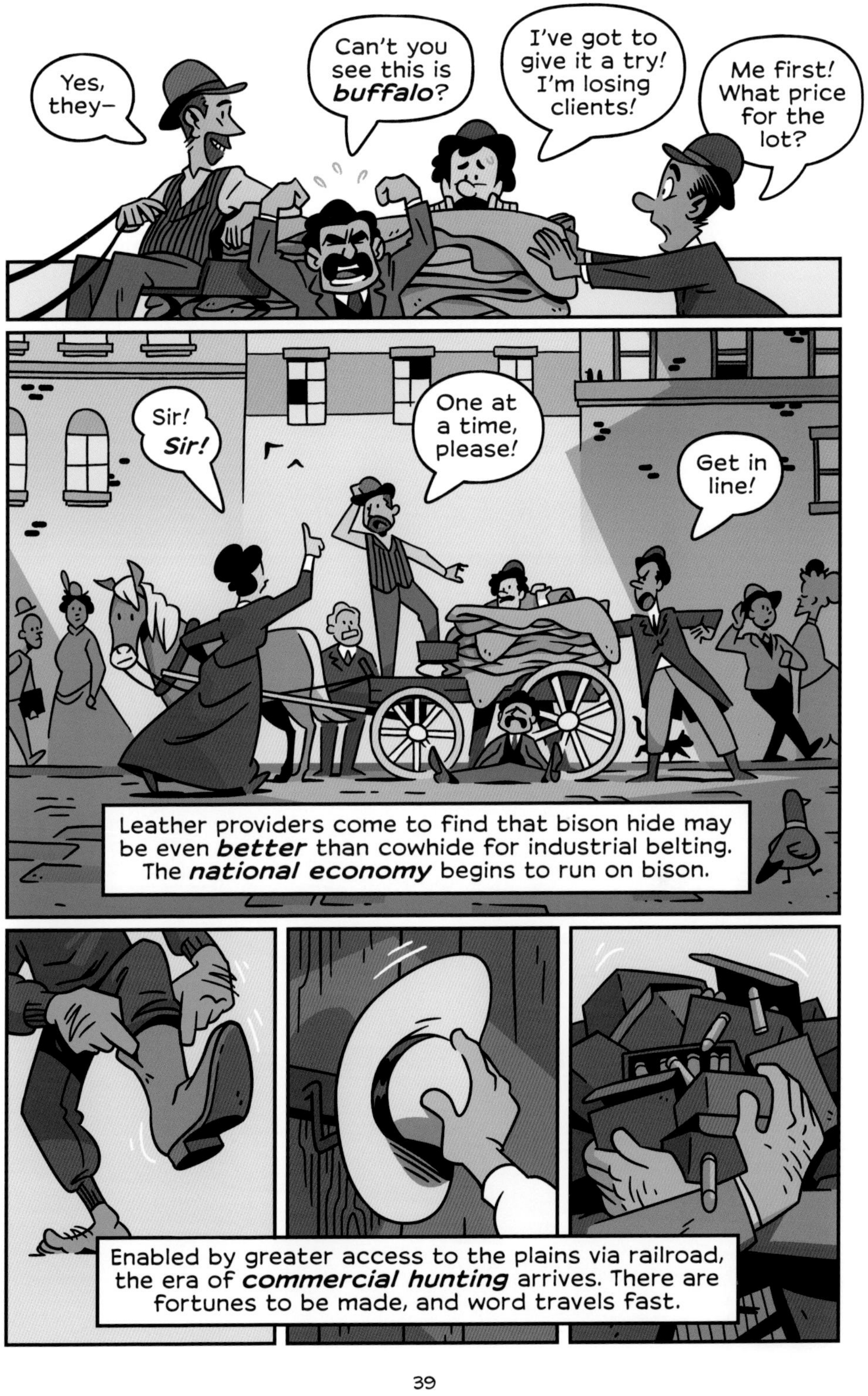
Yes, they–
Can't you see this is **buffalo**?
I've got to give it a try! I'm losing clients!
Me first! What price for the lot?
Sir! **Sir!**
One at a time, please!
Get in line!
Leather providers come to find that bison hide may be even ***better*** than cowhide for industrial belting. The ***national economy*** begins to run on bison.
Enabled by greater access to the plains via railroad, the era of ***commercial hunting*** arrives. There are fortunes to be made, and word travels fast.

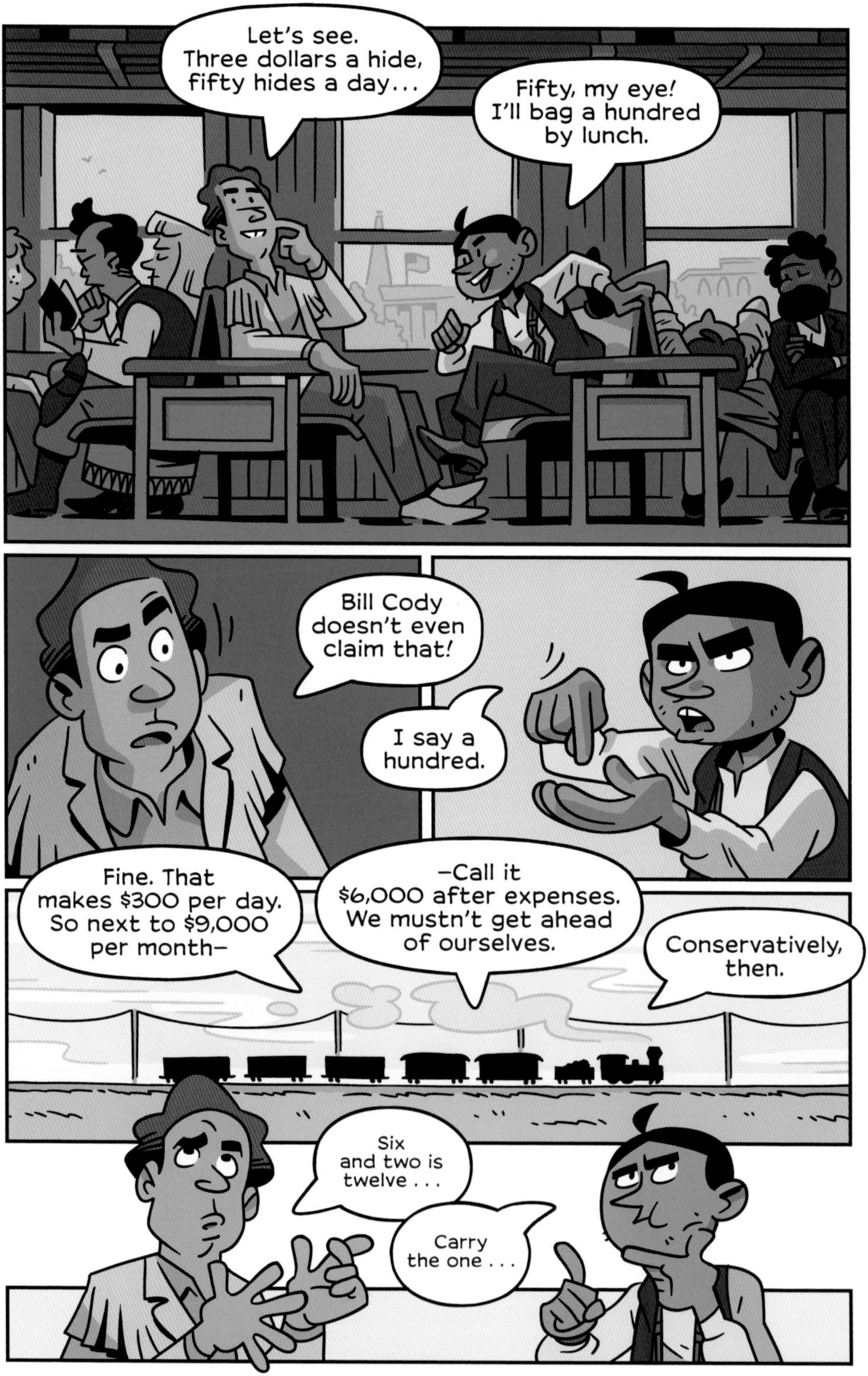

Let's see. Three dollars a hide, fifty hides a day...
Fifty, my eye! I'll bag a hundred by lunch.
Bill Cody doesn't even claim that!
I say a hundred.
Fine. That makes $300 per day. So next to $9,000 per month–
–Call it $6,000 after expenses. We mustn't get ahead of ourselves.
Conservatively, then.
Six and two is twelve . . .
Carry the one . . .

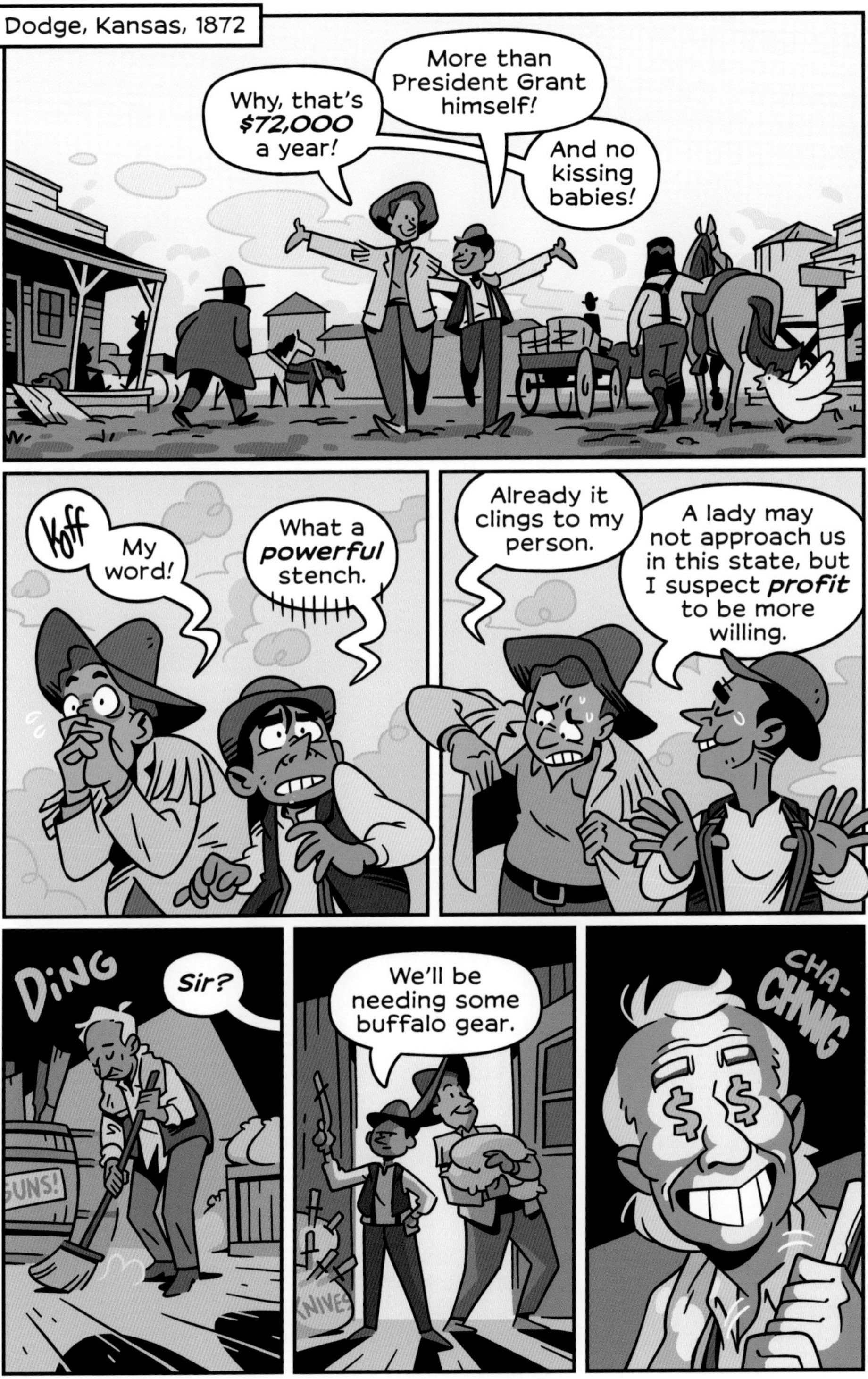
Dodge, Kansas, 1872
Why, that's $72,000 a year!
More than President Grant himself!
And no kissing babies!
Koff
My word!
What a powerful stench.
Already it clings to my person.
A lady may not approach us in this state, but I suspect profit to be more willing.
DING
Sir?
GUNS!
We'll be needing some buffalo gear.
KNIVES
CHA-CHING

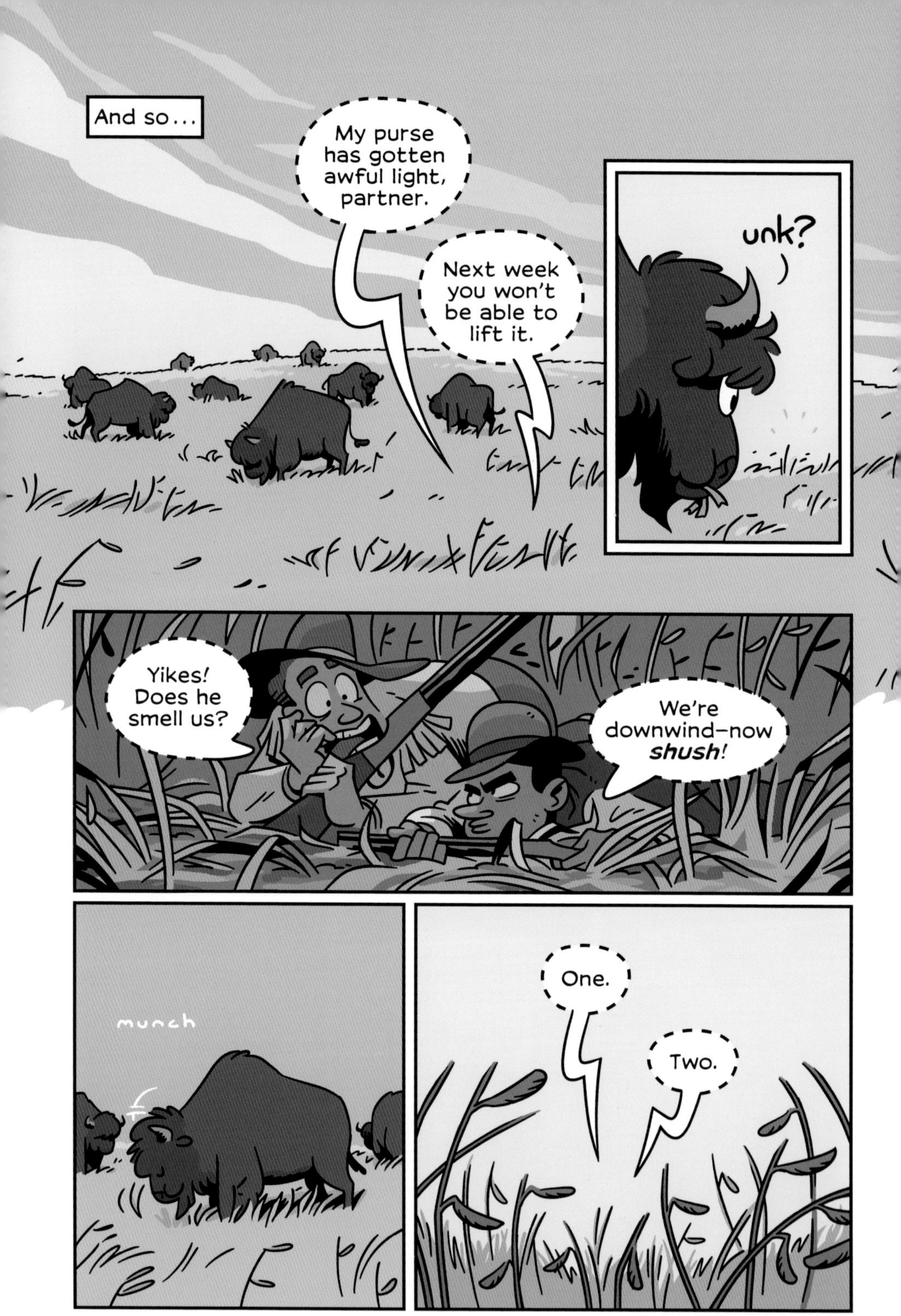
And so...
My purse has gotten awful light, partner.
Next week you won't be able to lift it.
unk?
Yikes! Does he smell us?
We're downwind—now ***shush***!
munch
One.
Two.

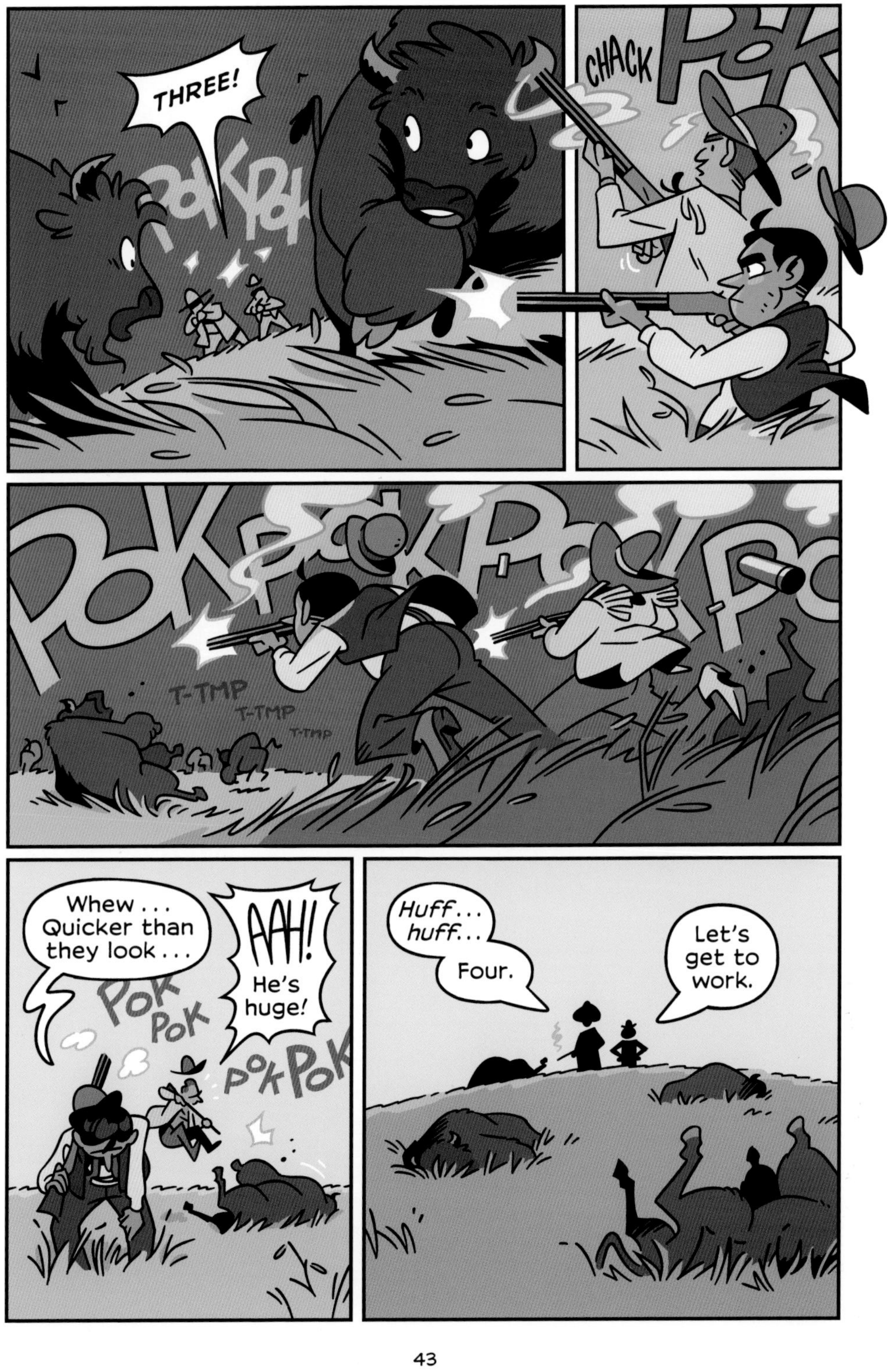
THREE!
POK POK
CHACK
POK
POK
T-TMP
T-TMP
T-TMP
Whew . . . Quicker than they look . . .
AAH! He's huge!
POK
POK
POK POK
Huff . . . huff . . .
Four.
Let's get to work.

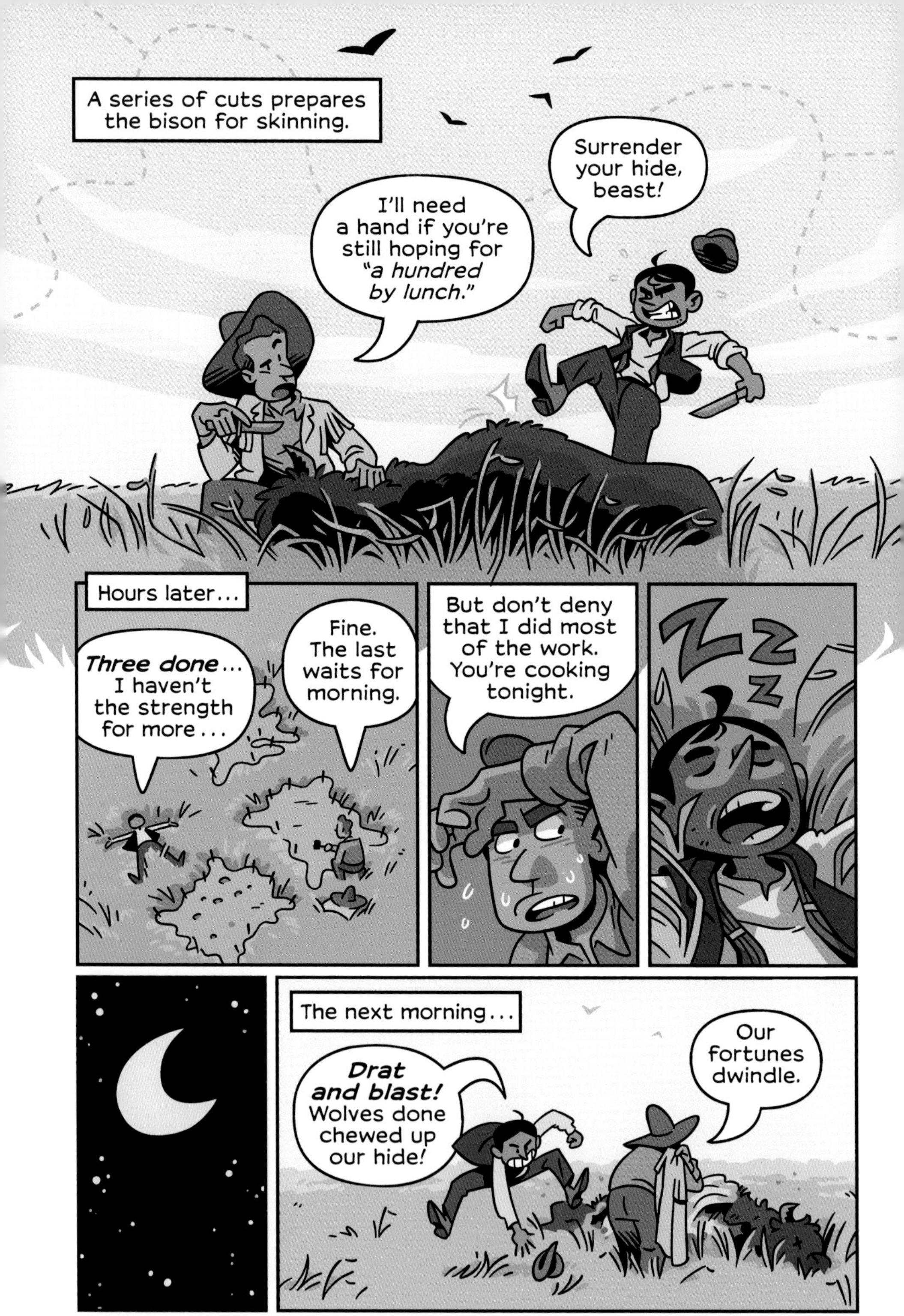
A series of cuts prepares the bison for skinning.
I'll need a hand if you're still hoping for *"a hundred by lunch."*
Surrender your hide, beast!
Hours later...
Three done... I haven't the strength for more...
Fine. The last waits for morning.
But don't deny that I did most of the work. You're cooking tonight.
ZZZ
The next morning...
Drat and blast! Wolves done chewed up our hide!
Our fortunes dwindle.

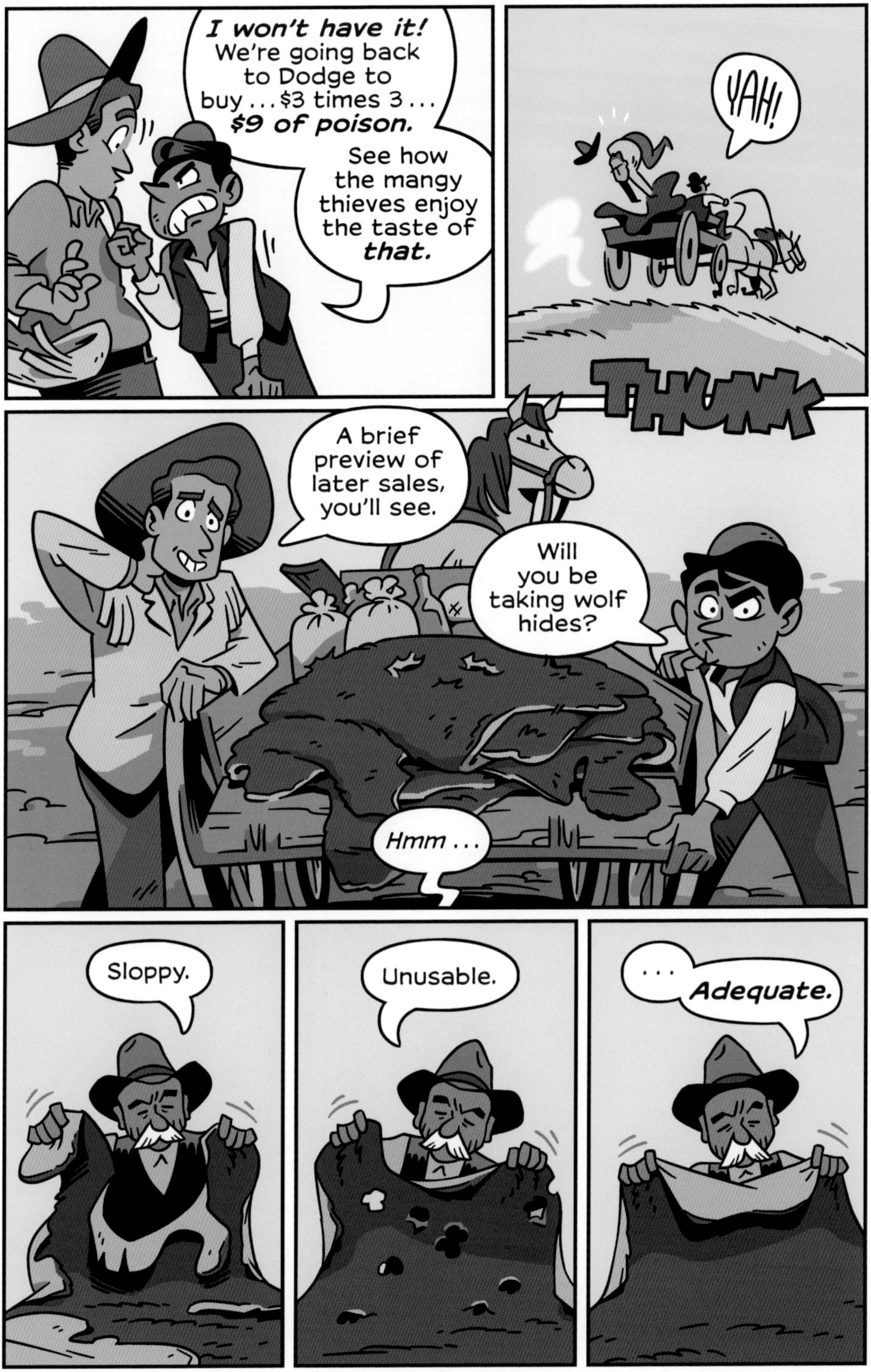
I won't have it! We're going back to Dodge to buy . . . $3 times 3 . . . ***$9 of poison.***
See how the mangy thieves enjoy the taste of ***that.***
YAH!
THUNK
A brief preview of later sales, you'll see.
Will you be taking wolf hides?
Hmm . . .
Sloppy.
Unusable.
. . . ***Adequate.***

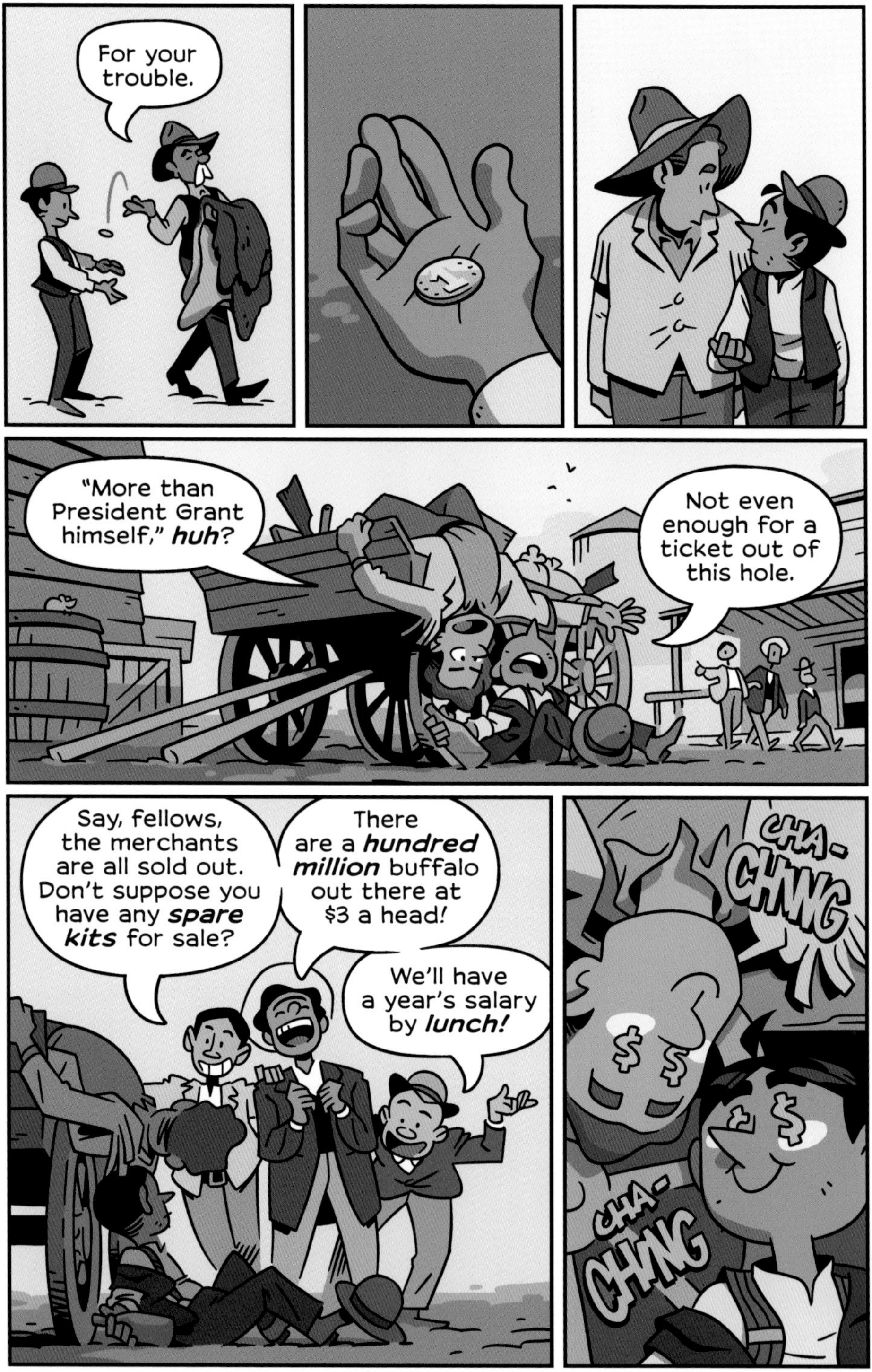
For your trouble.
"More than President Grant himself," *huh*?
Not even enough for a ticket out of this hole.
Say, fellows, the merchants are all sold out. Don't suppose you have any *spare kits* for sale?
There are a *hundred million* buffalo out there at $3 a head!
We'll have a year's salary by *lunch!*
CHA-CHING
CHA-CHING

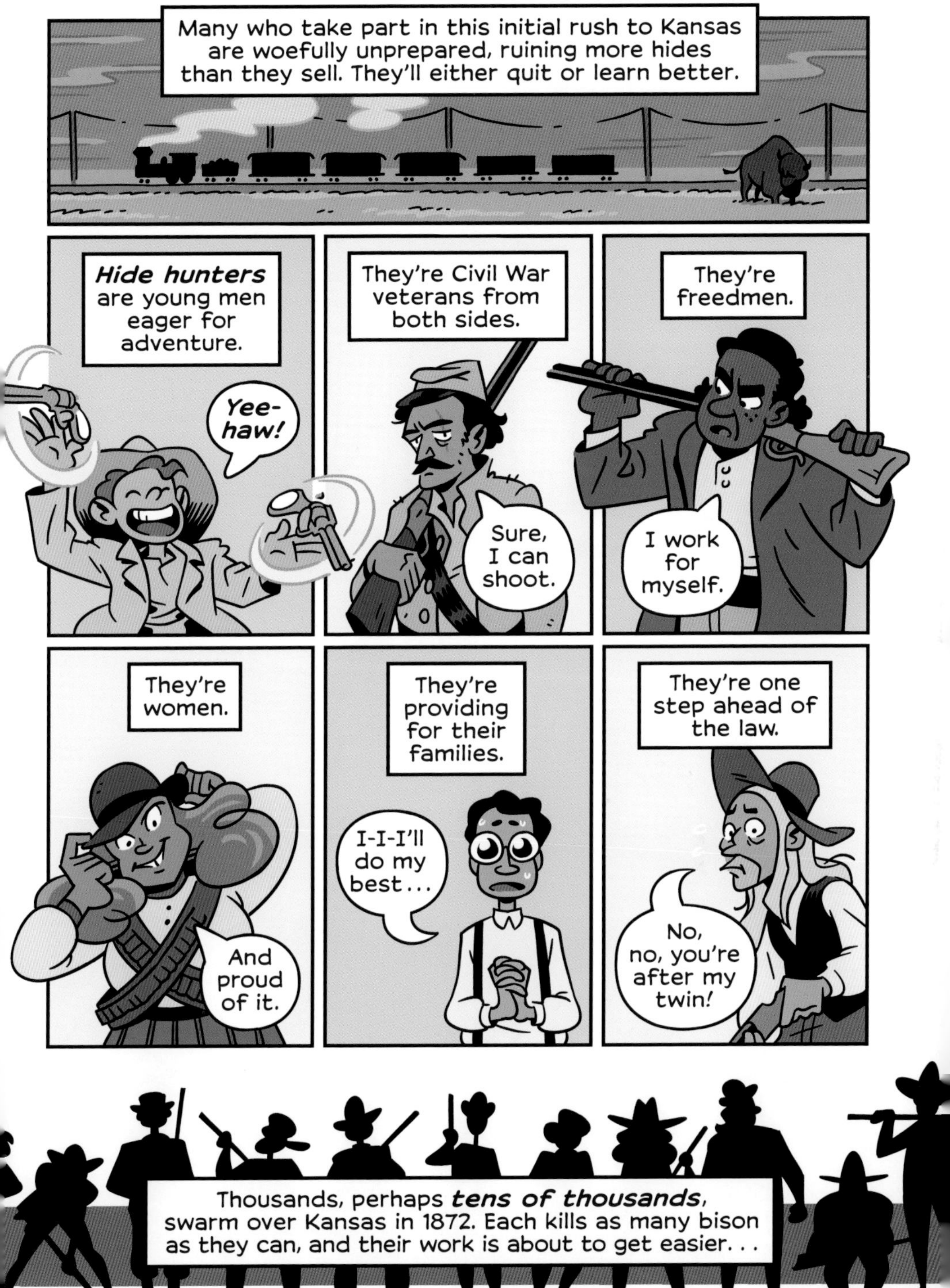

Many who take part in this initial rush to Kansas are woefully unprepared, ruining more hides than they sell. They'll either quit or learn better.
Hide hunters are young men eager for adventure.
Yee-haw!
They're Civil War veterans from both sides.
Sure, I can shoot.
They're freedmen.
I work for myself.
They're women.
And proud of it.
They're providing for their families.
I-I-I'll do my best...
They're one step ahead of the law.
No, no, you're after my twin!
Thousands, perhaps ***tens of thousands***, swarm over Kansas in 1872. Each kills as many bison as they can, and their work is about to get easier. . .

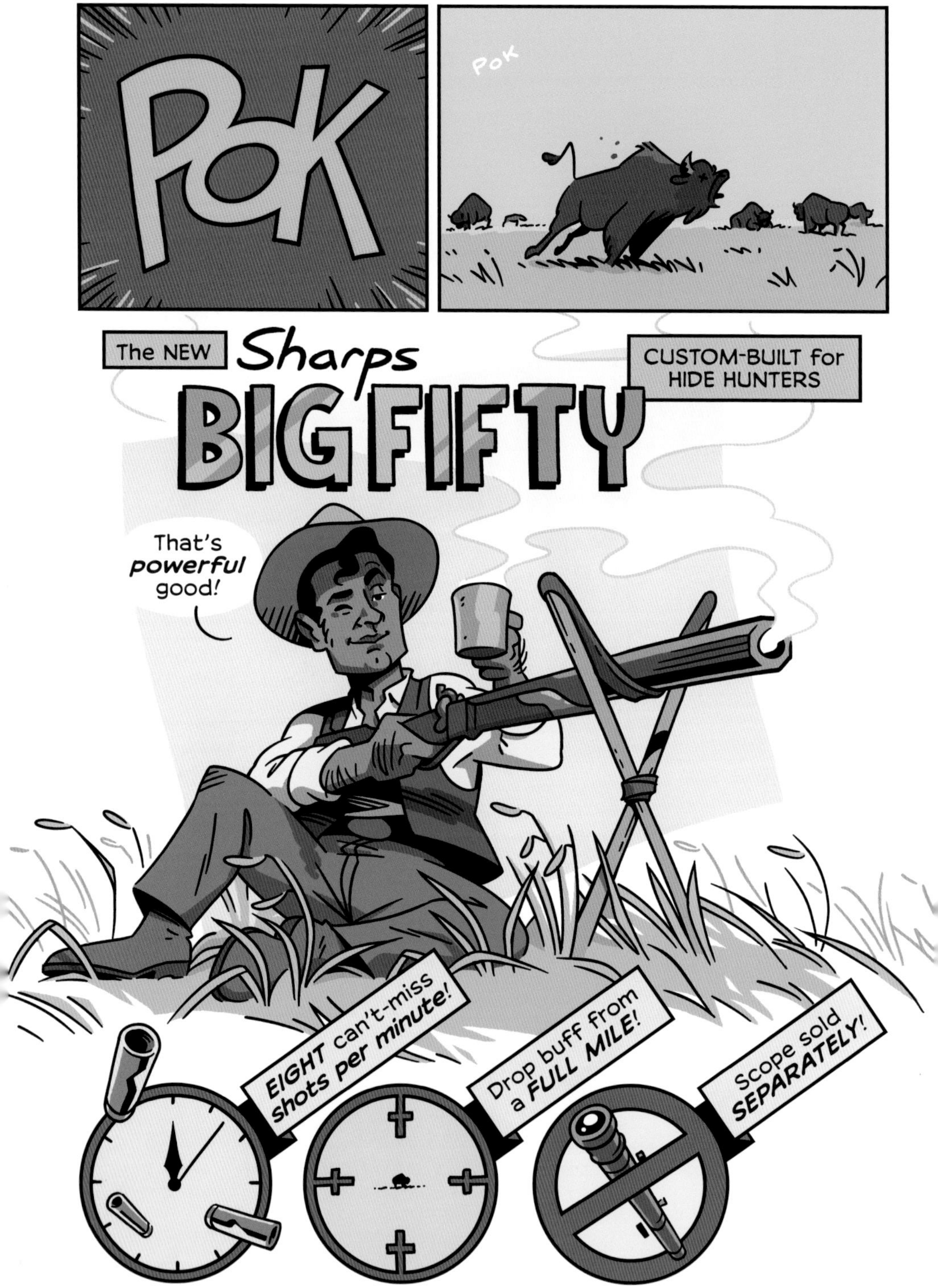

POK
POK
The NEW Sharps
BIG FIFTY
CUSTOM-BUILT for HIDE HUNTERS
That's *powerful* good!
EIGHT can't-miss *shots per minute!*
Drop buff from a *FULL MILE!*
Scope sold *SEPARATELY!*

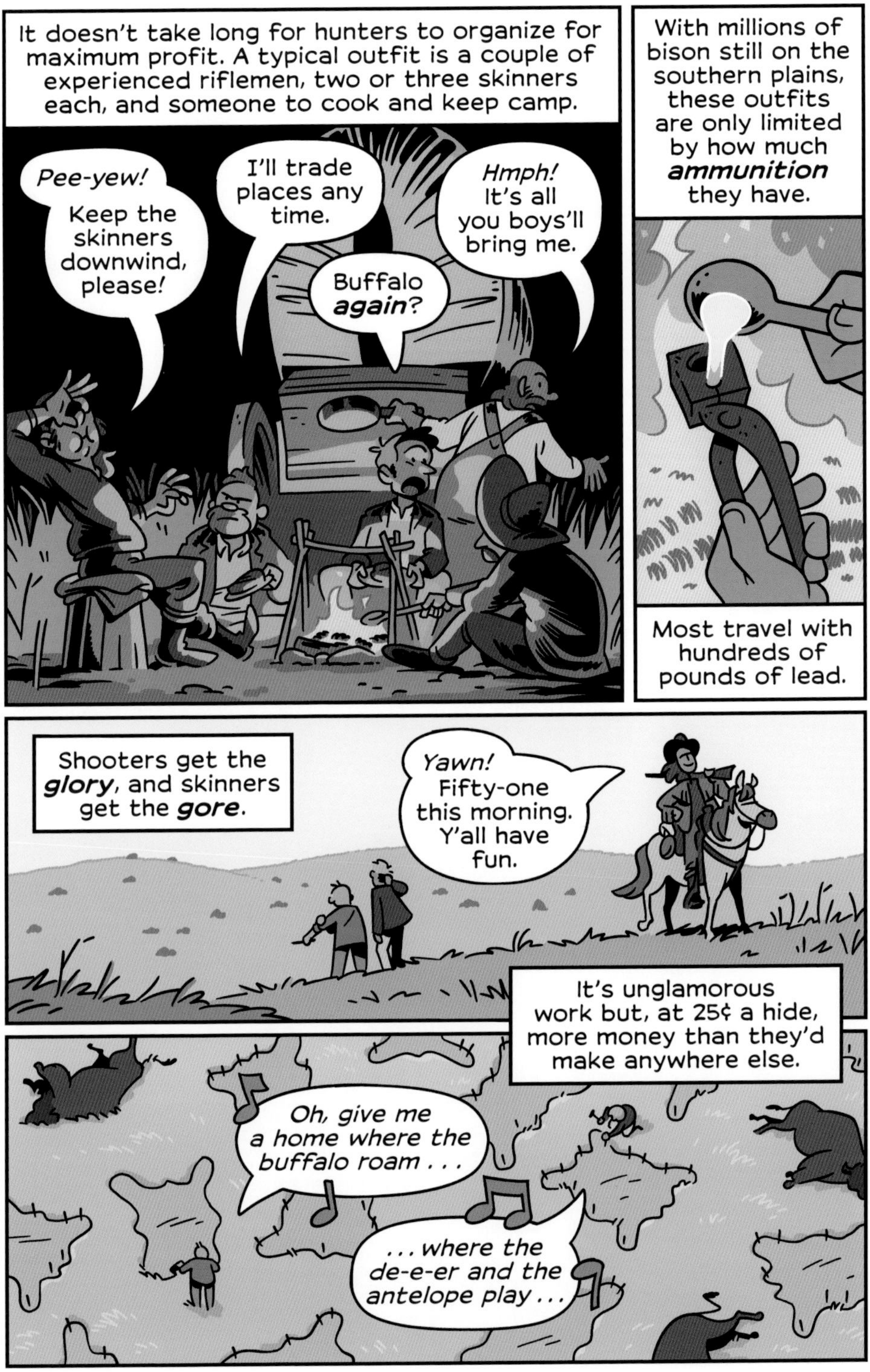
It doesn't take long for hunters to organize for maximum profit. A typical outfit is a couple of experienced riflemen, two or three skinners each, and someone to cook and keep camp.
Pee-yew! Keep the skinners downwind, *please!*
I'll trade places any time.
Buffalo ***again***?
Hmph! It's all you boys'll bring me.
With millions of bison still on the southern plains, these outfits are only limited by how much ***ammunition*** they have.
Most travel with hundreds of pounds of lead.
Shooters get the ***glory***, and skinners get the ***gore***.
Yawn! Fifty-one this morning. Y'all have fun.
It's unglamorous work but, at 25¢ a hide, more money than they'd make anywhere else.
Oh, give me a home where the buffalo roam . . .
. . . where the de-e-er and the antelope play . . .

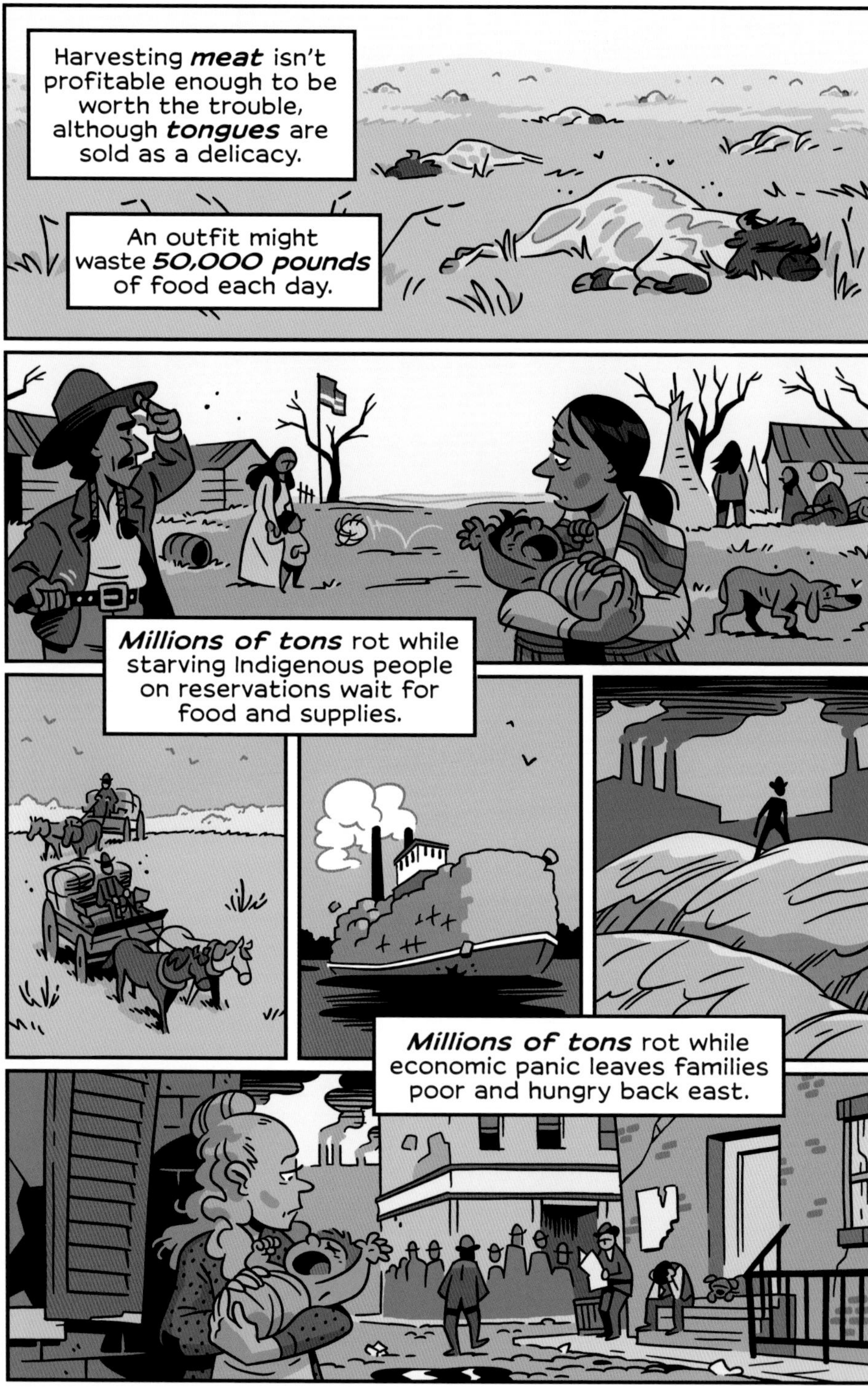
Harvesting ***meat*** isn't profitable enough to be worth the trouble, although ***tongues*** are sold as a delicacy.
An outfit might waste ***50,000 pounds*** of food each day.
Millions of tons rot while starving Indigenous people on reservations wait for food and supplies.
Millions of tons rot while economic panic leaves families poor and hungry back east.

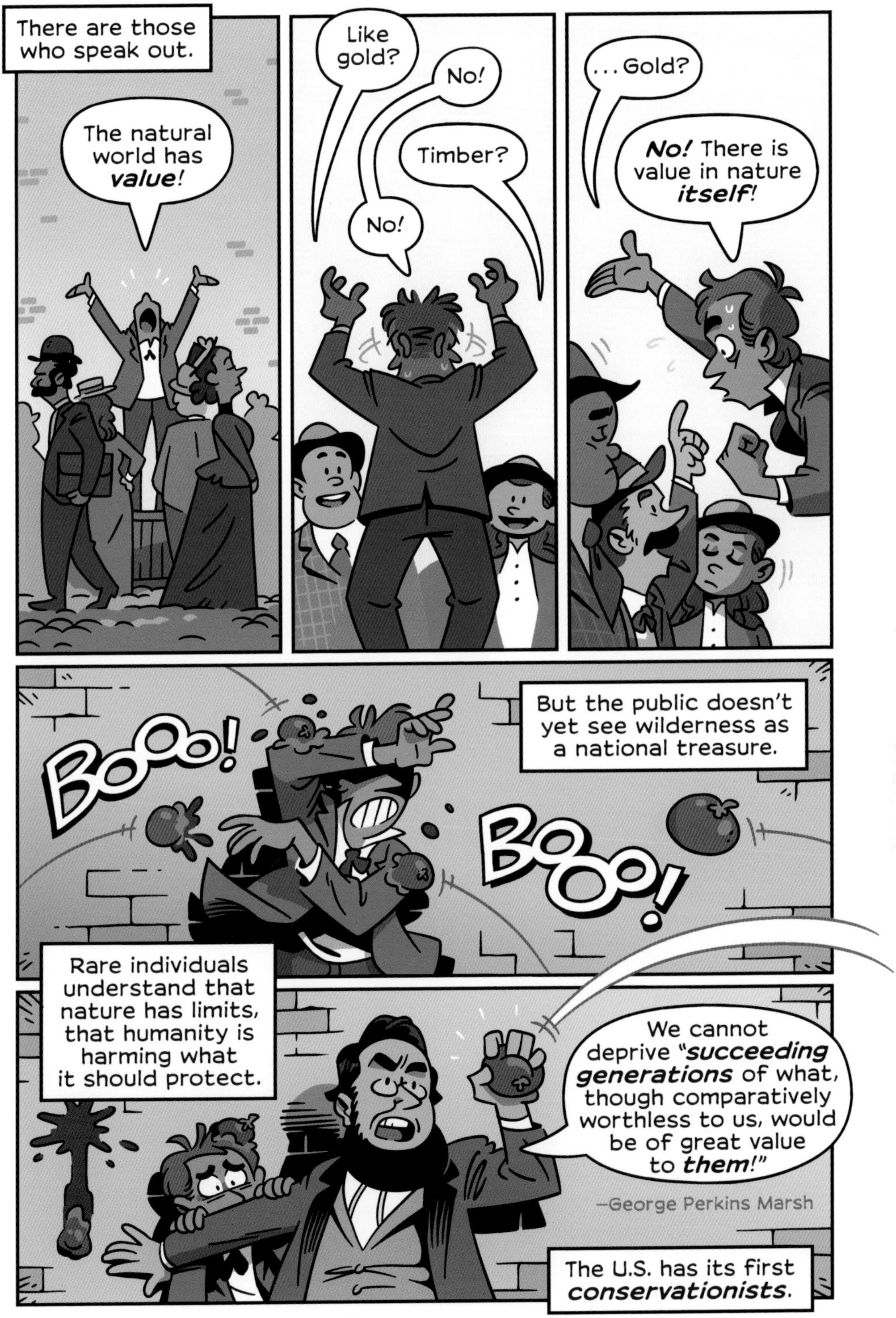

There are those who speak out.
The natural world has *value*!
Like gold?
No!
Timber?
No!
...Gold?
No! There is value in nature *itself*!
BOOoo!
But the public doesn't yet see wilderness as a national treasure.
BOOoo!
Rare individuals understand that nature has limits, that humanity is harming what it should protect.
We cannot deprive "*succeeding generations* of what, though comparatively worthless to us, would be of great value to *them*!"
—George Perkins Marsh
The U.S. has its first *conservationists*.

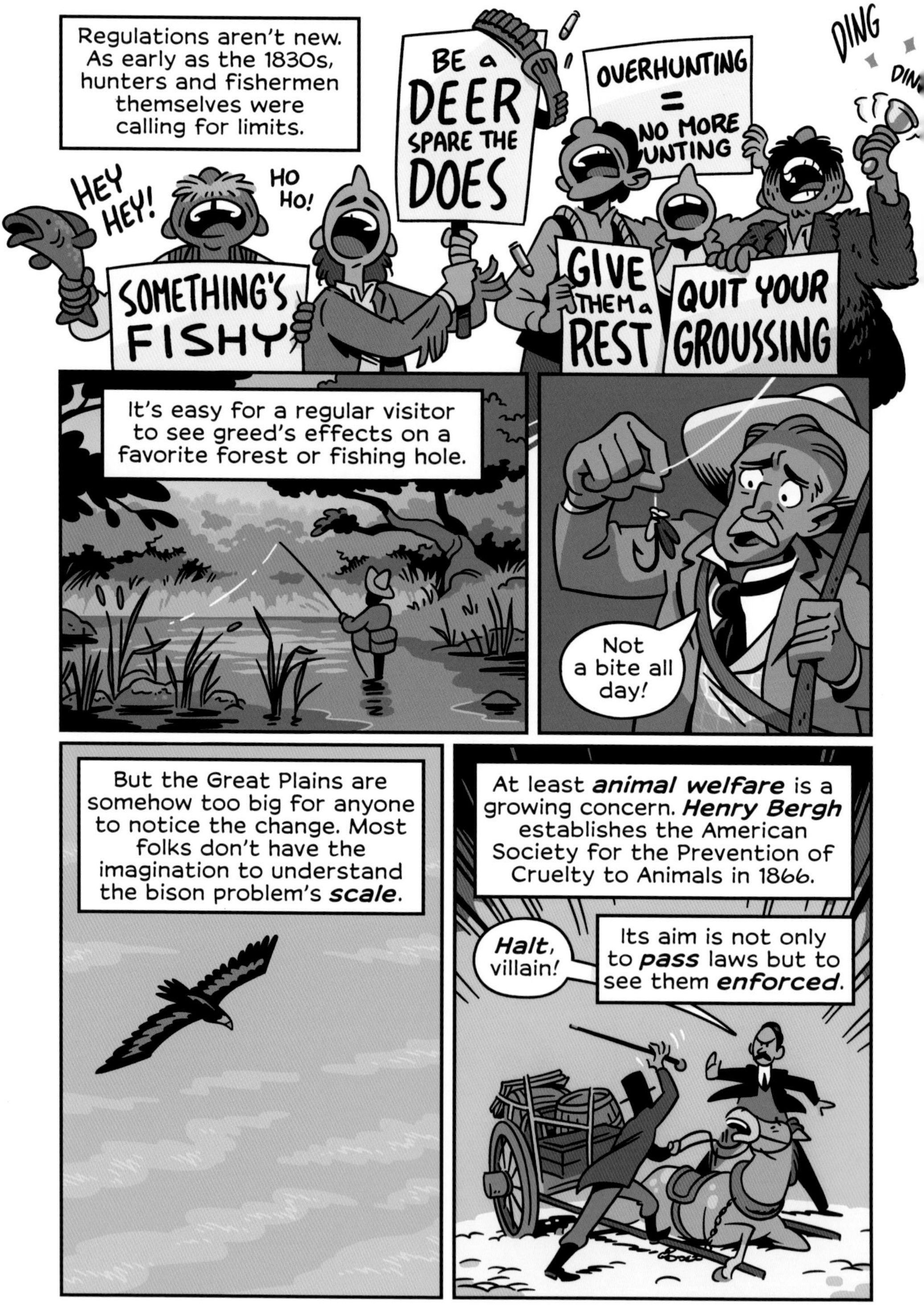

Regulations aren't new. As early as the 1830s, hunters and fishermen themselves were calling for limits.
HEY HEY!
HO HO!
SOMETHING'S FISHY
BE a DEER SPARE THE DOES
OVERHUNTING = NO MORE UNTING
DING
DIN
GIVE THEM a REST
QUIT YOUR GROUSSING
It's easy for a regular visitor to see greed's effects on a favorite forest or fishing hole.
Not a bite all day!
But the Great Plains are somehow too big for anyone to notice the change. Most folks don't have the imagination to understand the bison problem's *scale*.
At least ***animal welfare*** is a growing concern. ***Henry Bergh*** establishes the American Society for the Prevention of Cruelty to Animals in 1866.
Halt, villain!
Its aim is not only to ***pass*** laws but to see them ***enforced***.

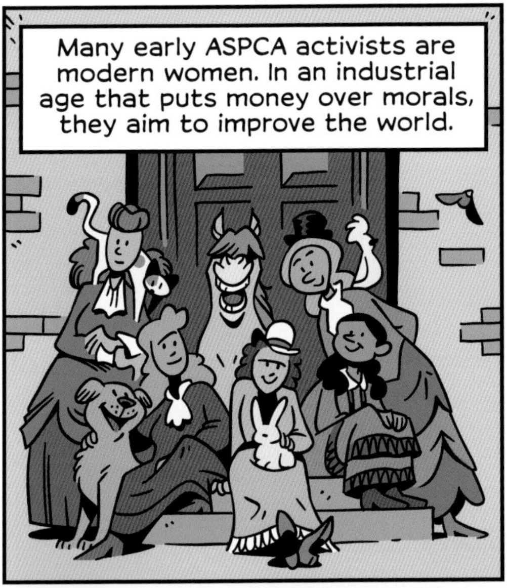
Many early ASPCA activists are modern women. In an industrial age that puts money over morals, they aim to improve the world.

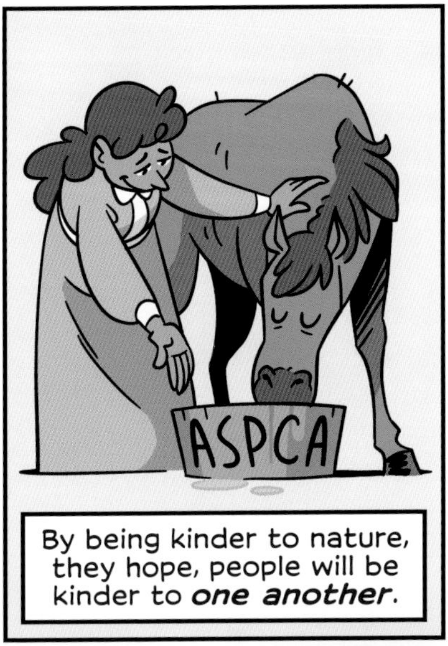
ASPCA
By being kinder to nature, they hope, people will be kinder to ***one another***.

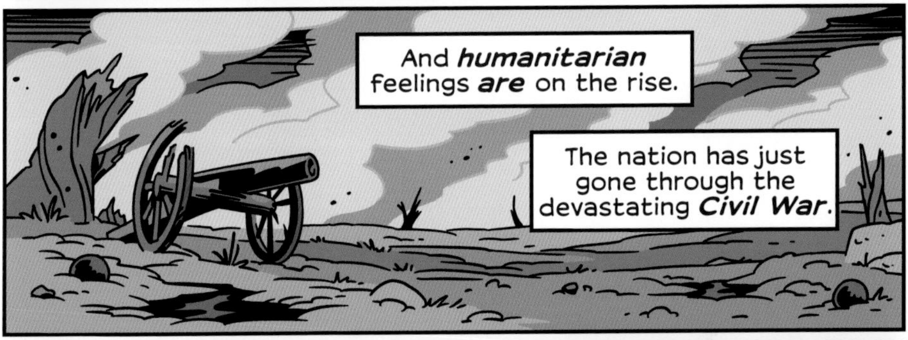
And ***humanitarian*** feelings ***are*** on the rise.
The nation has just gone through the devastating ***Civil War***.

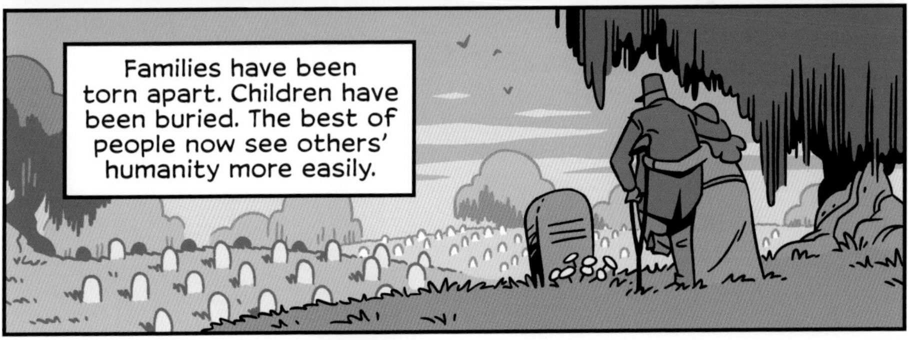
Families have been torn apart. Children have been buried. The best of people now see others' humanity more easily.

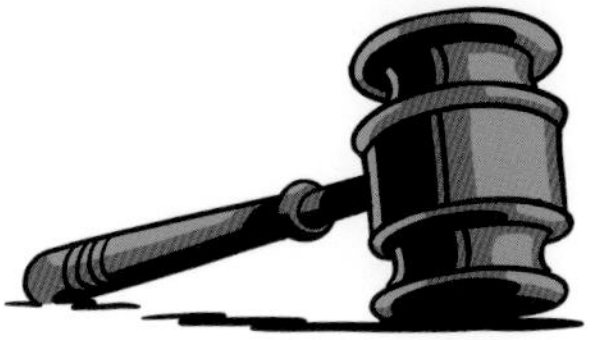

Unfortunately, the common tie among conservationists, animal welfare activists, and humanitarians is a historic ***lack of political power***.

That has to change, and ***fast***.

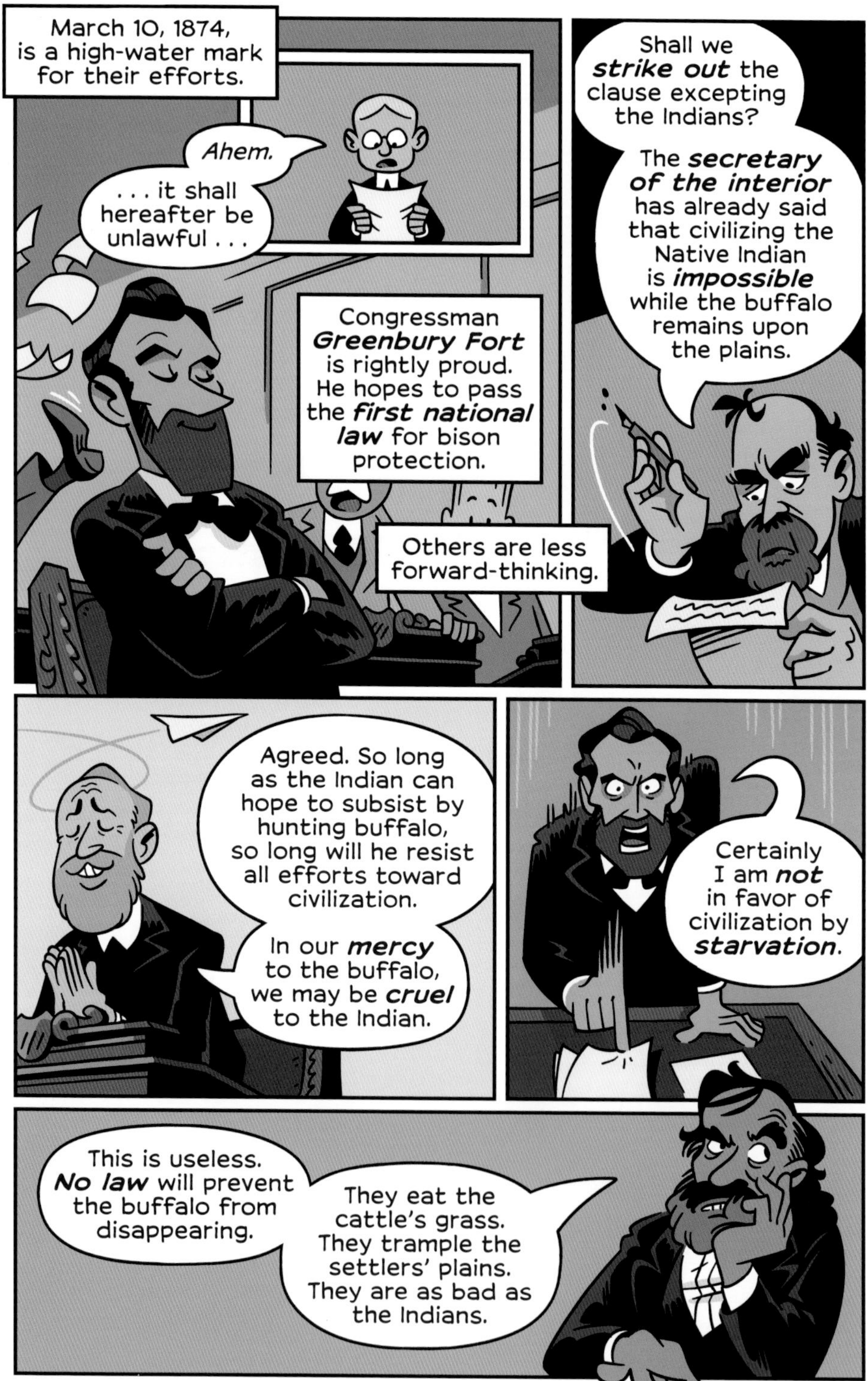
March 10, 1874, is a high-water mark for their efforts.
Ahem.
. . . it shall hereafter be unlawful . . .
Congressman ***Greenbury Fort*** is rightly proud. He hopes to pass the ***first national law*** for bison protection.
Others are less forward-thinking.
Shall we ***strike out*** the clause excepting the Indians?
The ***secretary of the interior*** has already said that civilizing the Native Indian is ***impossible*** while the buffalo remains upon the plains.
Agreed. So long as the Indian can hope to subsist by hunting buffalo, so long will he resist all efforts toward civilization.
In our ***mercy*** to the buffalo, we may be ***cruel*** to the Indian.
Certainly I am ***not*** in favor of civilization by ***starvation***.
This is useless. ***No law*** will prevent the buffalo from disappearing.
They eat the cattle's grass. They trample the settlers' plains. They are as bad as the Indians.

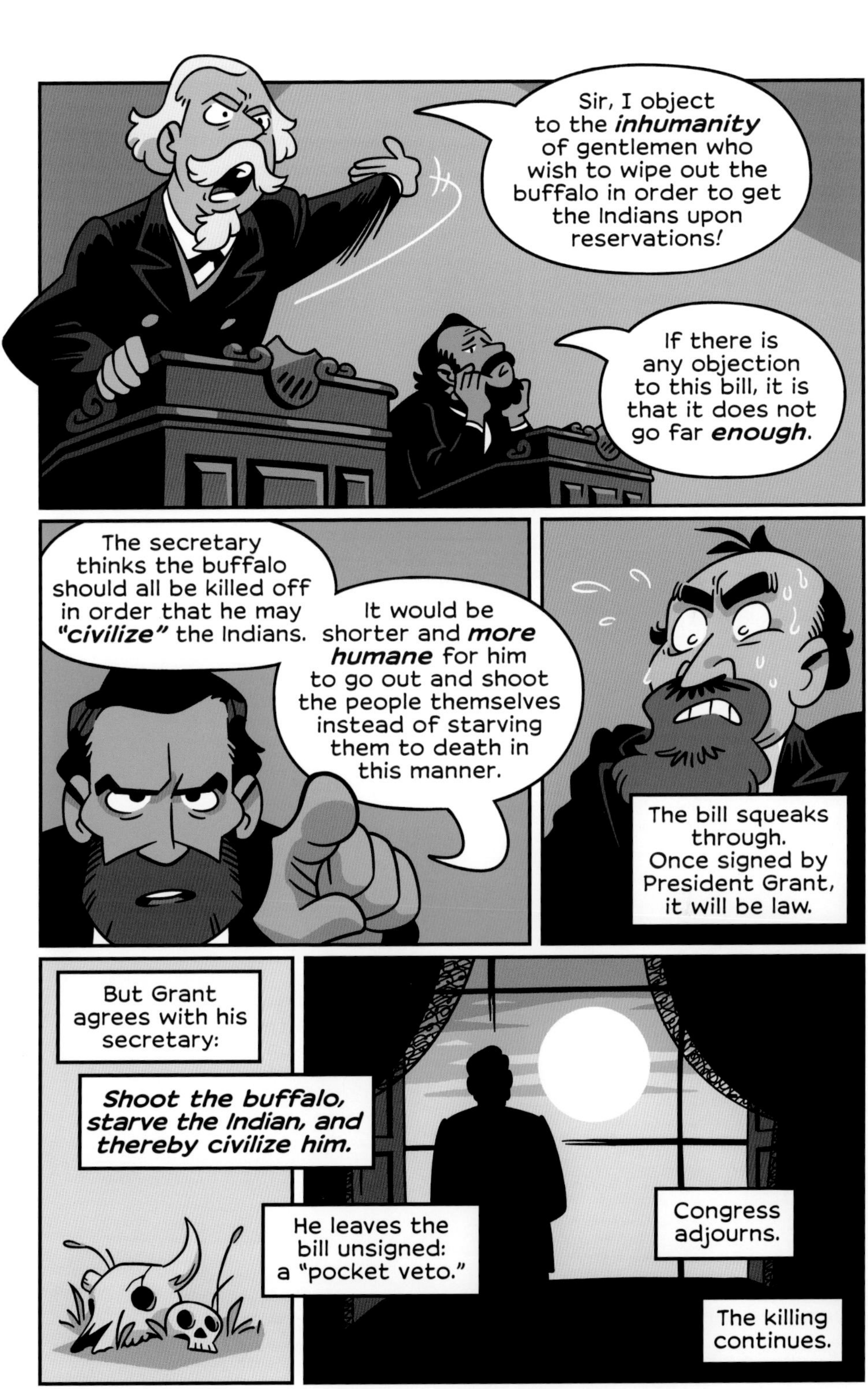
Sir, I object to the ***inhumanity*** of gentlemen who wish to wipe out the buffalo in order to get the Indians upon reservations!
If there is any objection to this bill, it is that it does not go far ***enough***.
The secretary thinks the buffalo should all be killed off in order that he may ***"civilize"*** the Indians.
It would be shorter and ***more humane*** for him to go out and shoot the people themselves instead of starving them to death in this manner.
The bill squeaks through. Once signed by President Grant, it will be law.
But Grant agrees with his secretary:
Shoot the buffalo, starve the Indian, and thereby civilize him.
He leaves the bill unsigned: a "pocket veto."
Congress adjourns.
The killing continues.

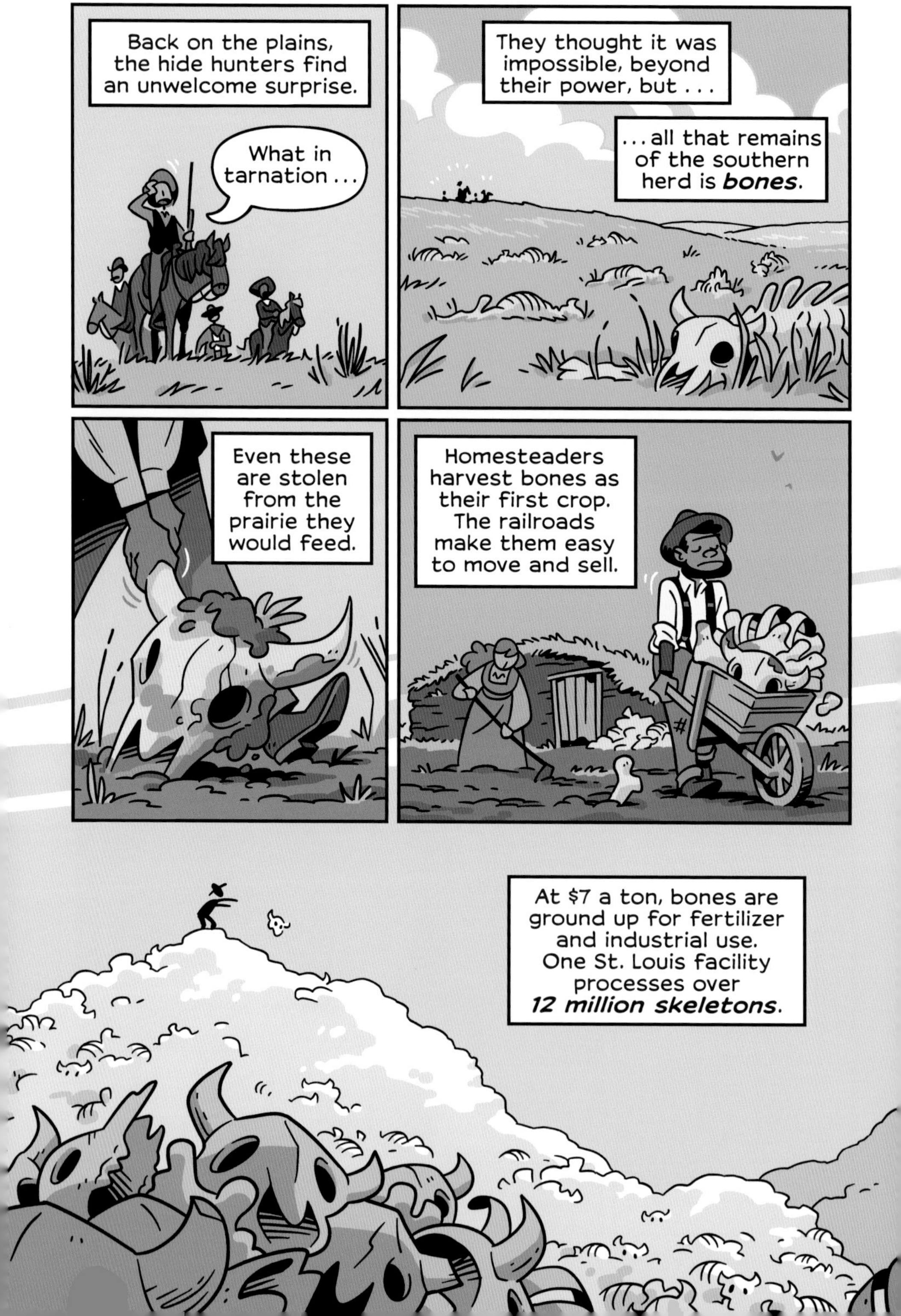
Back on the plains, the hide hunters find an unwelcome surprise.
What in tarnation . . .
They thought it was impossible, beyond their power, but . . .
. . . all that remains of the southern herd is ***bones***.
Even these are stolen from the prairie they would feed.
Homesteaders harvest bones as their first crop. The railroads make them easy to move and sell.
At $7 a ton, bones are ground up for fertilizer and industrial use. One St. Louis facility processes over ***12 million skeletons***.

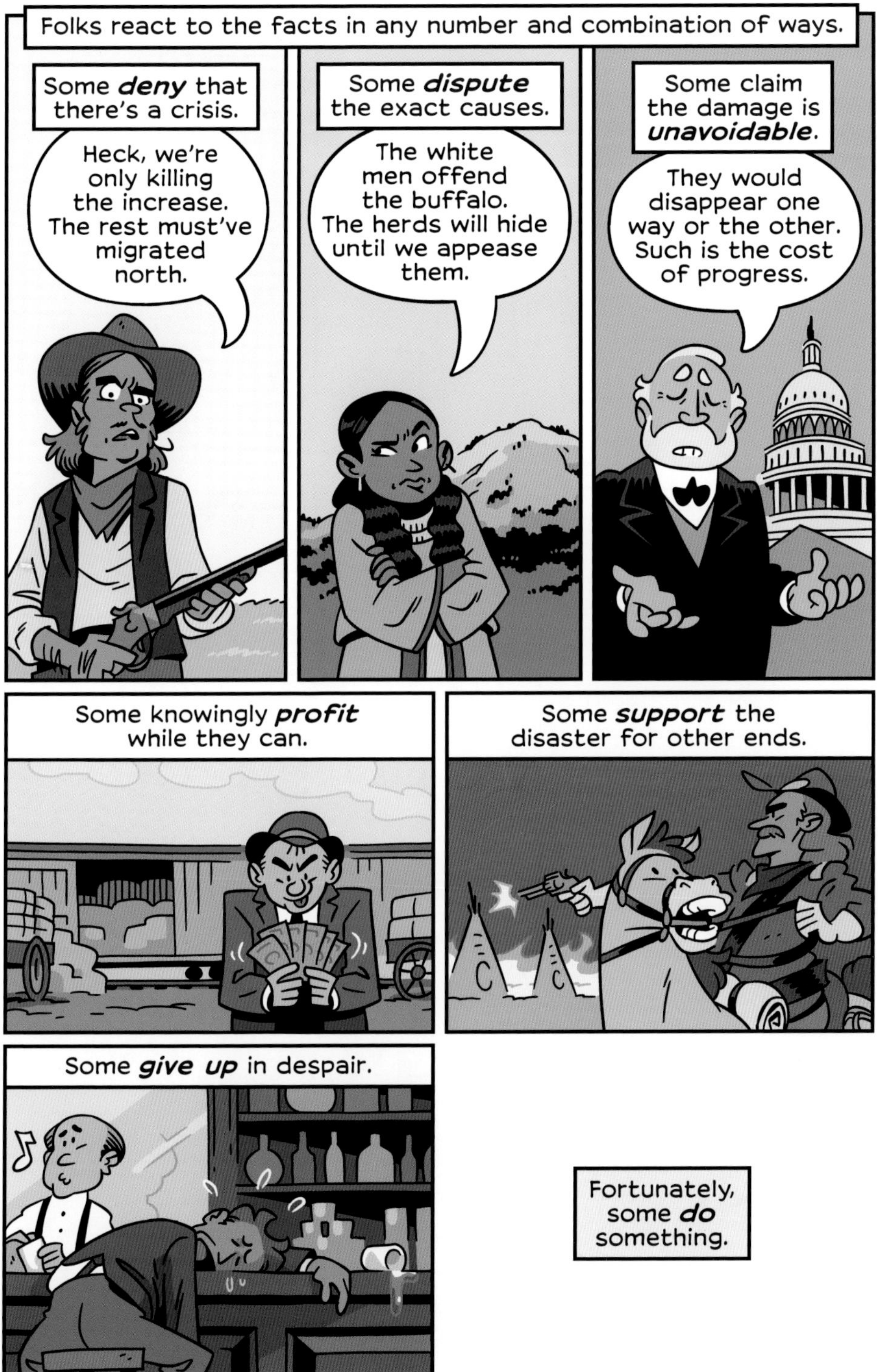

Folks react to the facts in any number and combination of ways.
Some *deny* that there's a crisis.
Heck, we're only killing the increase. The rest must've migrated north.
Some *dispute* the exact causes.
The white men offend the buffalo. The herds will hide until we appease them.
Some claim the damage is *unavoidable*.
They would disappear one way or the other. Such is the cost of progress.
Some knowingly *profit* while they can.
Some *support* the disaster for other ends.
Some *give up* in despair.
Fortunately, some *do* something.

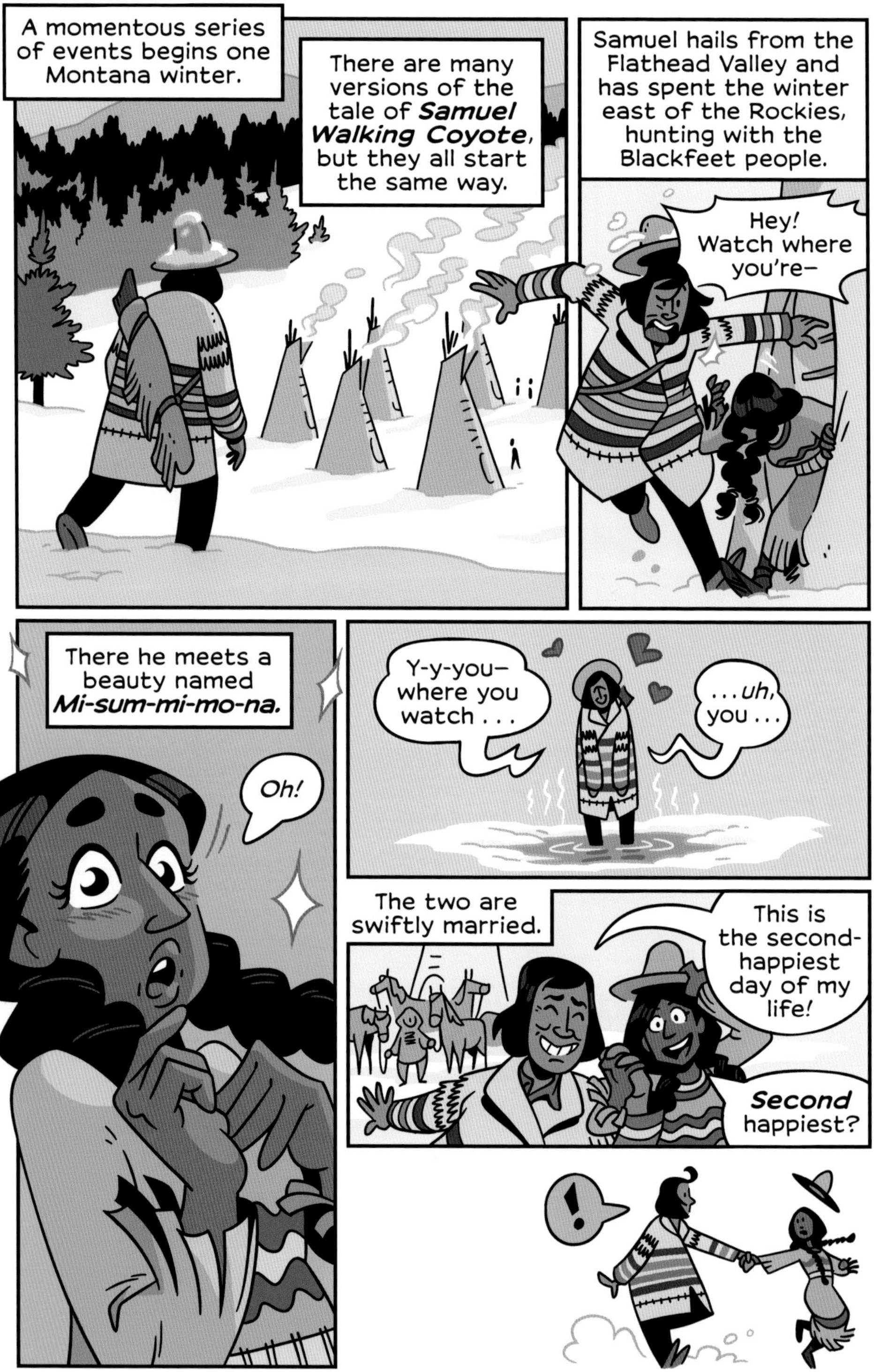
A momentous series of events begins one Montana winter.
There are many versions of the tale of **Samuel Walking Coyote**, but they all start the same way.
Samuel hails from the Flathead Valley and has spent the winter east of the Rockies, hunting with the Blackfeet people.
Hey! Watch where you're–
There he meets a beauty named ***Mi-sum-mi-mo-na.***
Oh!
Y-y-you– where you watch . . .
. . . uh, you . . .
The two are swiftly married.
This is the second-happiest day of my life!
Second happiest?
!

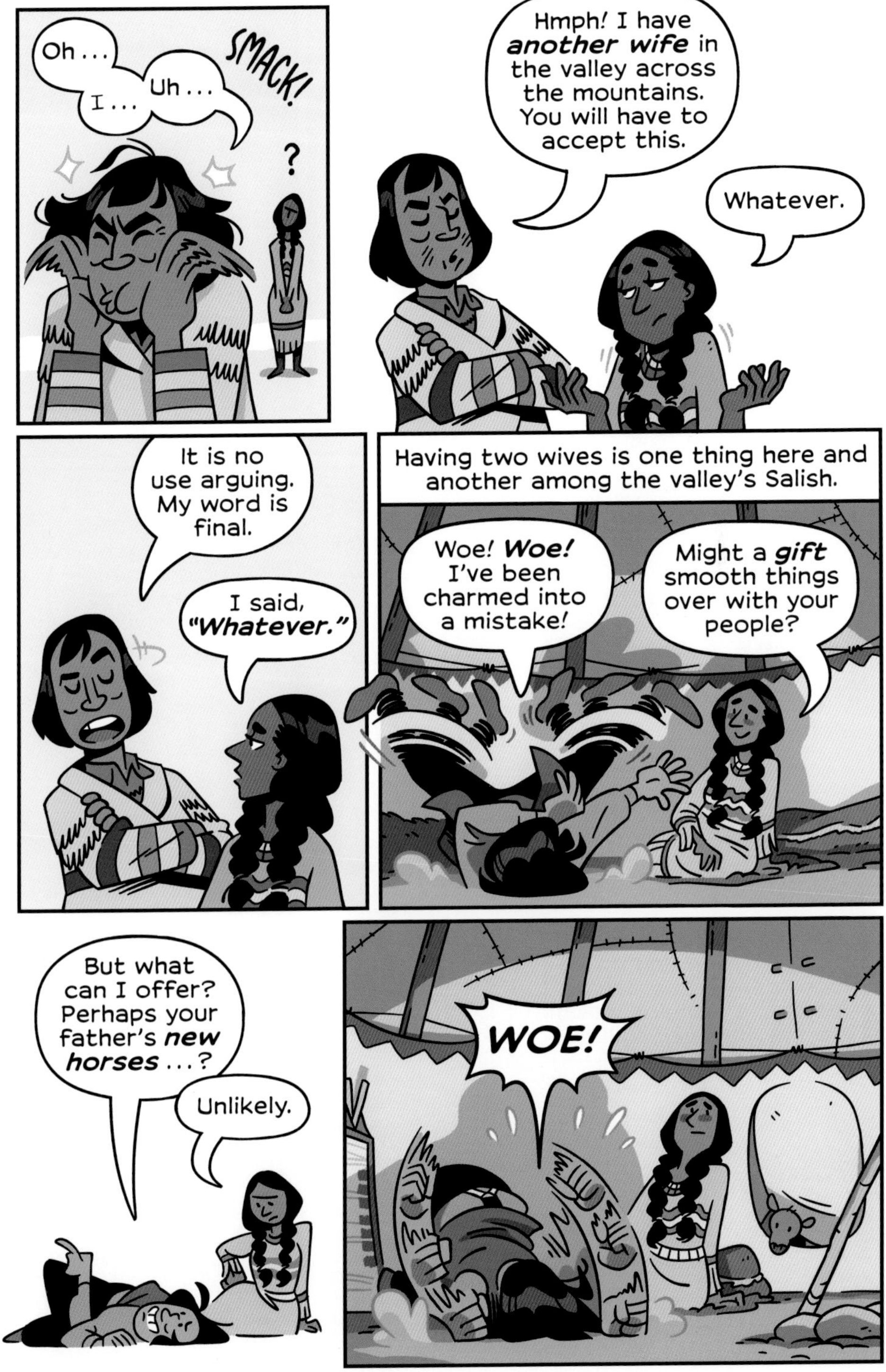
Oh . . .
I . . .
Uh . . .
SMACK!
?
Hmph! I have **another wife** in the valley across the mountains. You will have to accept this.
Whatever.
It is no use arguing. My word is final.
I said, **"Whatever."**
Having two wives is one thing here and another among the valley's Salish.
Woe! **Woe!** I've been charmed into a mistake!
Might a **gift** smooth things over with your people?
But what can I offer? Perhaps your father's **new horses** . . . ?
Unlikely.
WOE!

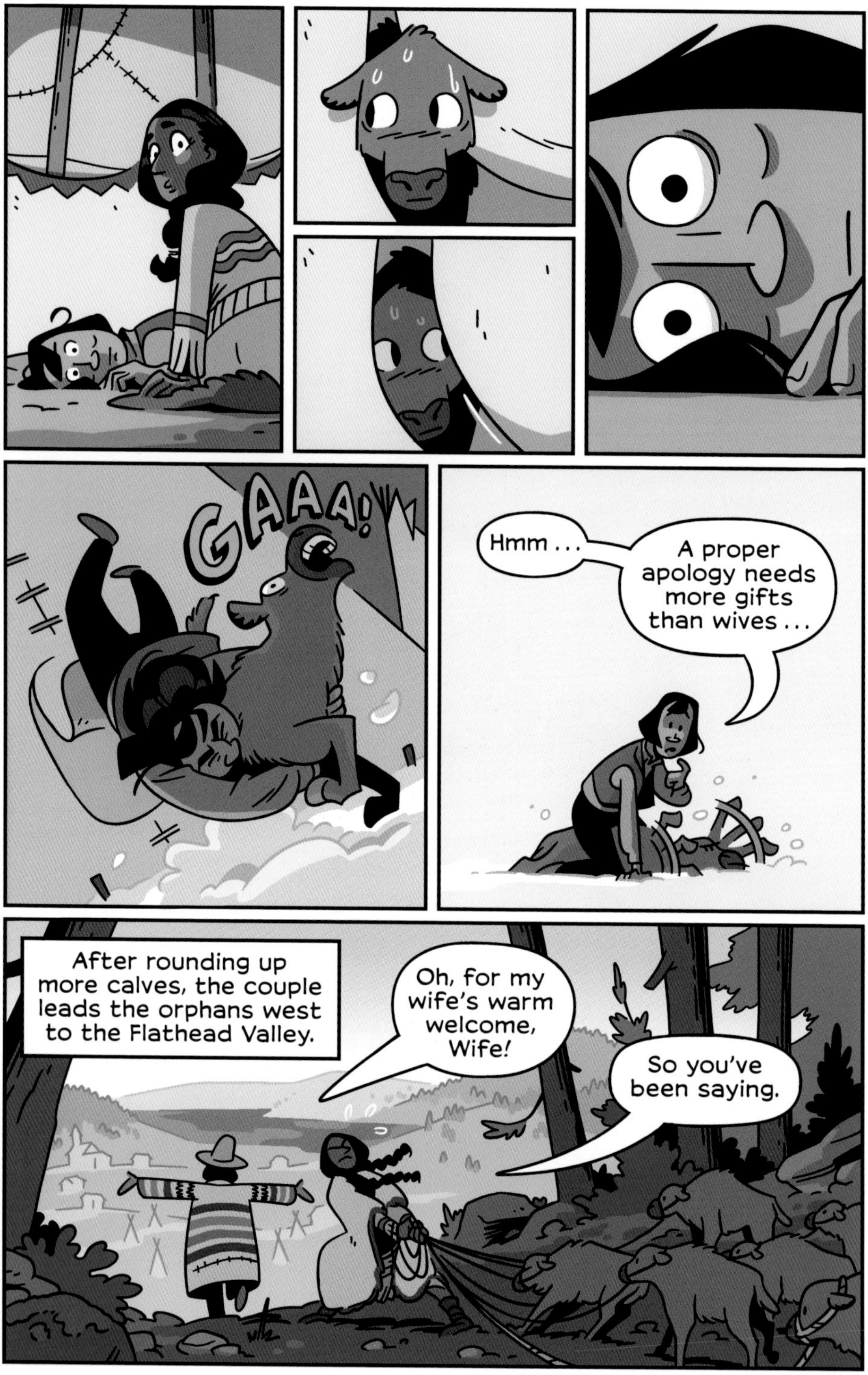
GAAA!
Hmm . . .
A proper apology needs more gifts than wives . . .
After rounding up more calves, the couple leads the orphans west to the Flathead Valley.
Oh, for my wife's warm welcome, Wife!
So you've been saying.

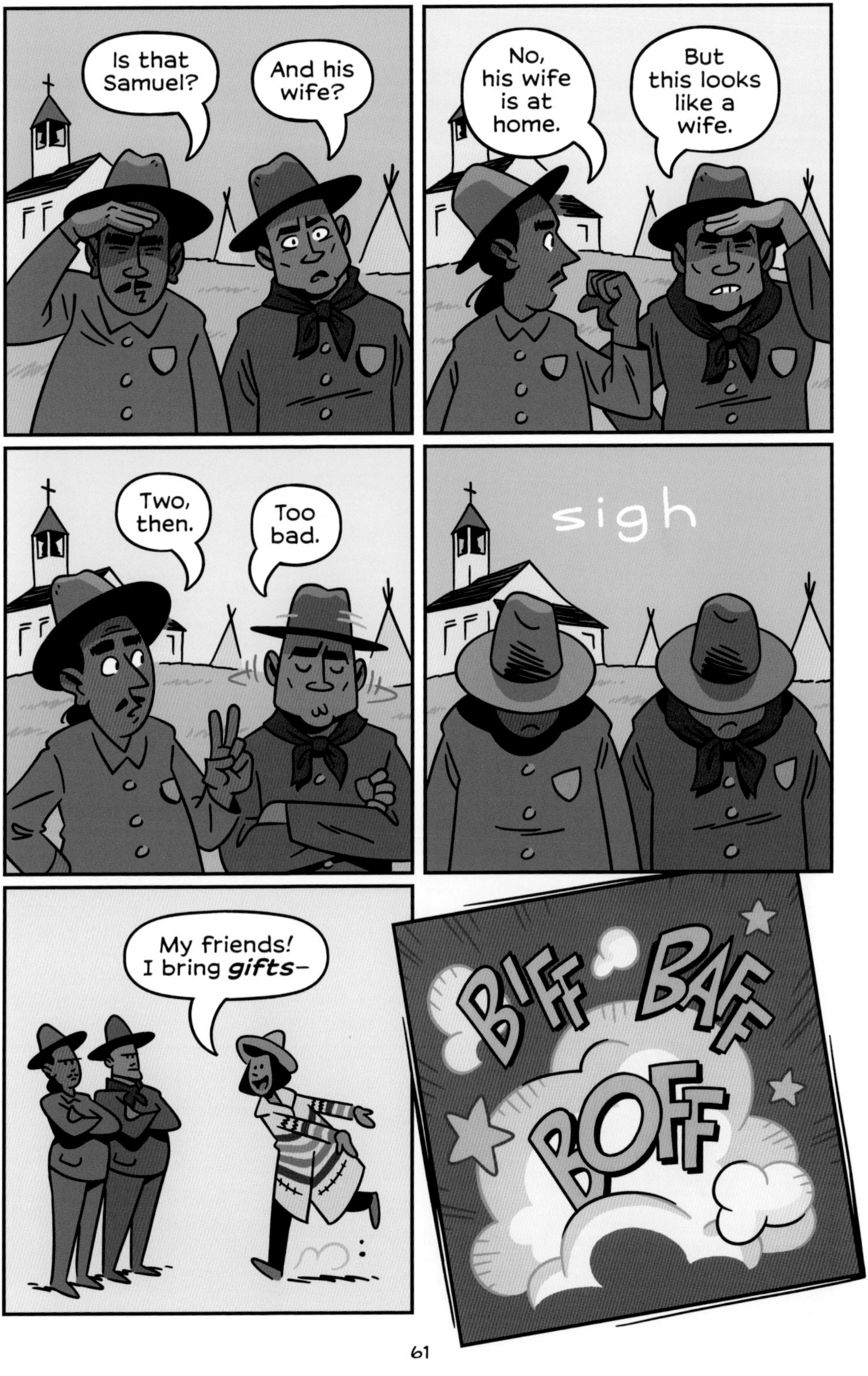
Is that Samuel?
And his wife?
No, his wife is at home.
But this looks like a wife.
Two, then.
Too bad.
sigh
My friends! I bring ***gifts***–
BIFF BAFF
BOFF

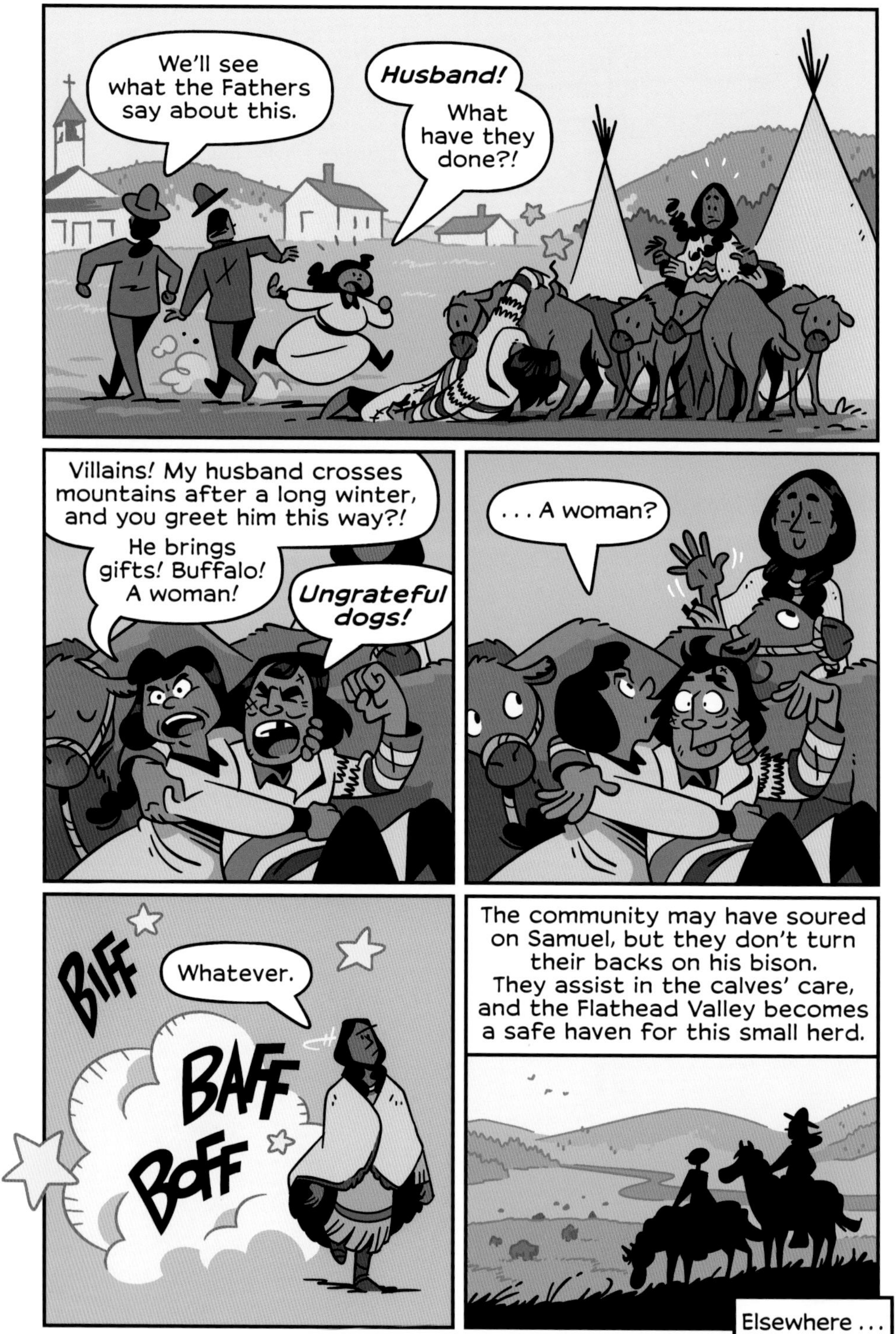

We'll see what the Fathers say about this.
Husband!
What have they done?!
Villains! My husband crosses mountains after a long winter, and you greet him this way?!
He brings gifts! Buffalo! A woman!
Ungrateful dogs!
. . . A woman?
BIFF
Whatever.
BAFF
BOFF
The community may have soured on Samuel, but they don't turn their backs on his bison. They assist in the calves' care, and the Flathead Valley becomes a safe haven for this small herd.
Elsewhere . . .

The southern hide hunters are at a loss. They'd expected the bison to last a lifetime, yet most are out of work by 1875.

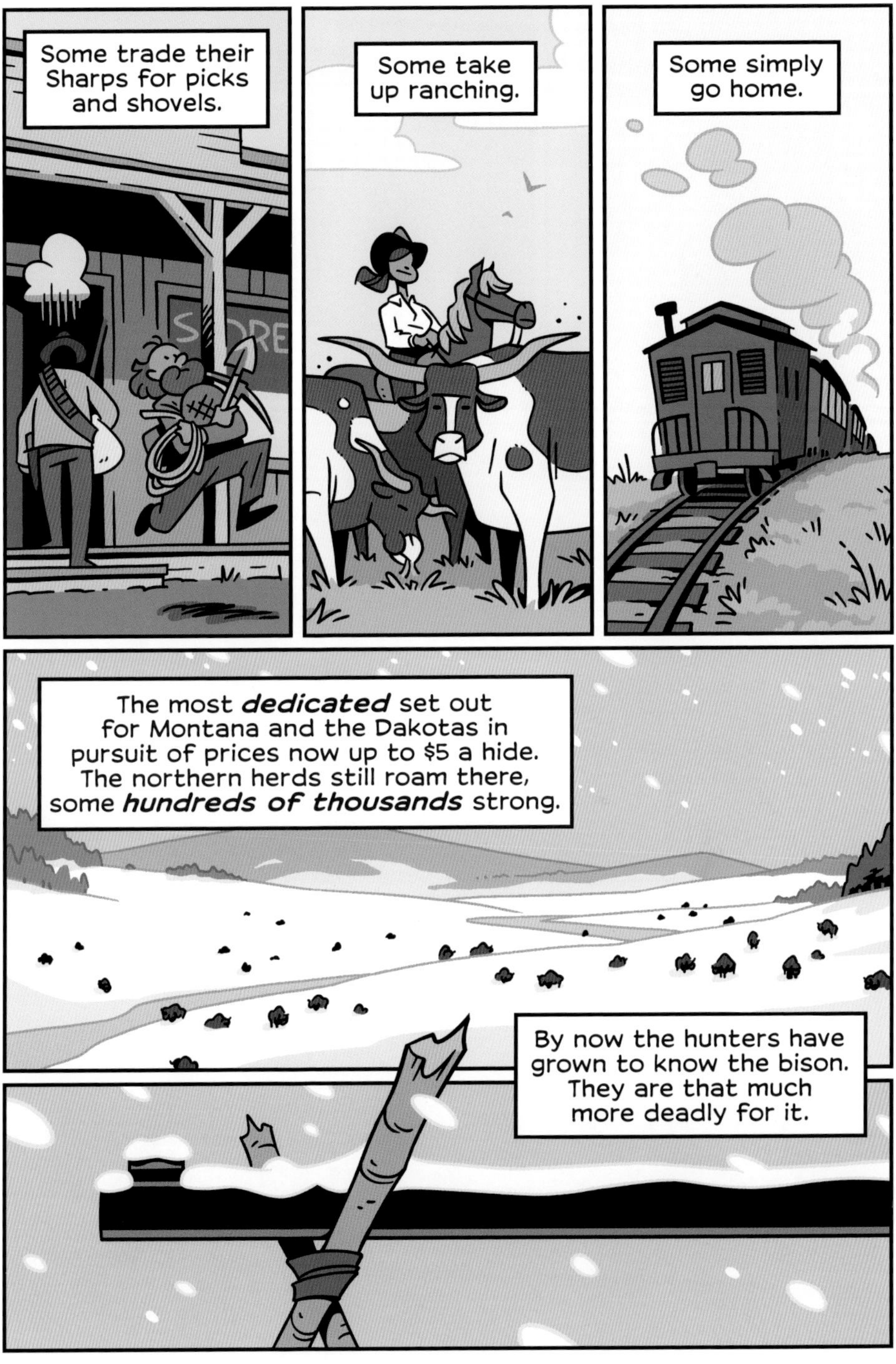
Some trade their Sharps for picks and shovels.
STORE
Some take up ranching.
Some simply go home.
The most dedicated set out for Montana and the Dakotas in pursuit of prices now up to $5 a hide. The northern herds still roam there, some hundreds of thousands strong.
By now the hunters have grown to know the bison. They are that much more deadly for it.

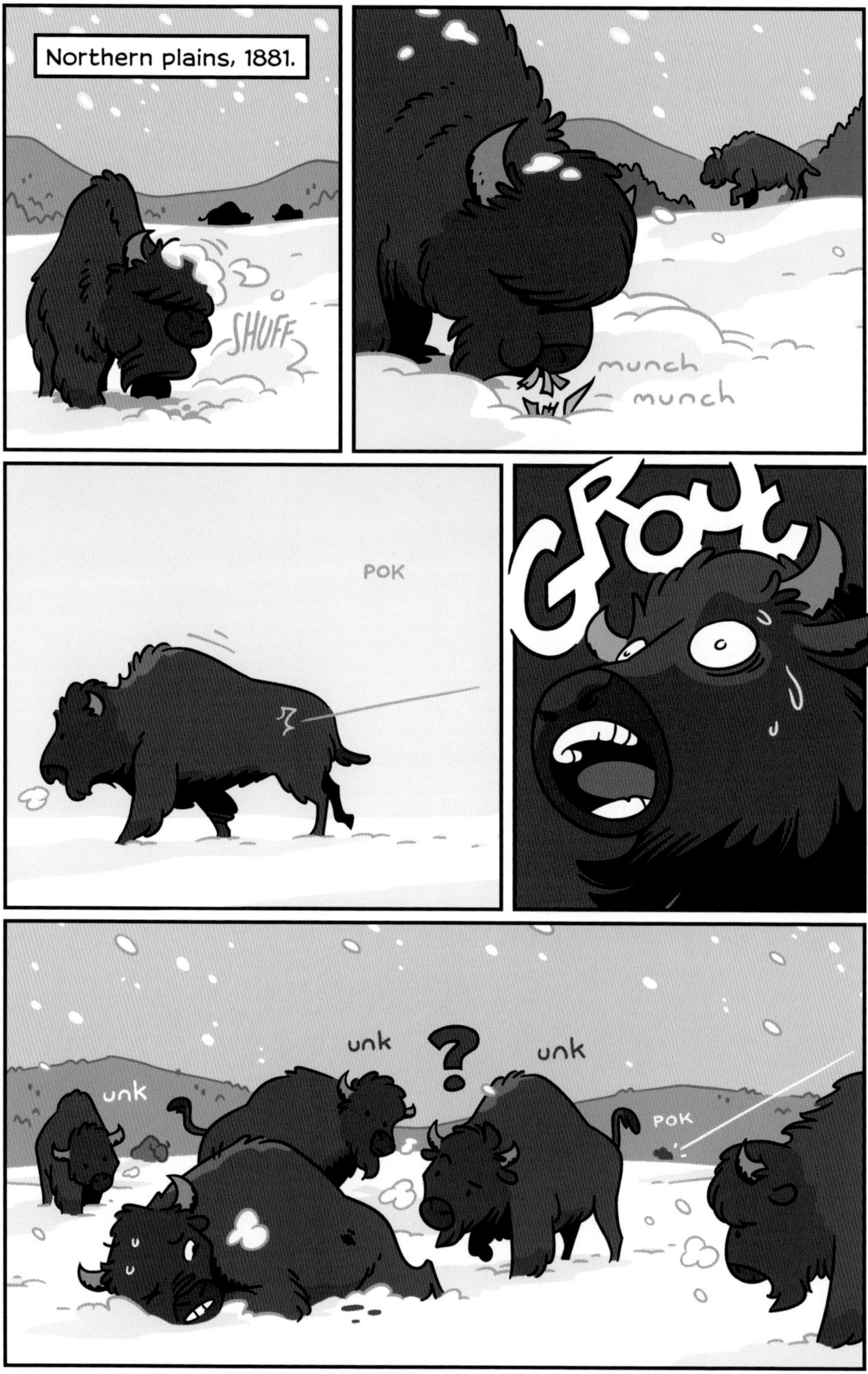
Northern plains, 1881.
SHUFF
munch
munch
POK
GROU
unk
unk
?
unk
POK

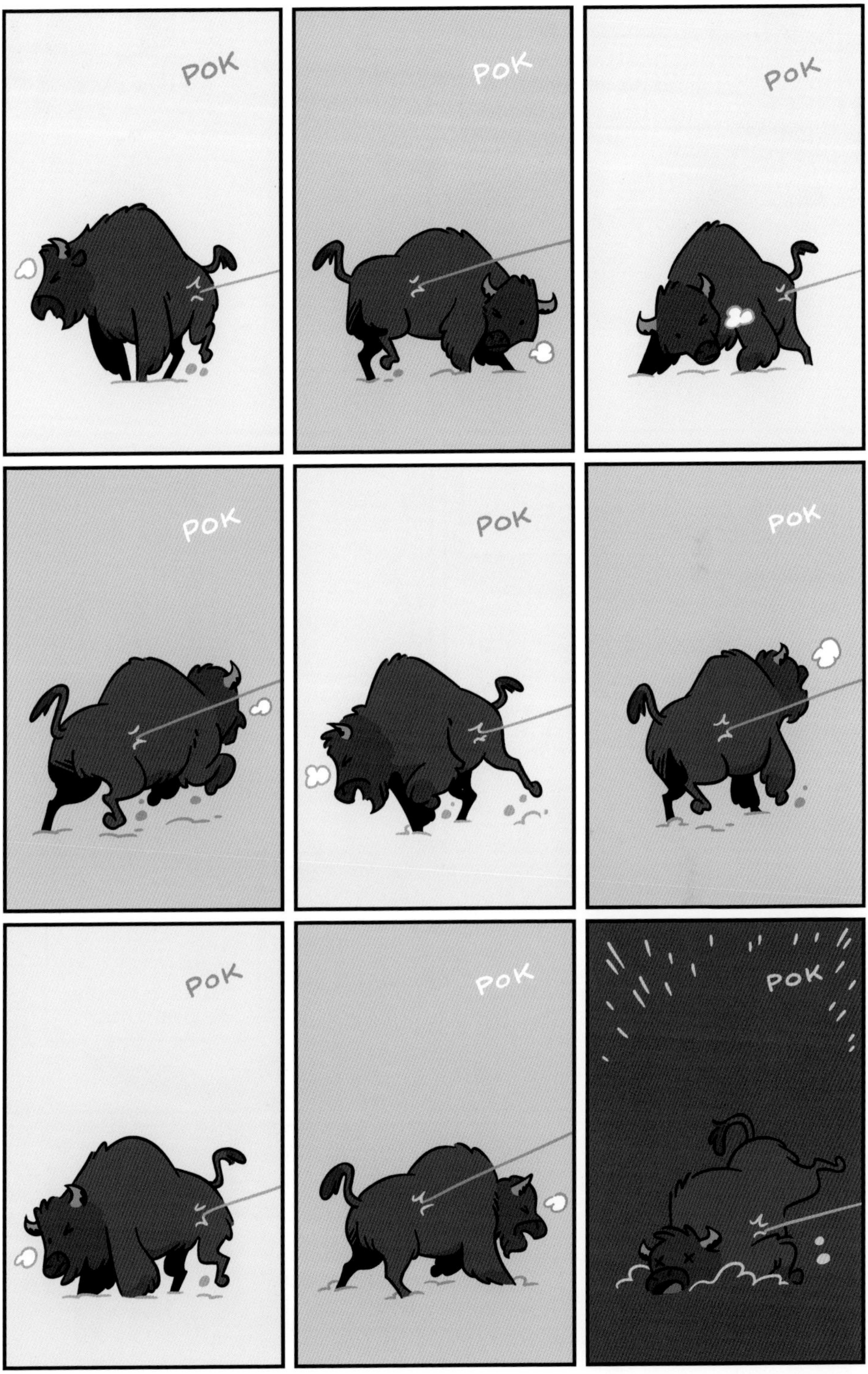
POK
POK
POK
POK
POK
POK
POK
POK
POK

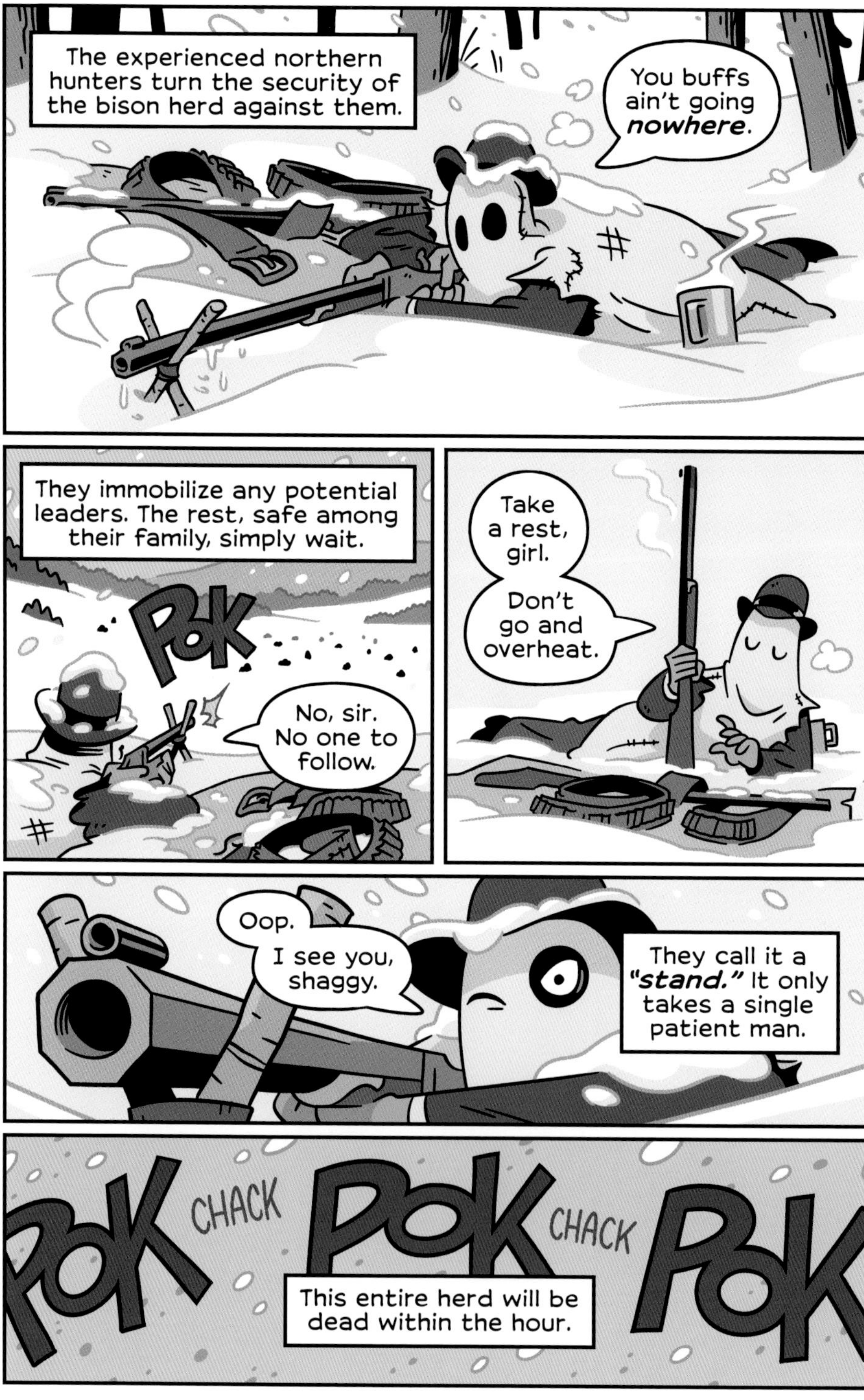

The experienced northern hunters turn the security of the bison herd against them.
You buffs ain't going *nowhere*.
They immobilize any potential leaders. The rest, safe among their family, simply wait.
POK
No, sir. No one to follow.
Take a rest, girl.
Don't go and overheat.
Oop.
I see you, shaggy.
They call it a ***"stand."*** It only takes a single patient man.
POK
CHACK
POK
CHACK
POK
This entire herd will be dead within the hour.

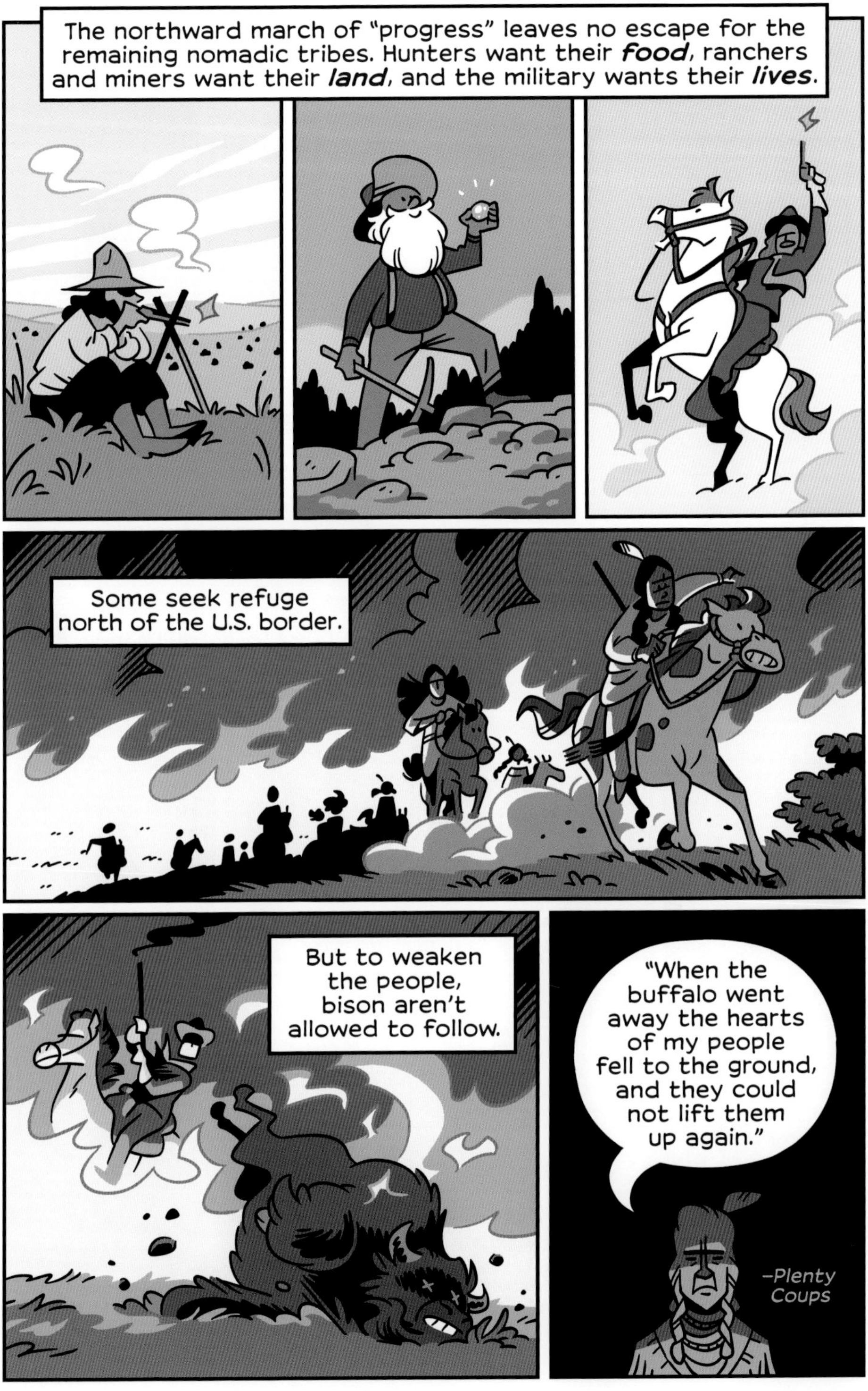
The northward march of "progress" leaves no escape for the remaining nomadic tribes. Hunters want their *food*, ranchers and miners want their *land*, and the military wants their *lives*.
Some seek refuge north of the U.S. border.
But to weaken the people, bison aren't allowed to follow.
"When the buffalo went away the hearts of my people fell to the ground, and they could not lift them up again."
–Plenty Coups

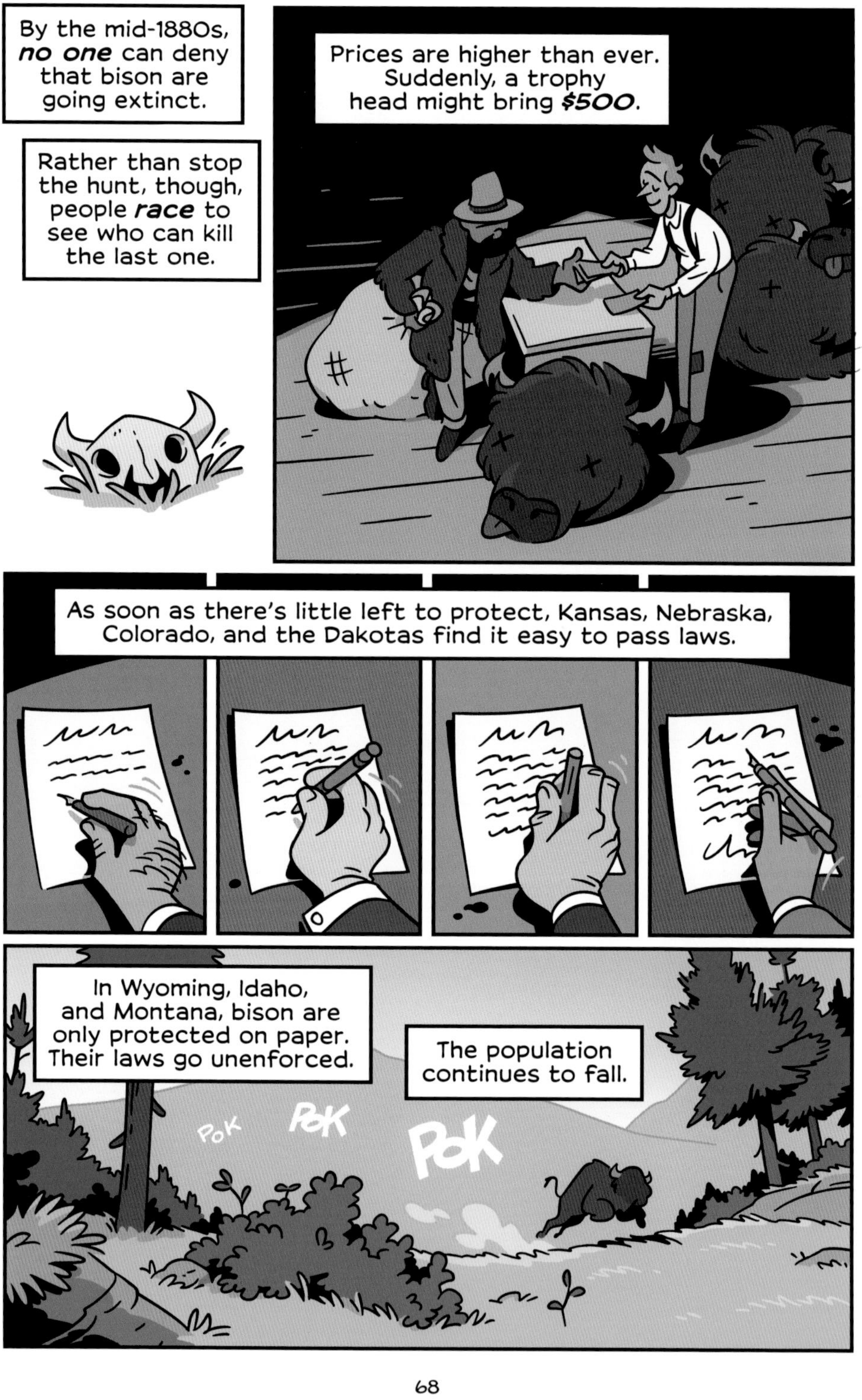
By the mid-1880s, ***no one*** can deny that bison are going extinct.
Rather than stop the hunt, though, people ***race*** to see who can kill the last one.
Prices are higher than ever. Suddenly, a trophy head might bring ***$500***.
As soon as there's little left to protect, Kansas, Nebraska, Colorado, and the Dakotas find it easy to pass laws.
In Wyoming, Idaho, and Montana, bison are only protected on paper. Their laws go unenforced.
The population continues to fall.
PoK
PoK
PoK

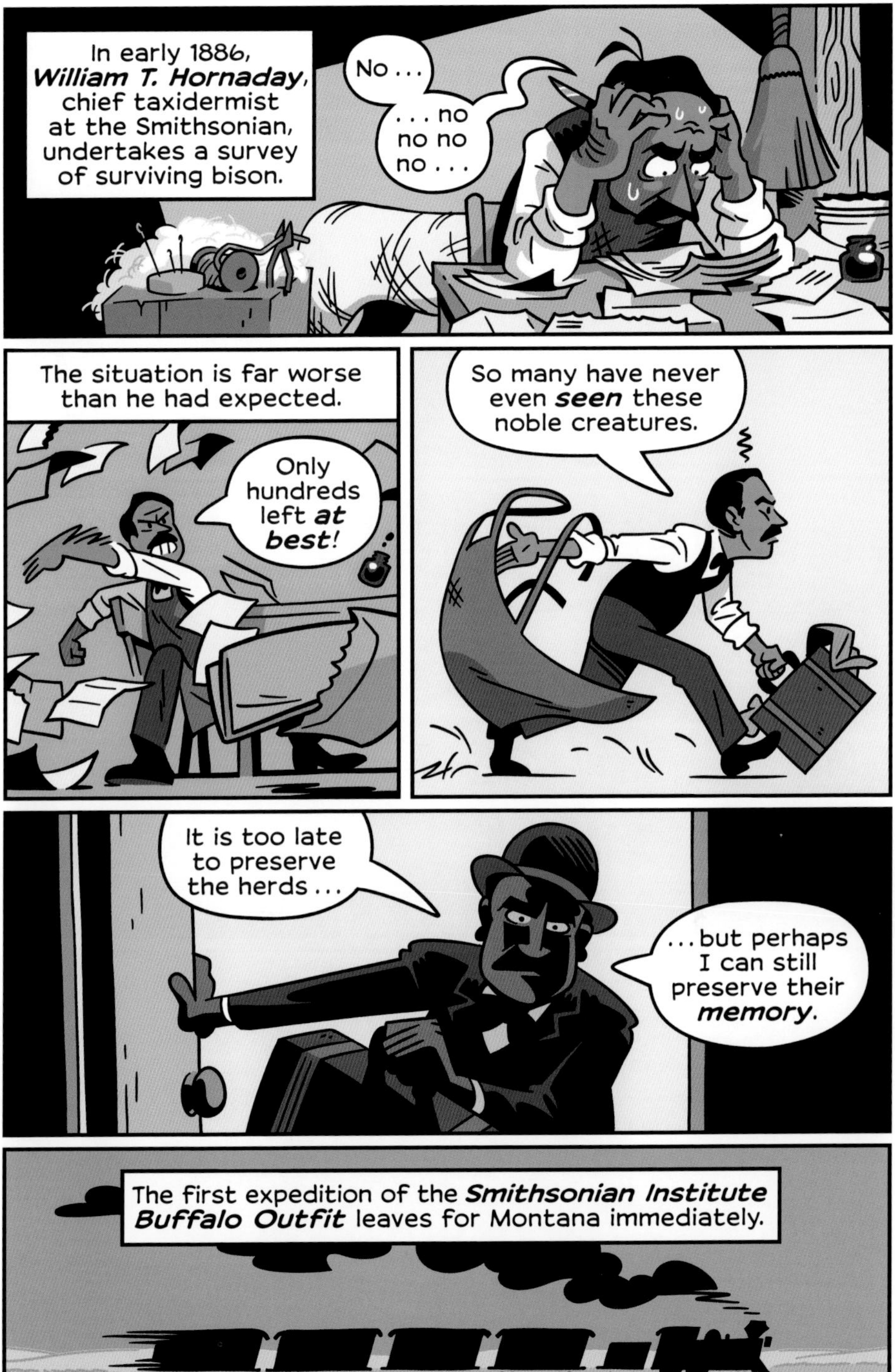
In early 1886, ***William T. Hornaday***, chief taxidermist at the Smithsonian, undertakes a survey of surviving bison.
No . . .
. . . no no no no . . .
The situation is far worse than he had expected.
Only hundreds left ***at best***!
So many have never even ***seen*** these noble creatures.
It is too late to preserve the herds . . .
. . . but perhaps I can still preserve their ***memory***.
The first expedition of the ***Smithsonian Institute Buffalo Outfit*** leaves for Montana immediately.

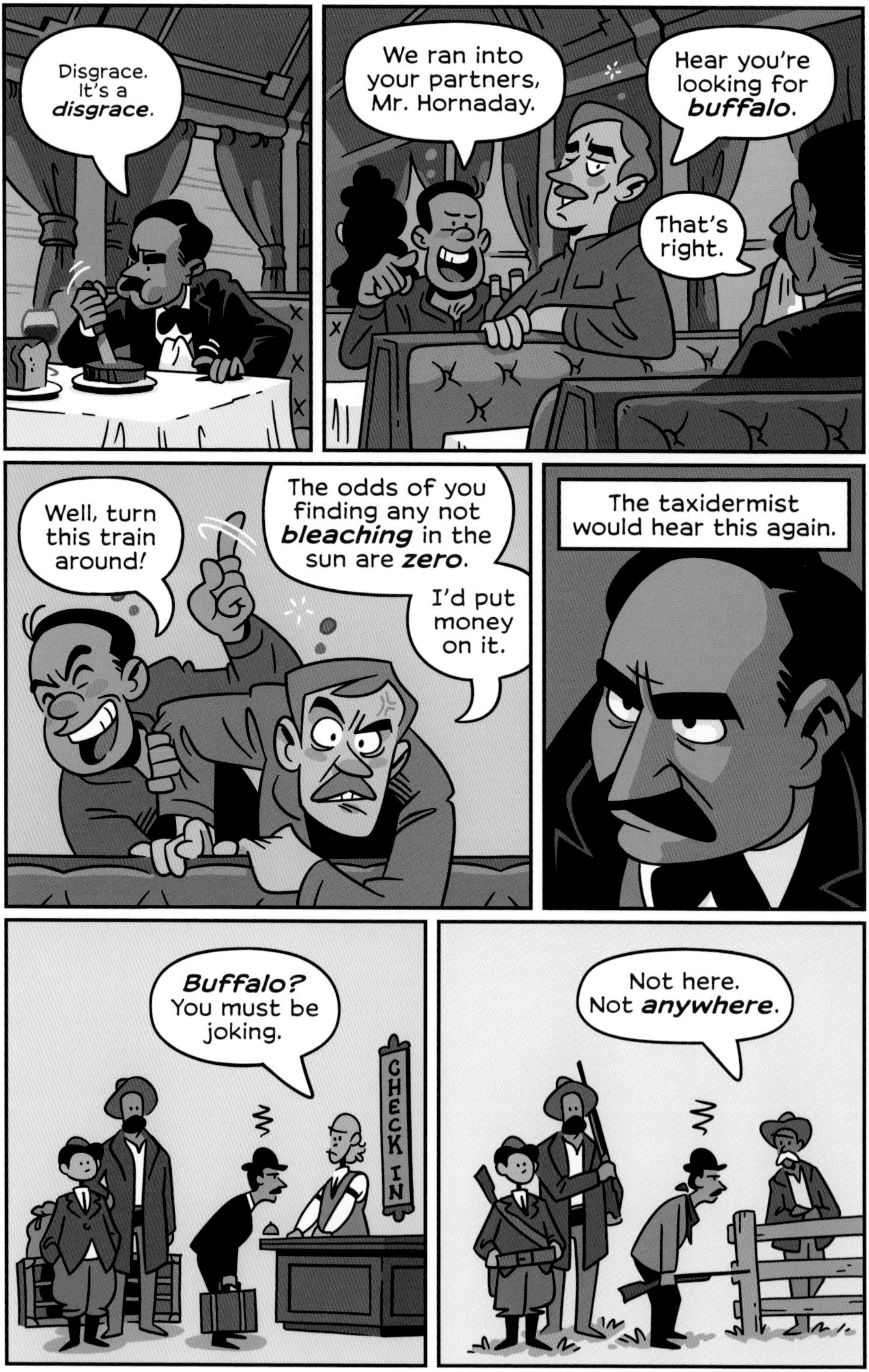
Disgrace. It's a *disgrace*.
We ran into your partners, Mr. Hornaday.
Hear you're looking for **buffalo**.
That's right.
Well, turn this train around!
The odds of you finding any not ***bleaching*** in the sun are ***zero***.
I'd put money on it.
The taxidermist would hear this again.
Buffalo? You must be joking.
CHECK IN
Not here. Not ***anywhere***.

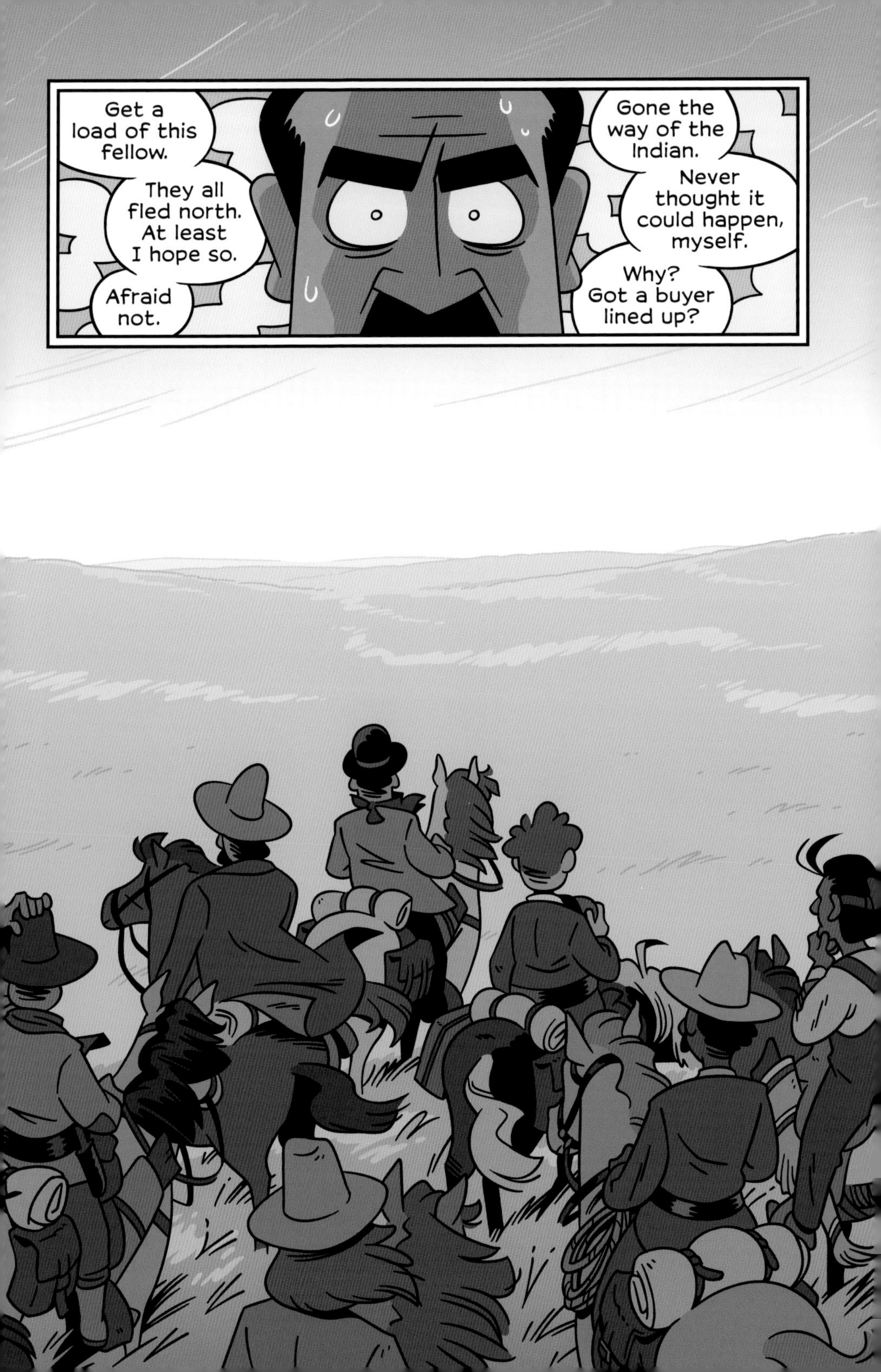
Get a load of this fellow.
Gone the way of the Indian.
They all fled north. At least I hope so.
Never thought it could happen, myself.
Why? Got a buyer lined up?
Afraid not.

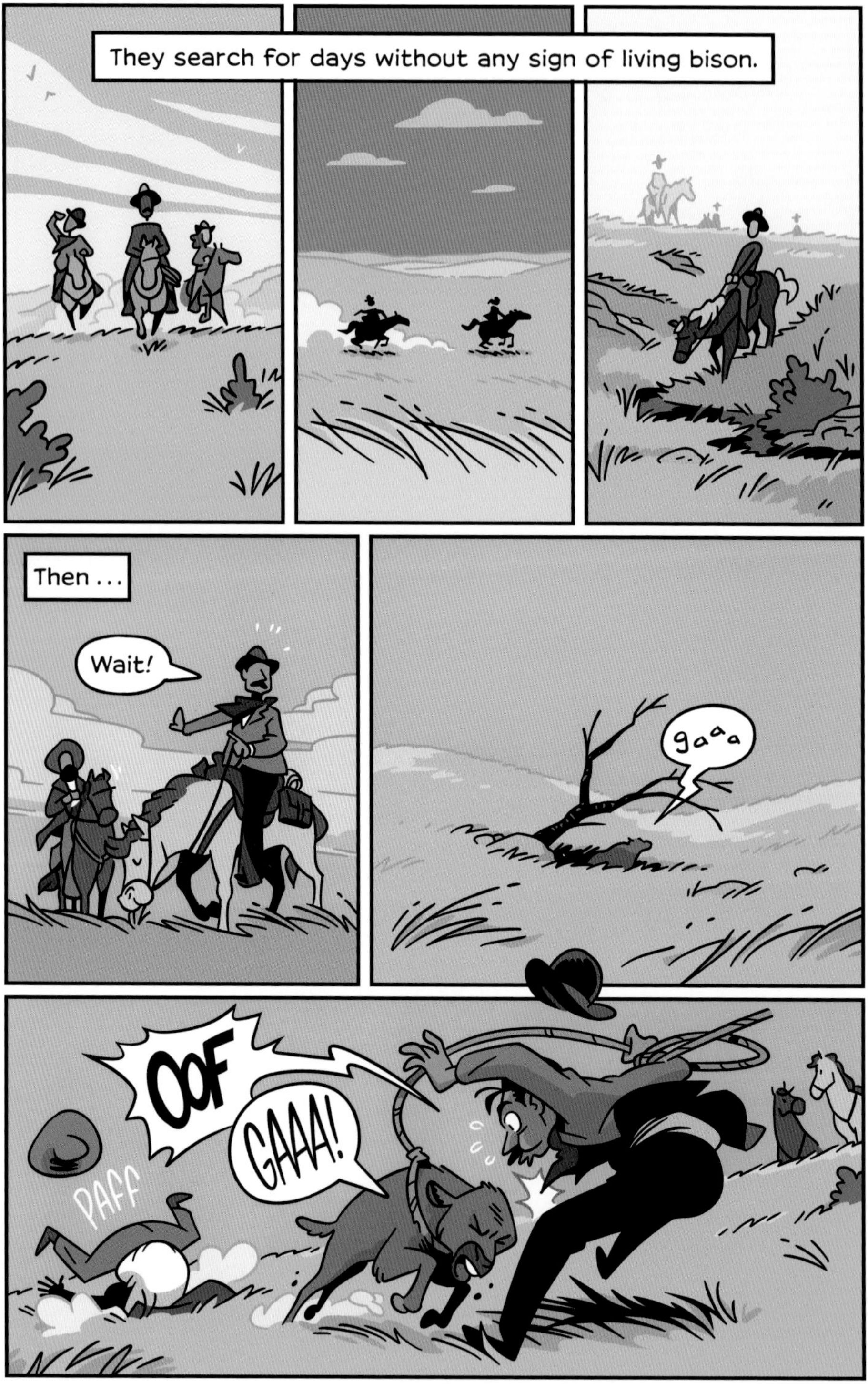
They search for days without any sign of living bison.
Then . . .
Wait!
gaaa
OOF
GAAA!
PAFF

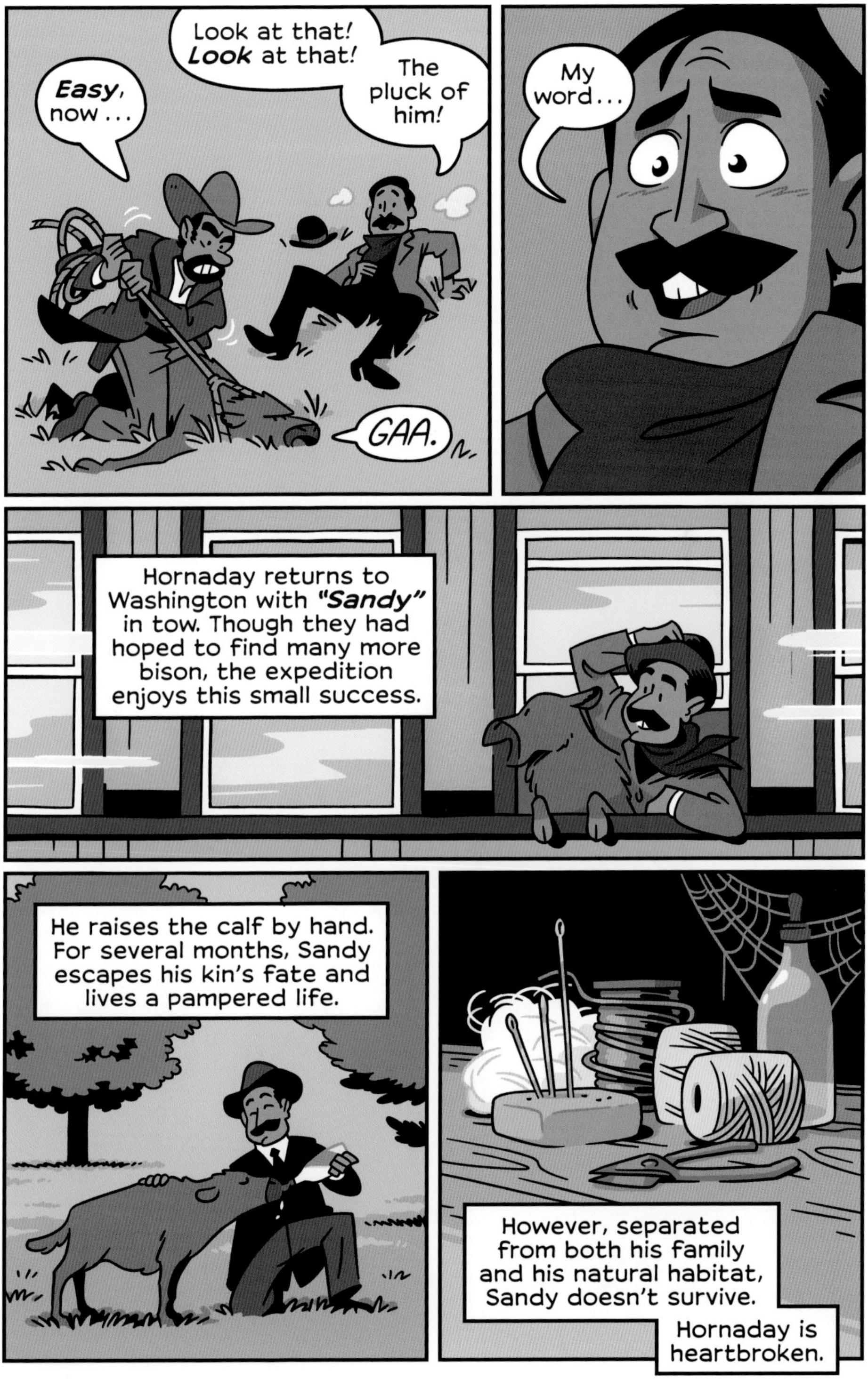

Easy, now . . .
Look at that! Look at that!
The pluck of him!
GAA.
My word . . .
Hornaday returns to Washington with "Sandy" in tow. Though they had hoped to find many more bison, the expedition enjoys this small success.
He raises the calf by hand. For several months, Sandy escapes his kin's fate and lives a pampered life.
However, separated from both his family and his natural habitat, Sandy doesn't survive.
Hornaday is heartbroken.

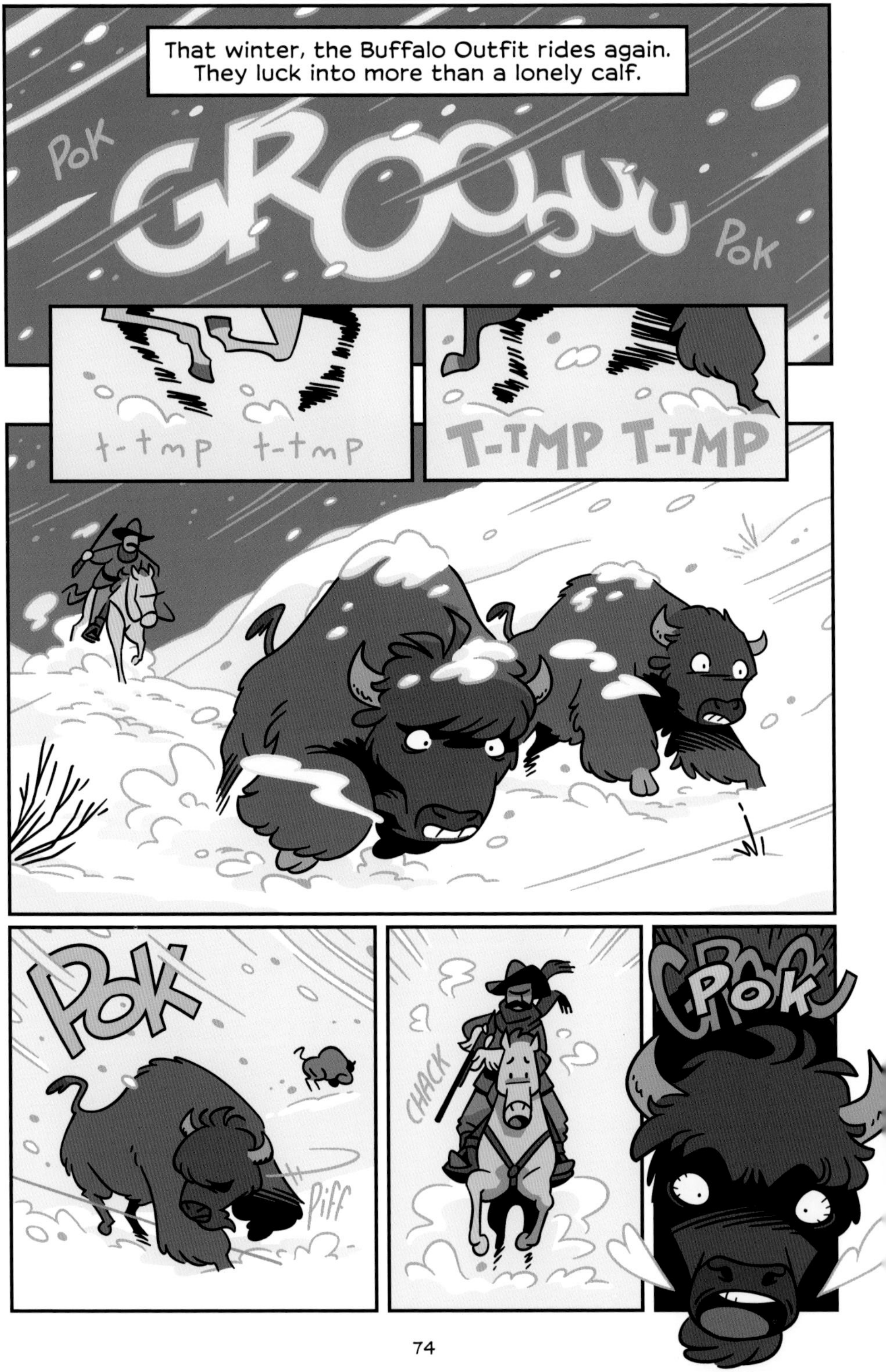

That winter, the Buffalo Outfit rides again.
They luck into more than a lonely calf.
Pok
GROOouu
Pok
t-tmp t-tmp
T-TMP T-TMP
POK
Piff
CHACK
POK

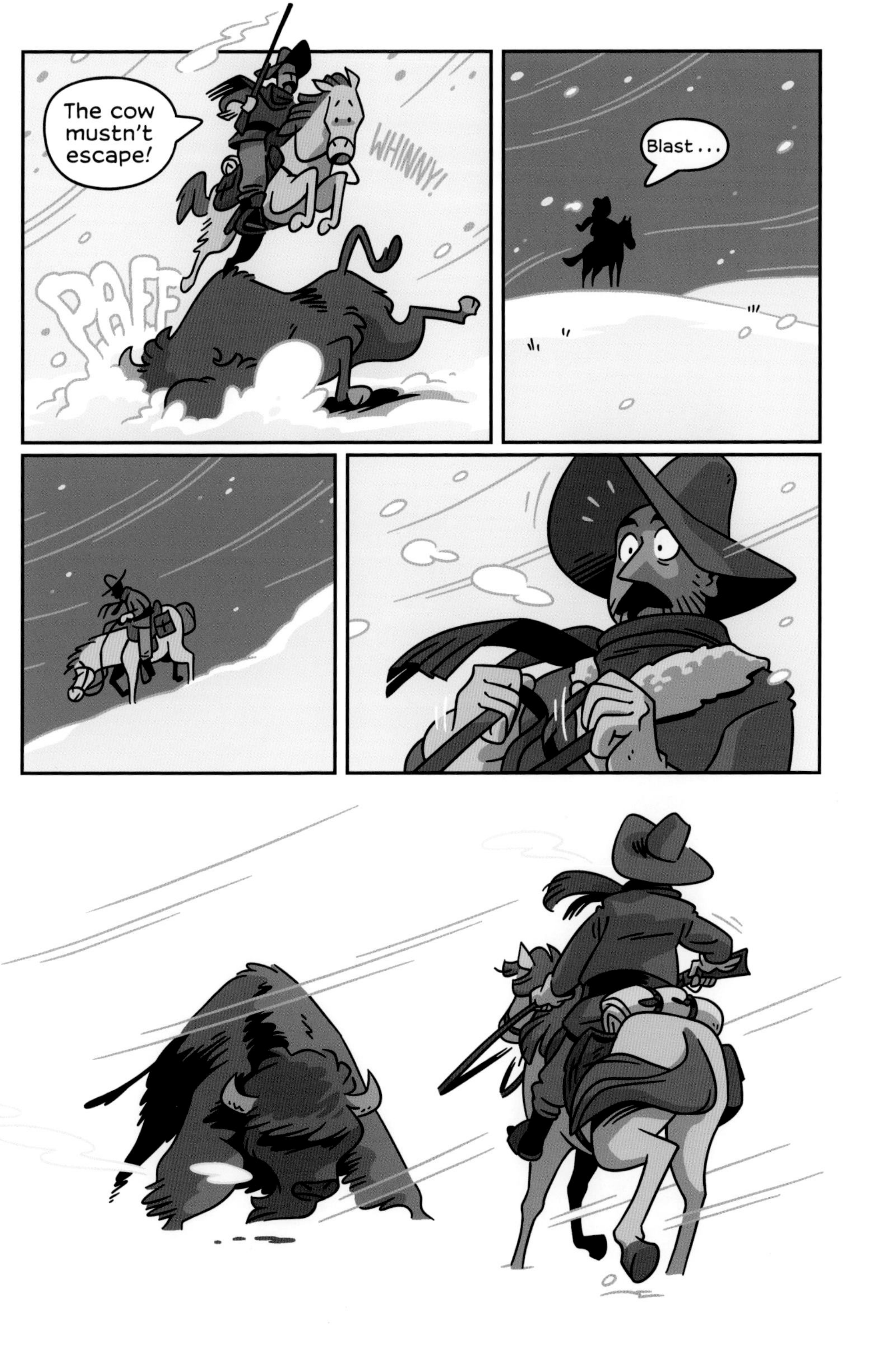
The cow mustn't escape!
WHINNY!
PAFF
Blast...

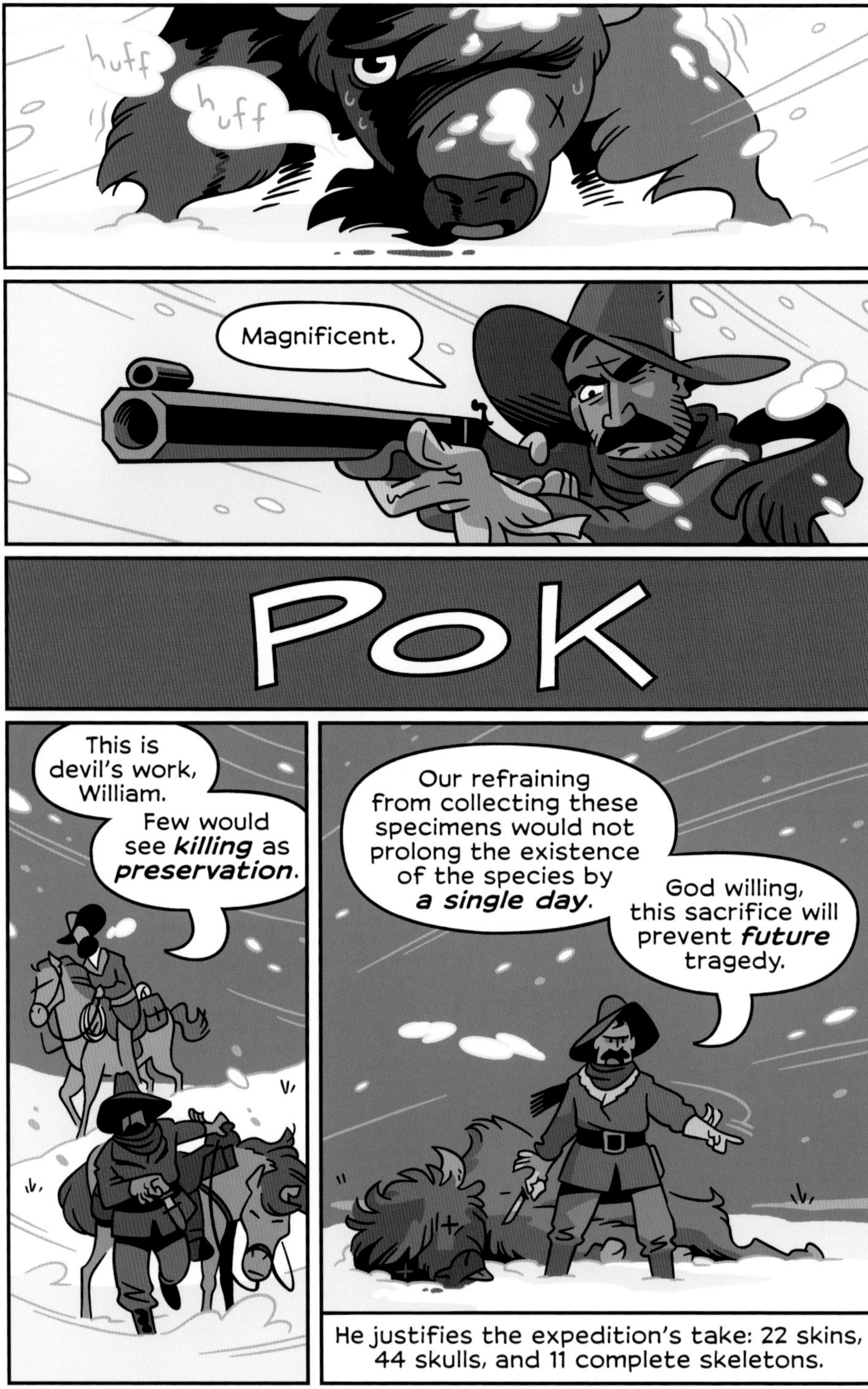
huff
huff
Magnificent.
POK
This is devil's work, William.
Few would see *killing* as *preservation*.
Our refraining from collecting these specimens would not prolong the existence of the species by *a single day*.
God willing, this sacrifice will prevent *future* tragedy.
He justifies the expedition's take: 22 skins, 44 skulls, and 11 complete skeletons.

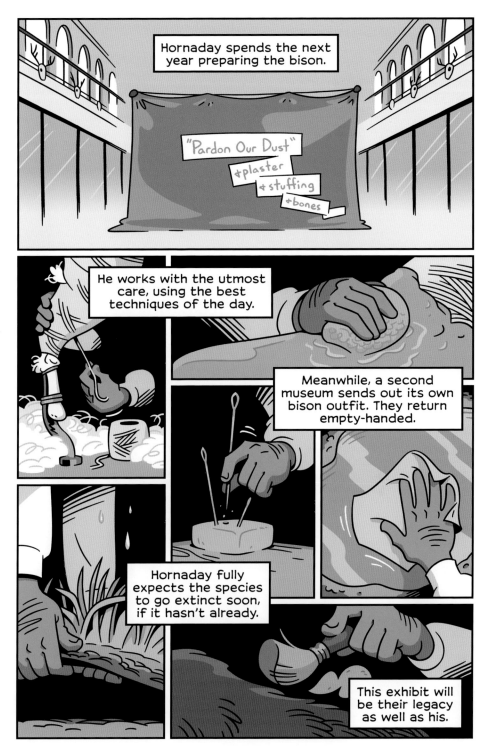

Hornaday spends the next year preparing the bison.

"Pardon Our Dust"
+ plaster
+ stuffing
+ bones

He works with the utmost care, using the best techniques of the day.

Meanwhile, a second museum sends out its own bison outfit. They return empty-handed.

Hornaday fully expects the species to go extinct soon, if it hasn't already.

This exhibit will be their legacy as well as his.

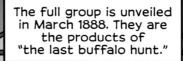

The full group is unveiled
in March 1888. They are
the products of
"the last buffalo hunt."

The mighty bull who stood his ground.
Two cows ready for motherhood.
A young "spike" bull with his straight horns.
A yearling, hair darkening with age.
And little Sandy preserved along with them.

Tens of millions
of museum visitors will
see Hornaday's warning.

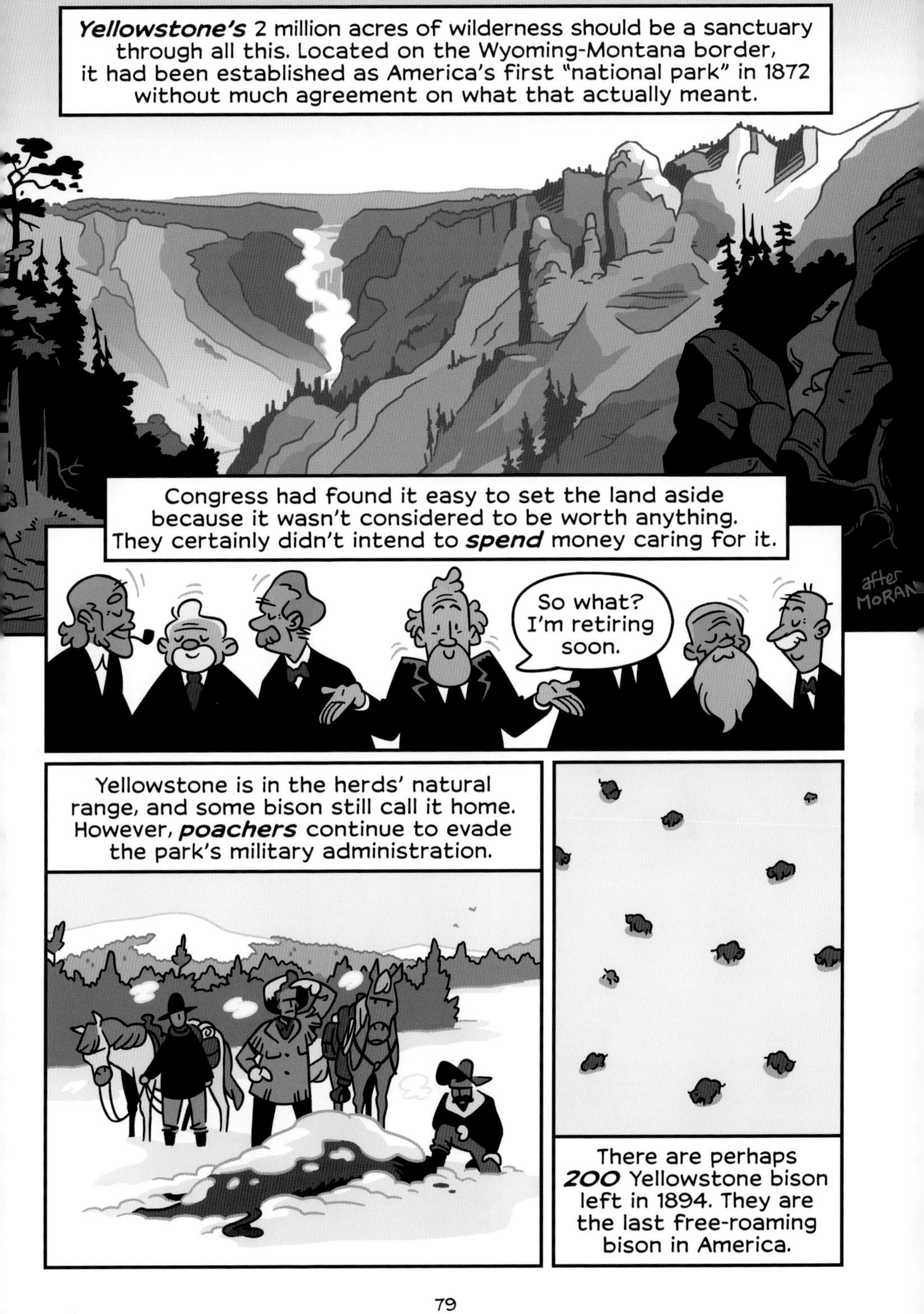

Yellowstone's 2 million acres of wilderness should be a sanctuary through all this. Located on the Wyoming-Montana border, it had been established as America's first "national park" in 1872 without much agreement on what that actually meant.
after MORAN
Congress had found it easy to set the land aside because it wasn't considered to be worth anything. They certainly didn't intend to ***spend*** money caring for it.
So what? I'm retiring soon.
Yellowstone is in the herds' natural range, and some bison still call it home. However, ***poachers*** continue to evade the park's military administration.
There are perhaps ***200*** Yellowstone bison left in 1894. They are the last free-roaming bison in America.

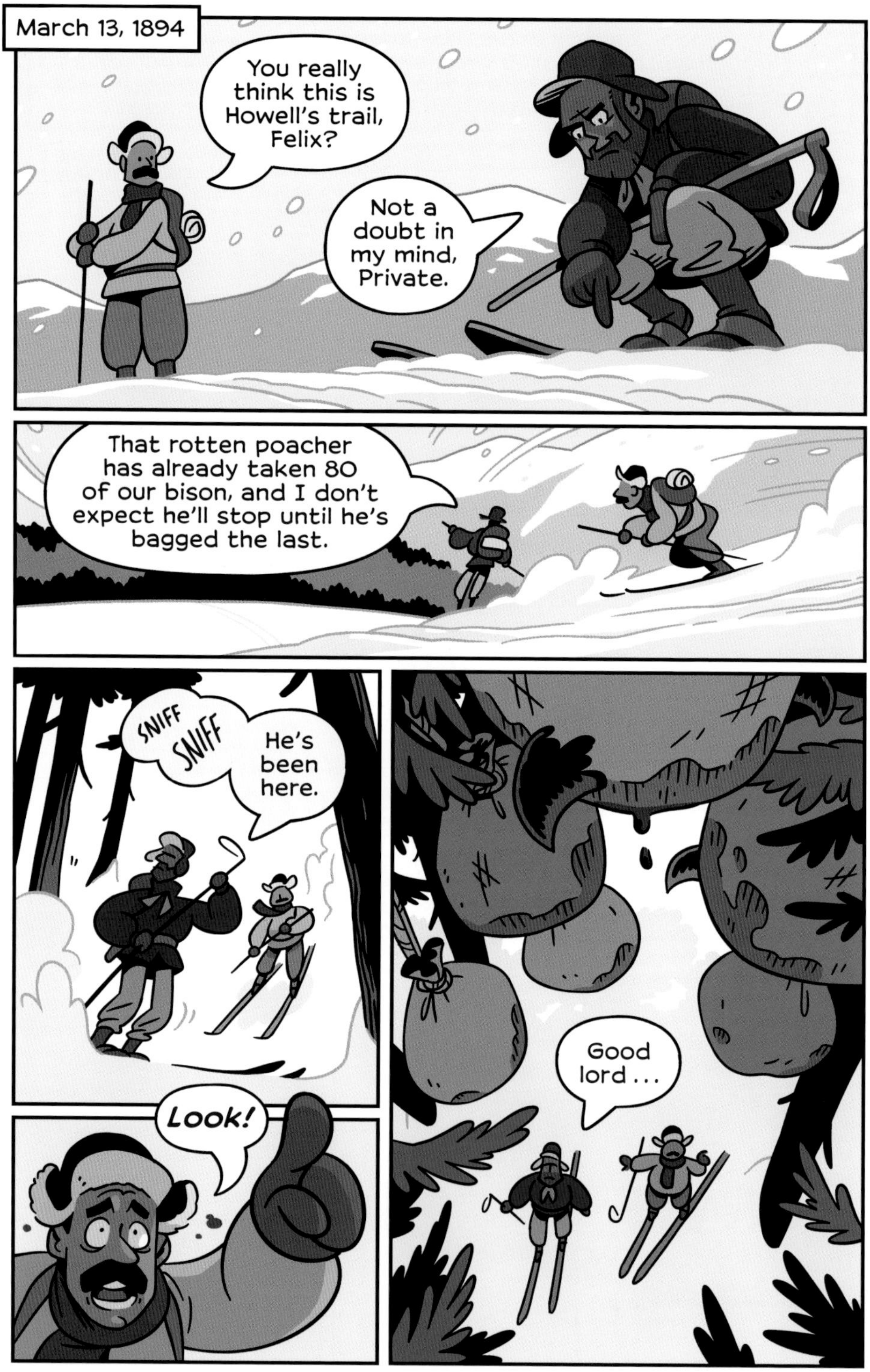
March 13, 1894
You really think this is Howell's trail, Felix?
Not a doubt in my mind, Private.
That rotten poacher has already taken 80 of our bison, and I don't expect he'll stop until he's bagged the last.
SNIFF SNIFF
He's been here.
Look!
Good lord . . .

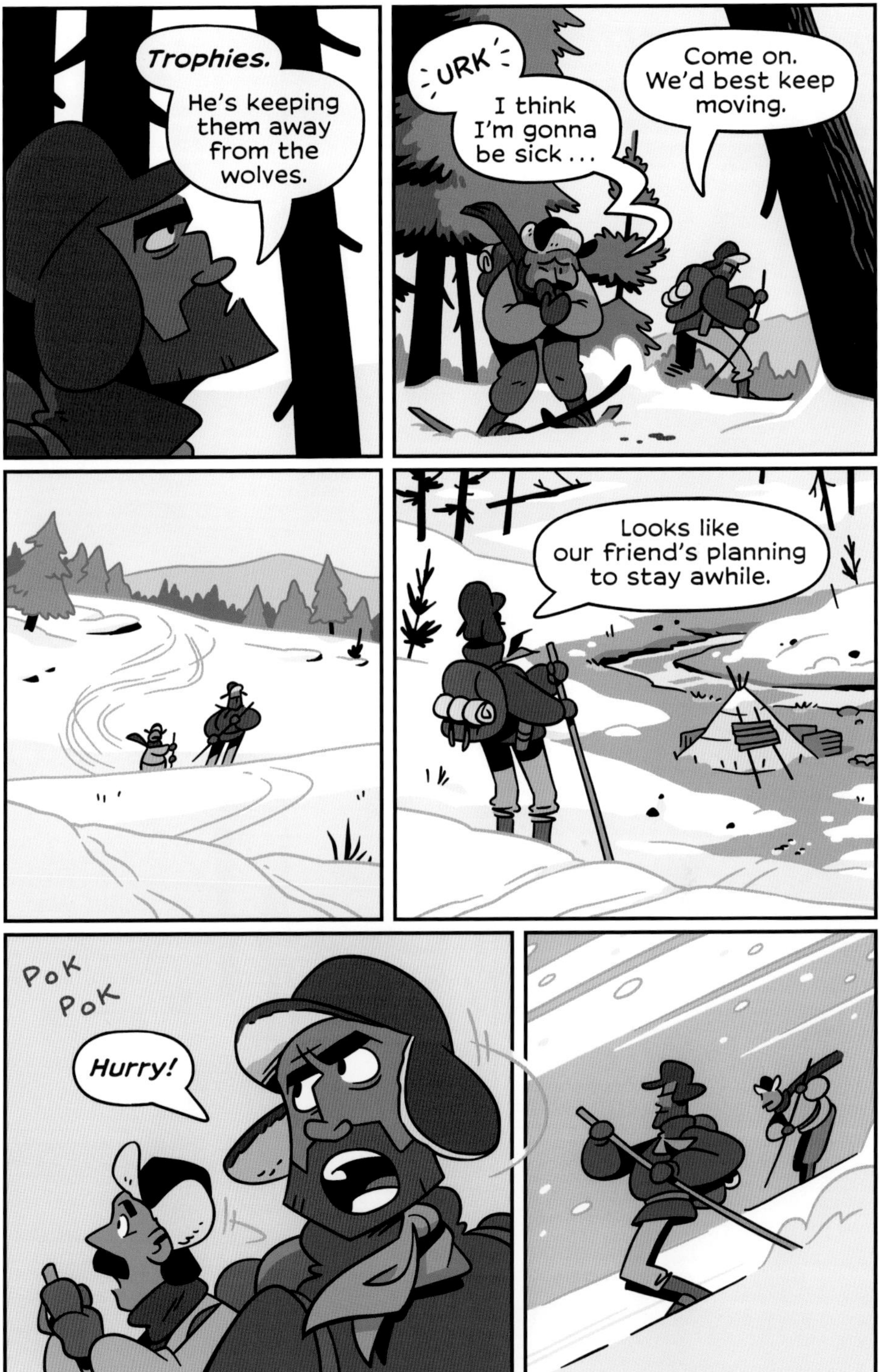
Trophies.
He's keeping them away from the wolves.
URK
I think I'm gonna be sick . . .
Come on. We'd best keep moving.
Looks like our friend's planning to stay awhile.
POK POK
Hurry!

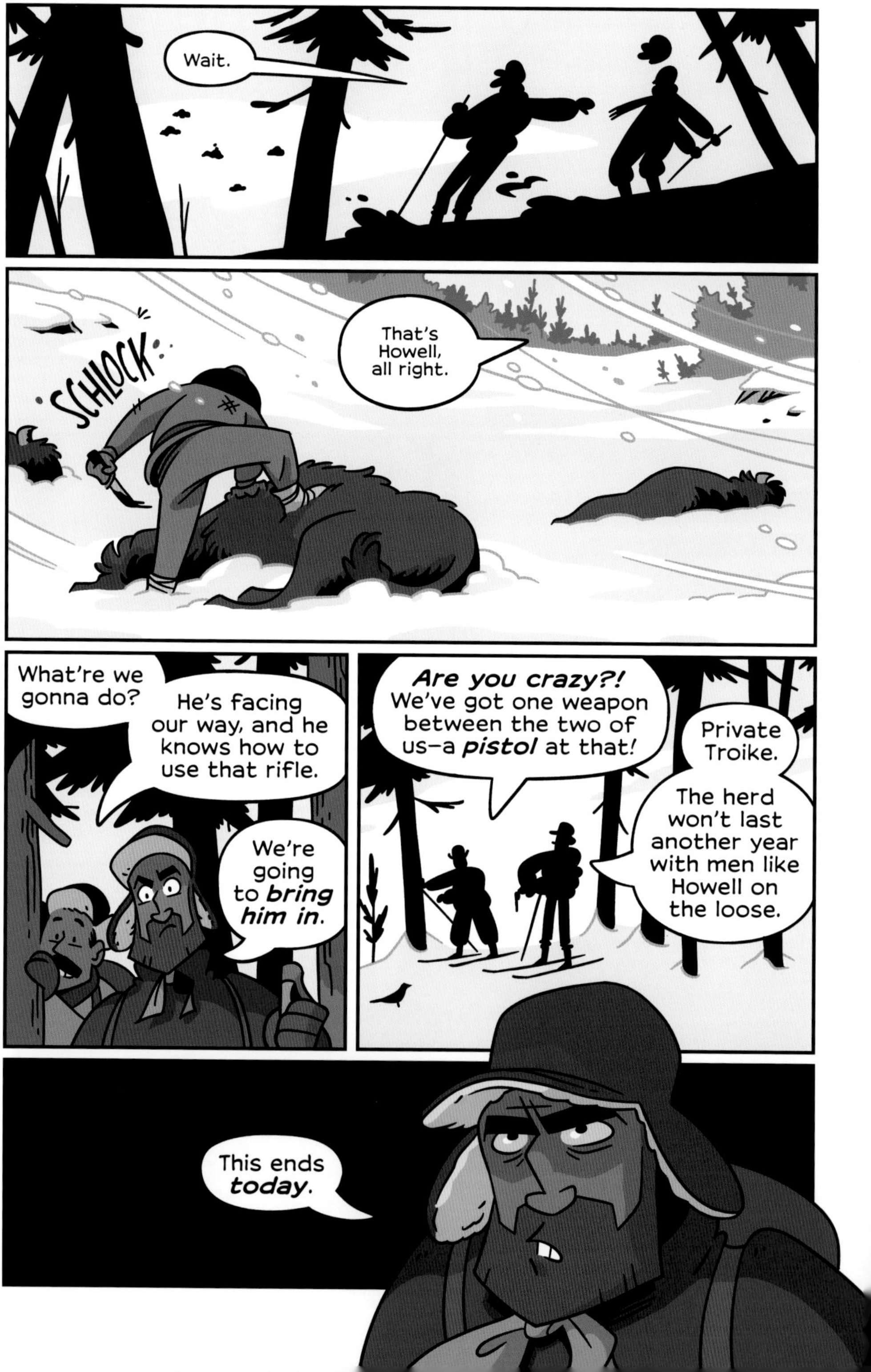
Wait.
That's Howell, all right.
SCHLOCK
What're we gonna do?
He's facing our way, and he knows how to use that rifle.
We're going to *bring him in*.
Are you crazy?! We've got one weapon between the two of us—a ***pistol*** at that!
Private Troike.
The herd won't last another year with men like Howell on the loose.
This ends ***today***.

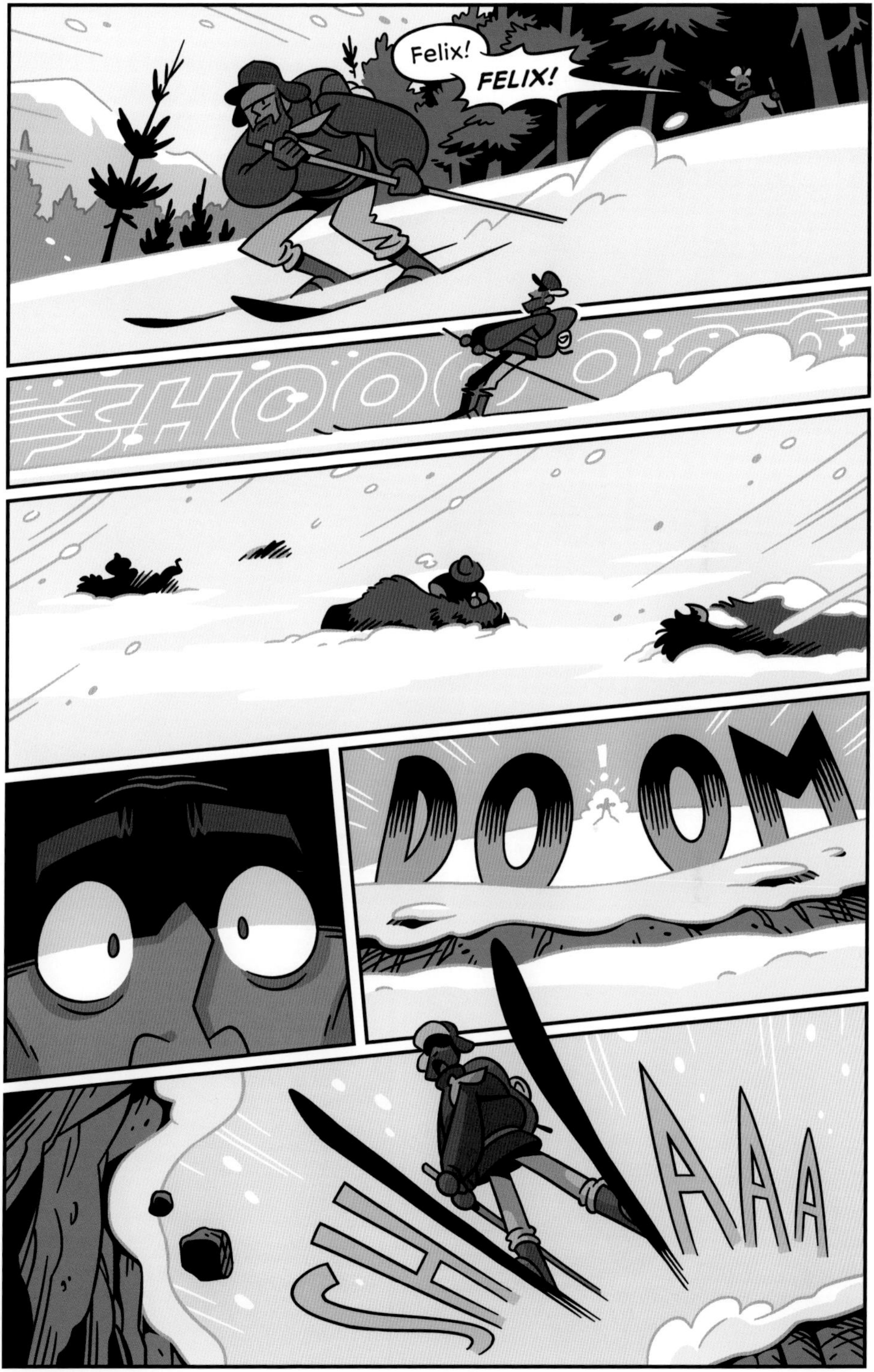
Felix!
FELIX!
!
DOOM
HAAAA

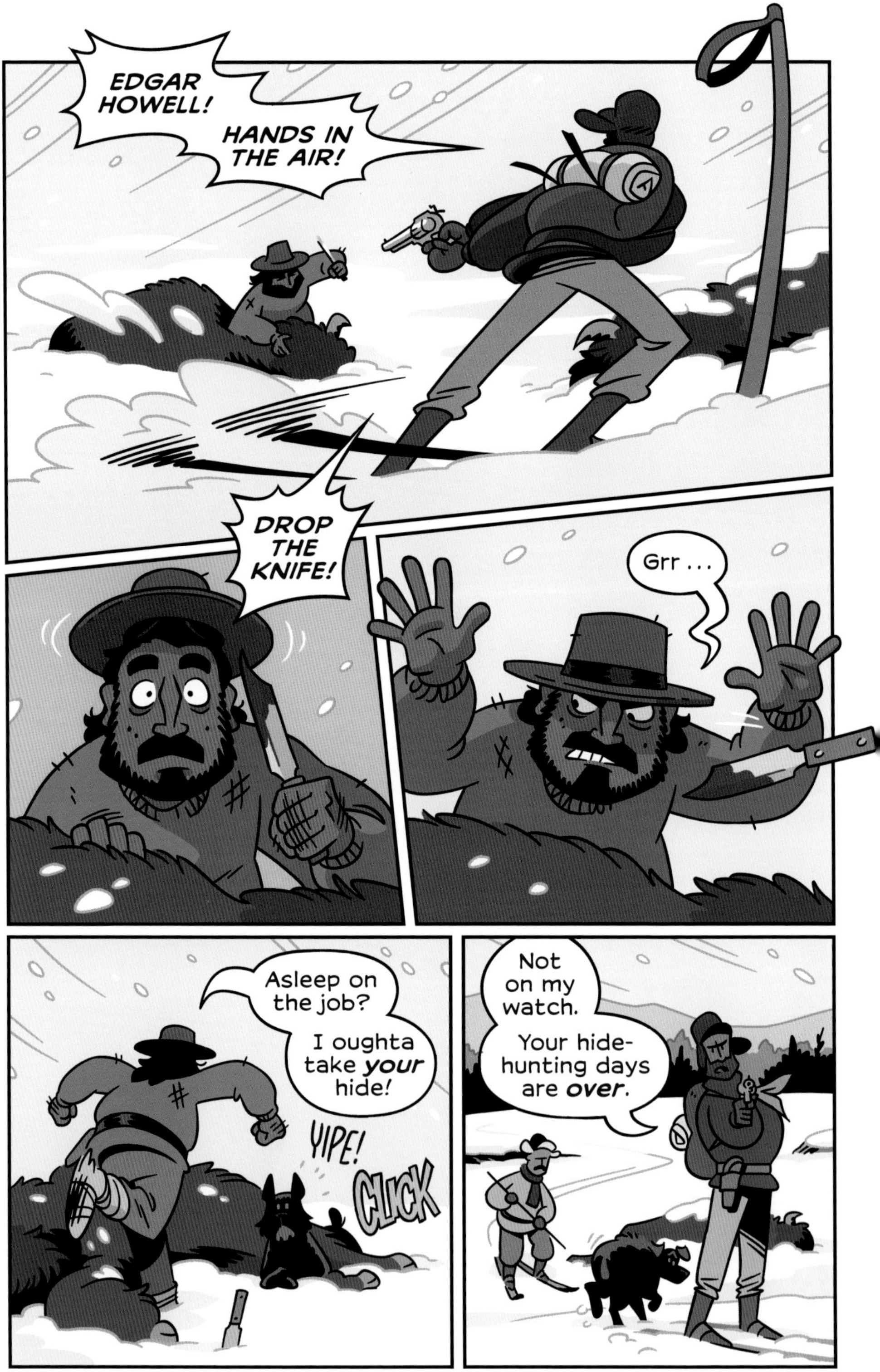
EDGAR HOWELL!
HANDS IN THE AIR!
DROP THE KNIFE!
Grr . . .
Asleep on the job?
I oughta take *your* hide!
YIPE!
CLICK
Not on my watch.
Your hide-hunting days are *over*.

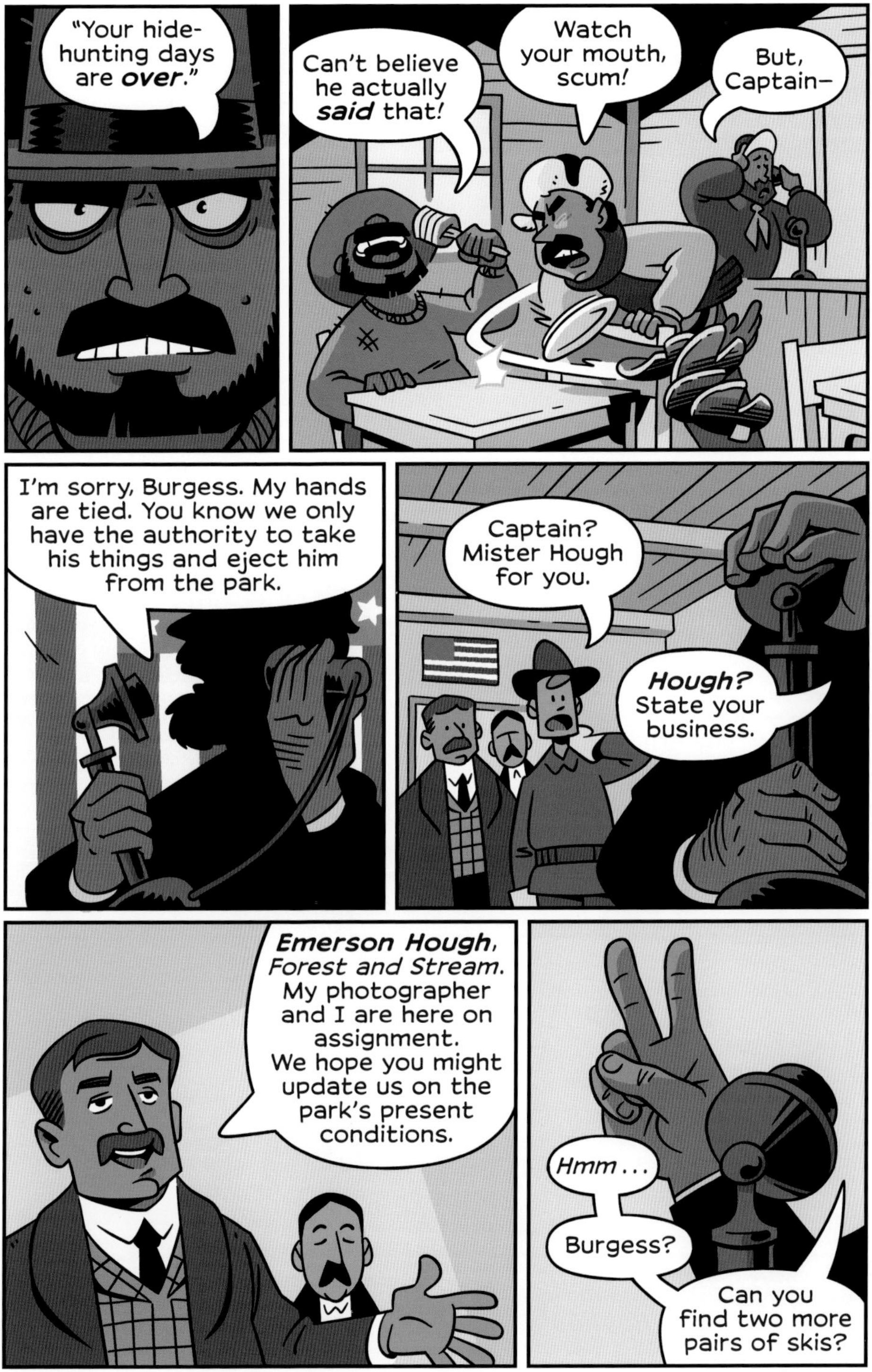
"Your hide-hunting days are *over*."
Can't believe he actually *said* that!
Watch your mouth, scum!
But, Captain—
I'm sorry, Burgess. My hands are tied. You know we only have the authority to take his things and eject him from the park.
Captain? Mister Hough for you.
Hough? State your business.
Emerson Hough, *Forest and Stream*. My photographer and I are here on assignment. We hope you might update us on the park's present conditions.
Hmm . . .
Burgess?
Can you find two more pairs of skis?

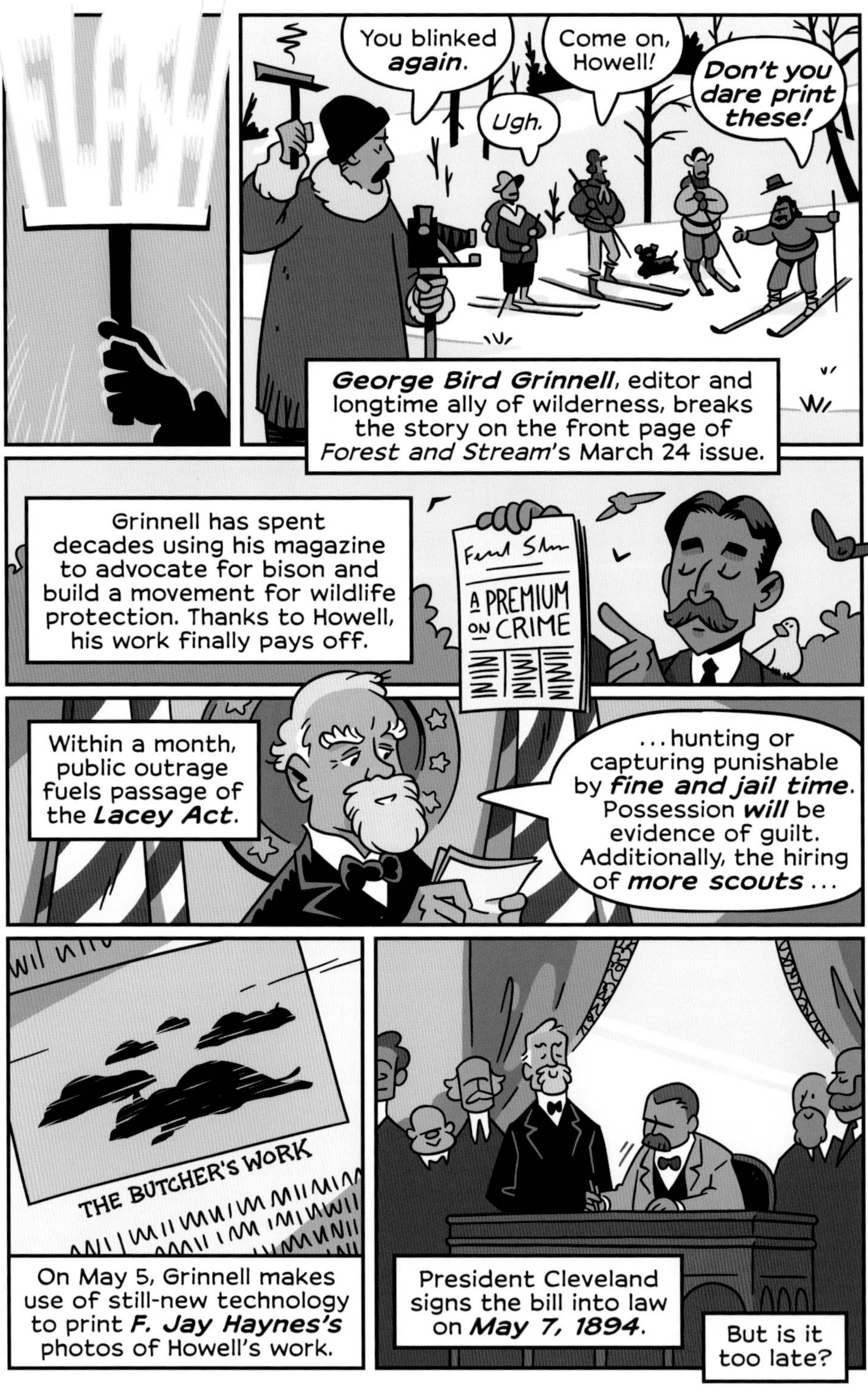
You blinked again.
Ugh.
Come on, Howell!
Don't you dare print these!
George Bird Grinnell, editor and longtime ally of wilderness, breaks the story on the front page of Forest and Stream's March 24 issue.
Grinnell has spent decades using his magazine to advocate for bison and build a movement for wildlife protection. Thanks to Howell, his work finally pays off.
A PREMIUM ON CRIME
Within a month, public outrage fuels passage of the Lacey Act.
...hunting or capturing punishable by fine and jail time. Possession will be evidence of guilt. Additionally, the hiring of more scouts...
THE BUTCHER'S WORK
On May 5, Grinnell makes use of still-new technology to print F. Jay Haynes's photos of Howell's work.
President Cleveland signs the bill into law on May 7, 1894.
But is it too late?

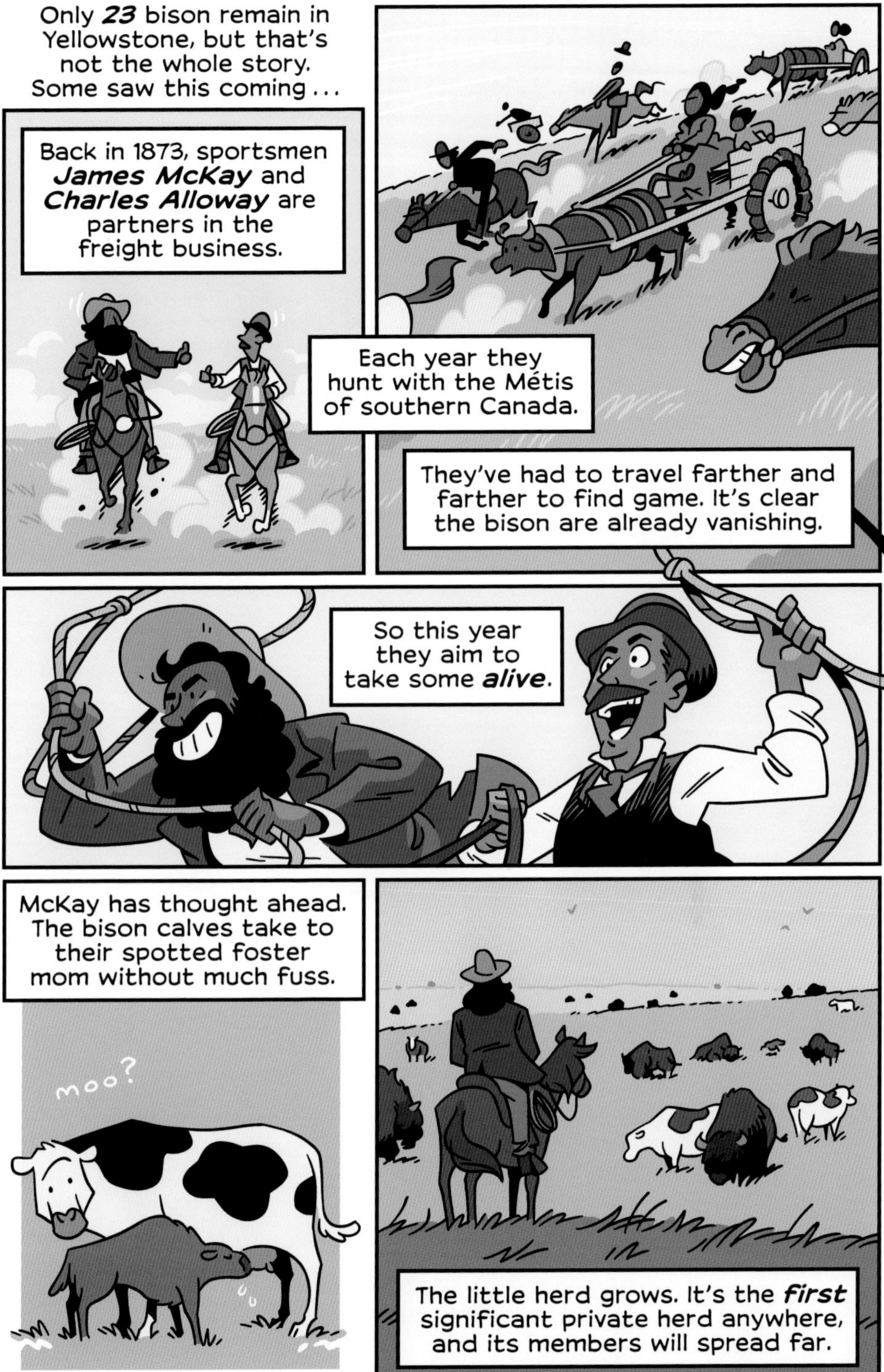
Only *23* bison remain in Yellowstone, but that's not the whole story. Some saw this coming . . .
Back in 1873, sportsmen *James McKay* and *Charles Alloway* are partners in the freight business.
Each year they hunt with the Métis of southern Canada.
They've had to travel farther and farther to find game. It's clear the bison are already vanishing.
So this year they aim to take some *alive*.
McKay has thought ahead. The bison calves take to their spotted foster mom without much fuss.
moo?
The little herd grows. It's the *first* significant private herd anywhere, and its members will spread far.

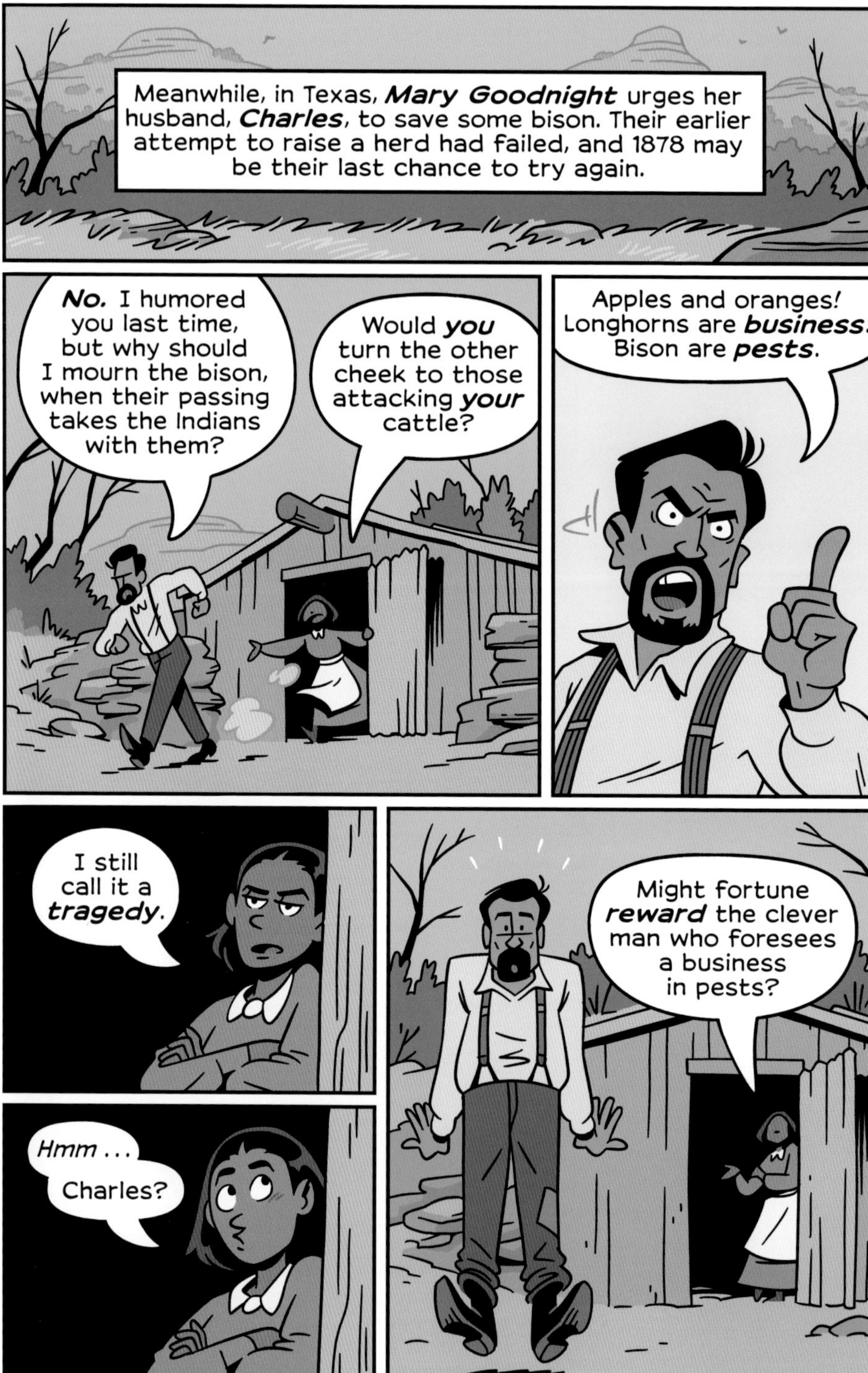

Meanwhile, in Texas, ***Mary Goodnight*** urges her husband, ***Charles***, to save some bison. Their earlier attempt to raise a herd had failed, and 1878 may be their last chance to try again.
No. I humored you last time, but why should I mourn the bison, when their passing takes the Indians with them?
Would ***you*** turn the other cheek to those attacking ***your*** cattle?
Apples and oranges! Longhorns are ***business***. Bison are ***pests***.
I still call it a ***tragedy***.
Hmm . . .
Charles?
Might fortune ***reward*** the clever man who foresees a business in pests?

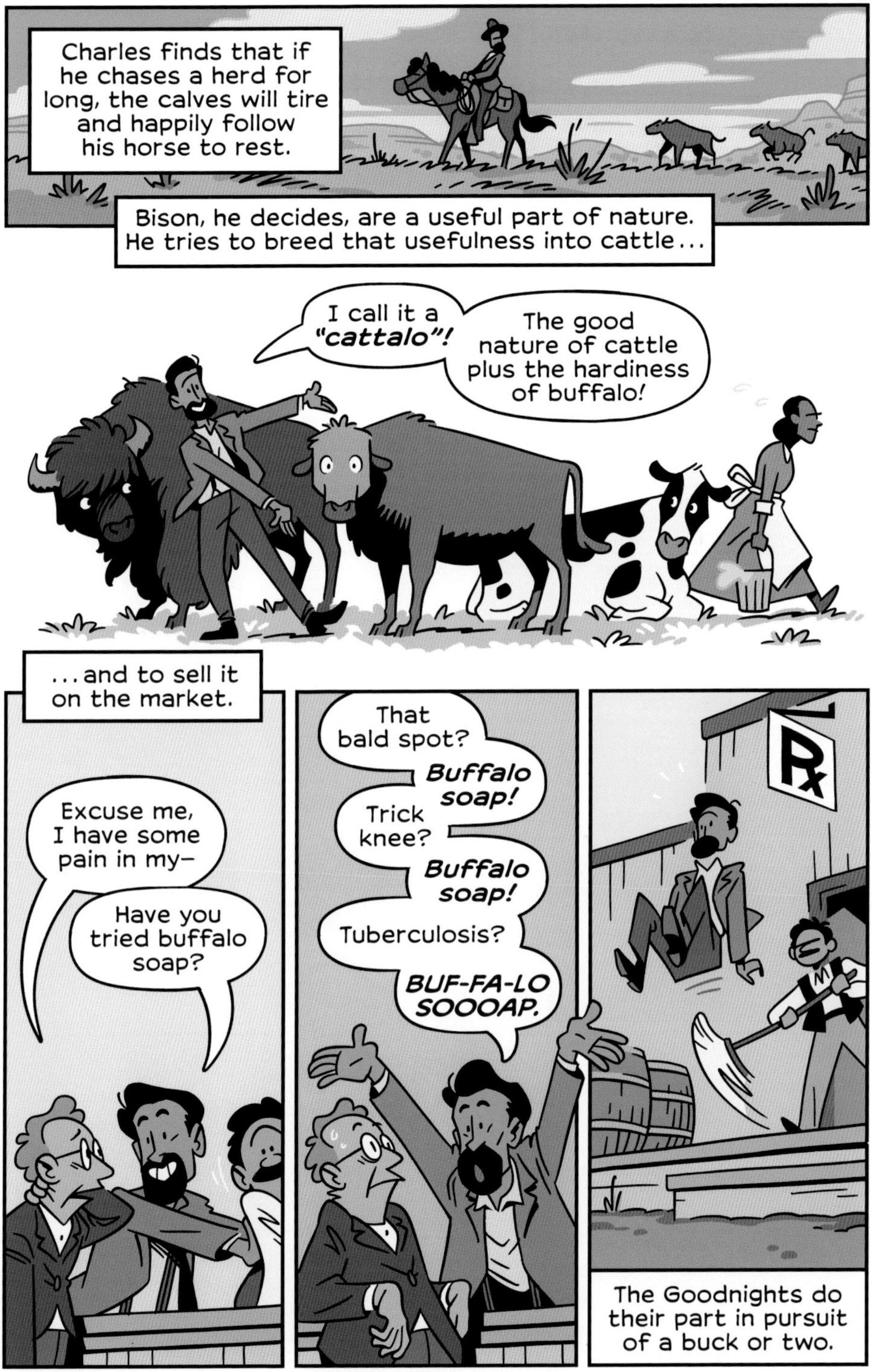
Charles finds that if he chases a herd for long, the calves will tire and happily follow his horse to rest.
Bison, he decides, are a useful part of nature. He tries to breed that usefulness into cattle...
I call it a "cattalo"!
The good nature of cattle plus the hardiness of buffalo!
...and to sell it on the market.
Excuse me, I have some pain in my–
Have you tried buffalo soap?
That bald spot?
Buffalo soap!
Trick knee?
Buffalo soap!
Tuberculosis?
BUF-FA-LO SOOOAP.
Rx
The Goodnights do their part in pursuit of a buck or two.

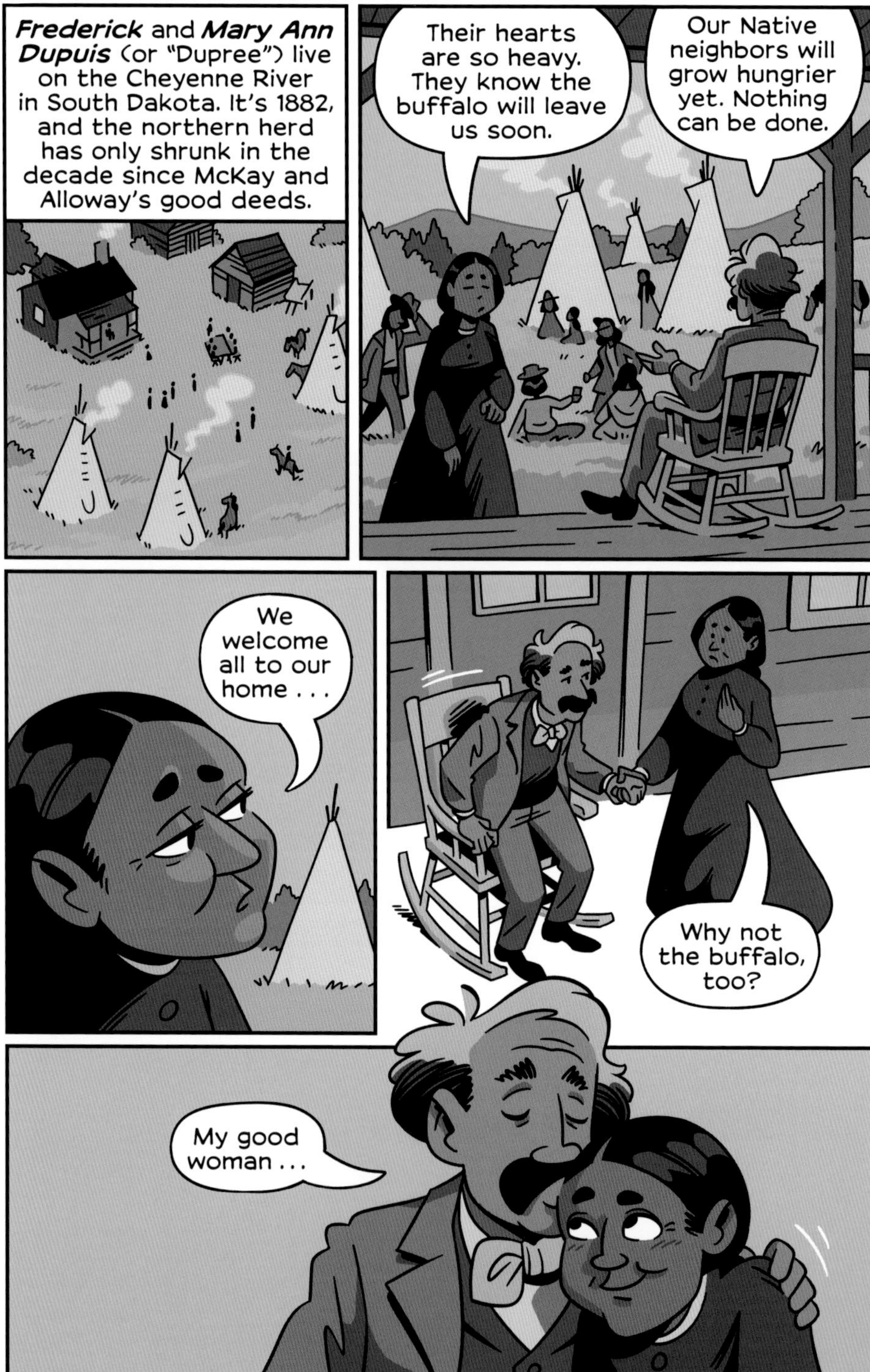

Frederick and ***Mary Ann Dupuis*** (or "Dupree") live on the Cheyenne River in South Dakota. It's 1882, and the northern herd has only shrunk in the decade since McKay and Alloway's good deeds.
Their hearts are so heavy. They know the buffalo will leave us soon.
Our Native neighbors will grow hungrier yet. Nothing can be done.
We welcome all to our home . . .
Why not the buffalo, too?
My good woman . . .

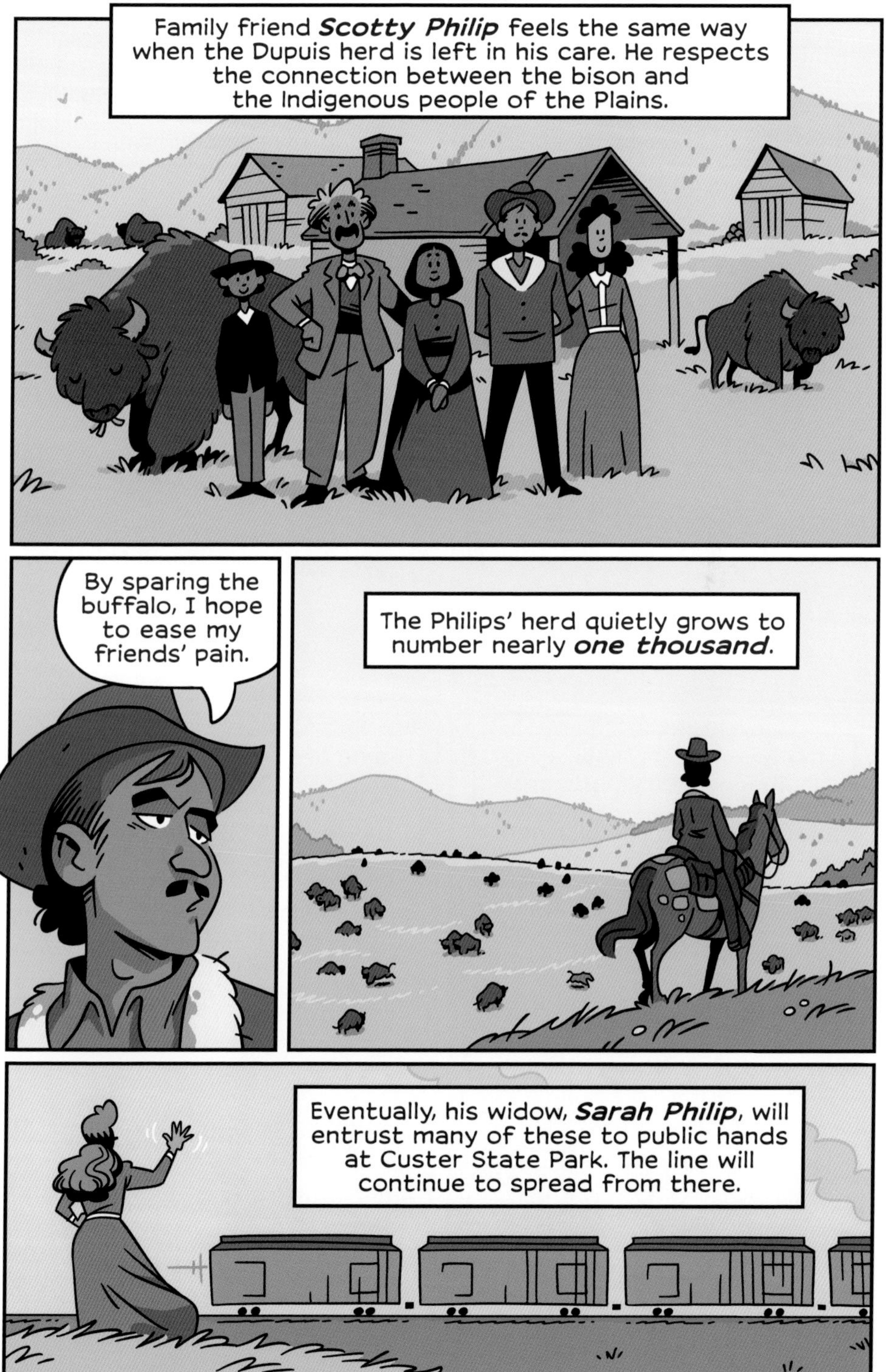
Family friend **Scotty Philip** feels the same way when the Dupuis herd is left in his care. He respects the connection between the bison and the Indigenous people of the Plains.
By sparing the buffalo, I hope to ease my friends' pain.
The Philips' herd quietly grows to number nearly ***one thousand***.
Eventually, his widow, **Sarah Philip**, will entrust many of these to public hands at Custer State Park. The line will continue to spread from there.

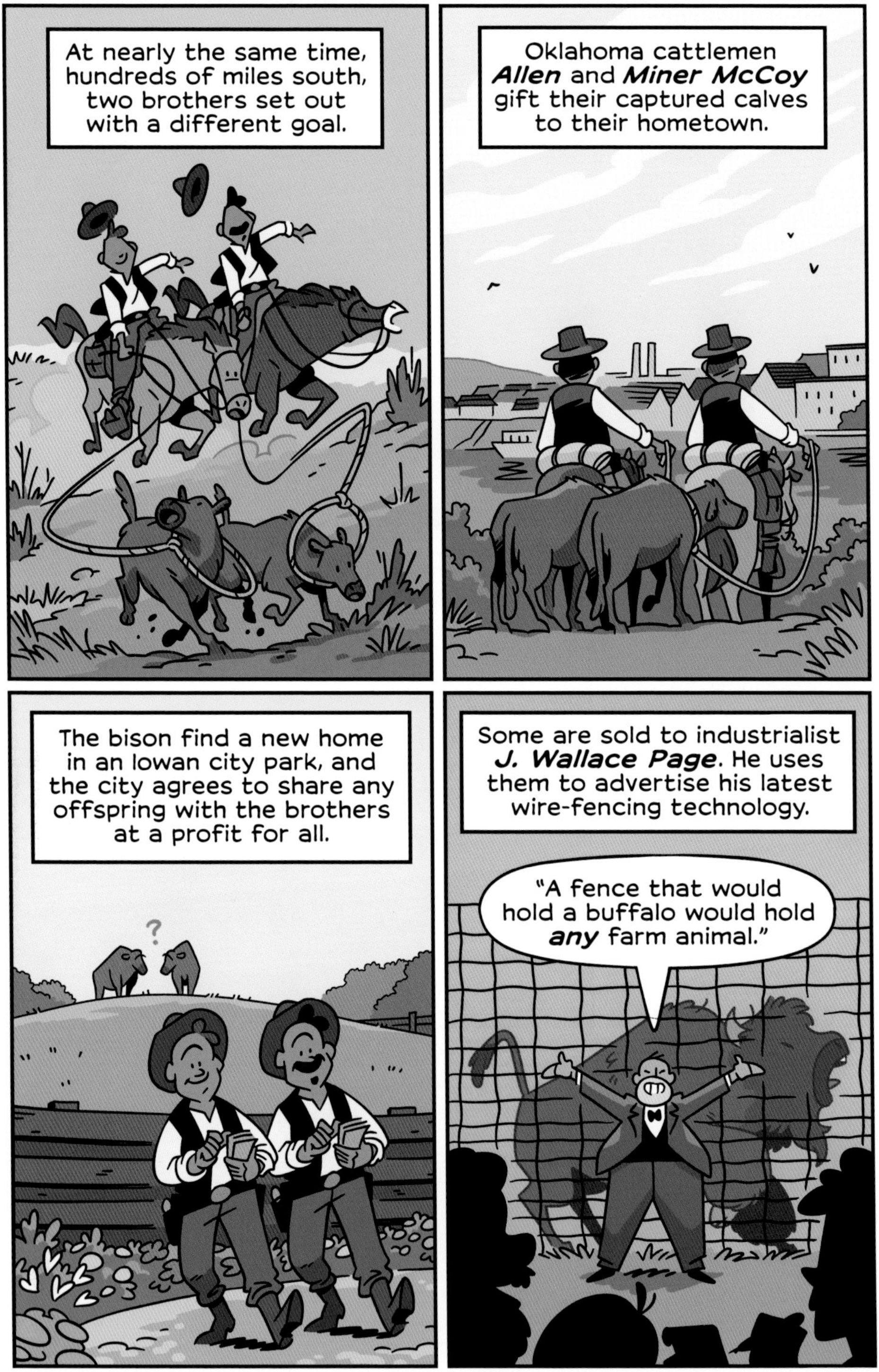
At nearly the same time, hundreds of miles south, two brothers set out with a different goal.
Oklahoma cattlemen *Allen* and *Miner McCoy* gift their captured calves to their hometown.
The bison find a new home in an Iowan city park, and the city agrees to share any offspring with the brothers at a profit for all.
?
Some are sold to industrialist *J. Wallace Page*. He uses them to advertise his latest wire-fencing technology.
"A fence that would hold a buffalo would hold *any* farm animal."

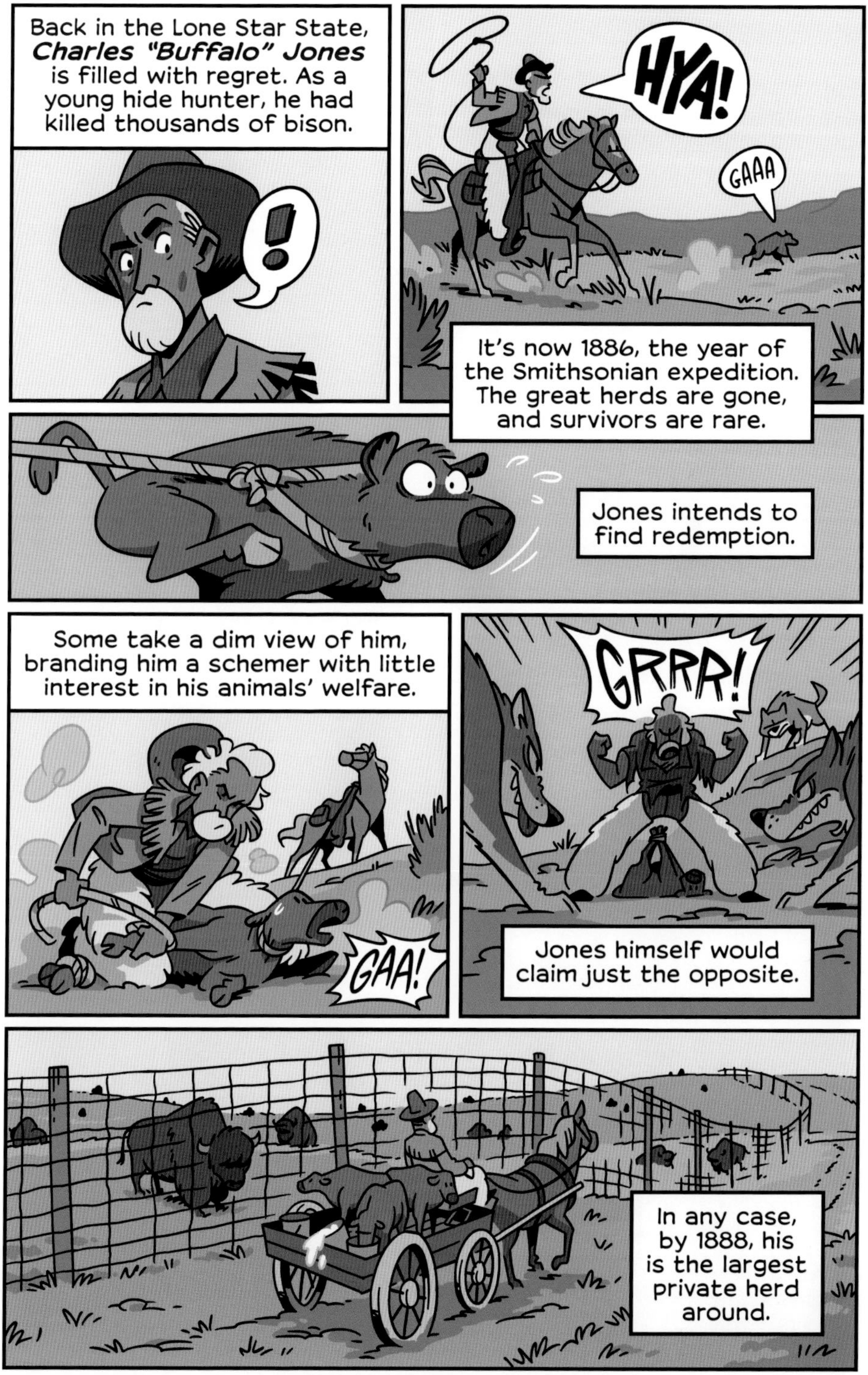
Back in the Lone Star State, ***Charles "Buffalo" Jones*** is filled with regret. As a young hide hunter, he had killed thousands of bison.
!
HYA!
GAAA
It's now 1886, the year of the Smithsonian expedition. The great herds are gone, and survivors are rare.
Jones intends to find redemption.
Some take a dim view of him, branding him a schemer with little interest in his animals' welfare.
GAA!
GRRR!
Jones himself would claim just the opposite.
In any case, by 1888, his is the largest private herd around.

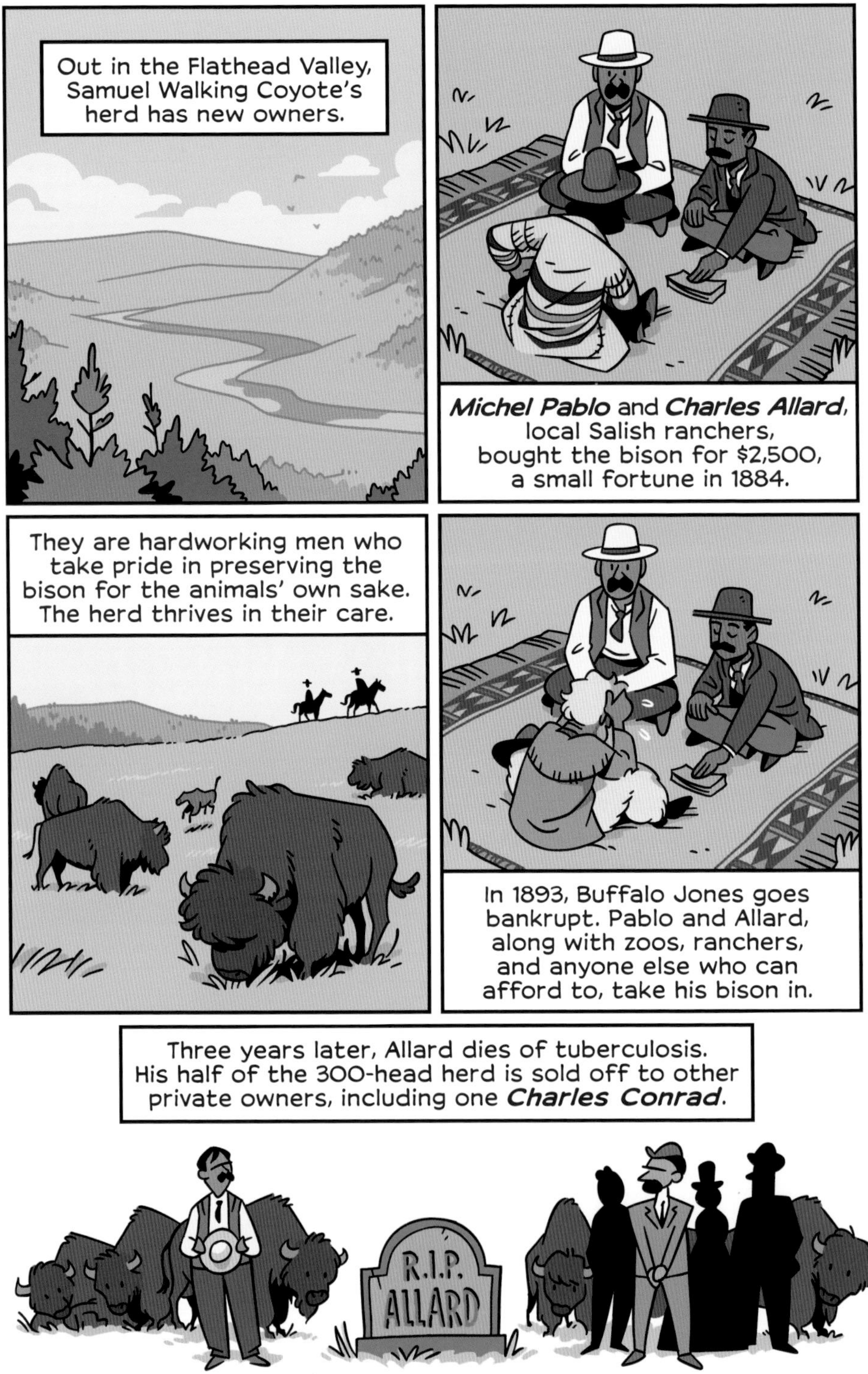
Out in the Flathead Valley, Samuel Walking Coyote's herd has new owners.
Michel Pablo and *Charles Allard*, local Salish ranchers, bought the bison for $2,500, a small fortune in 1884.
They are hardworking men who take pride in preserving the bison for the animals' own sake. The herd thrives in their care.
In 1893, Buffalo Jones goes bankrupt. Pablo and Allard, along with zoos, ranchers, and anyone else who can afford to, take his bison in.
Three years later, Allard dies of tuberculosis. His half of the 300-head herd is sold off to other private owners, including one *Charles Conrad*.
R.I.P. ALLARD

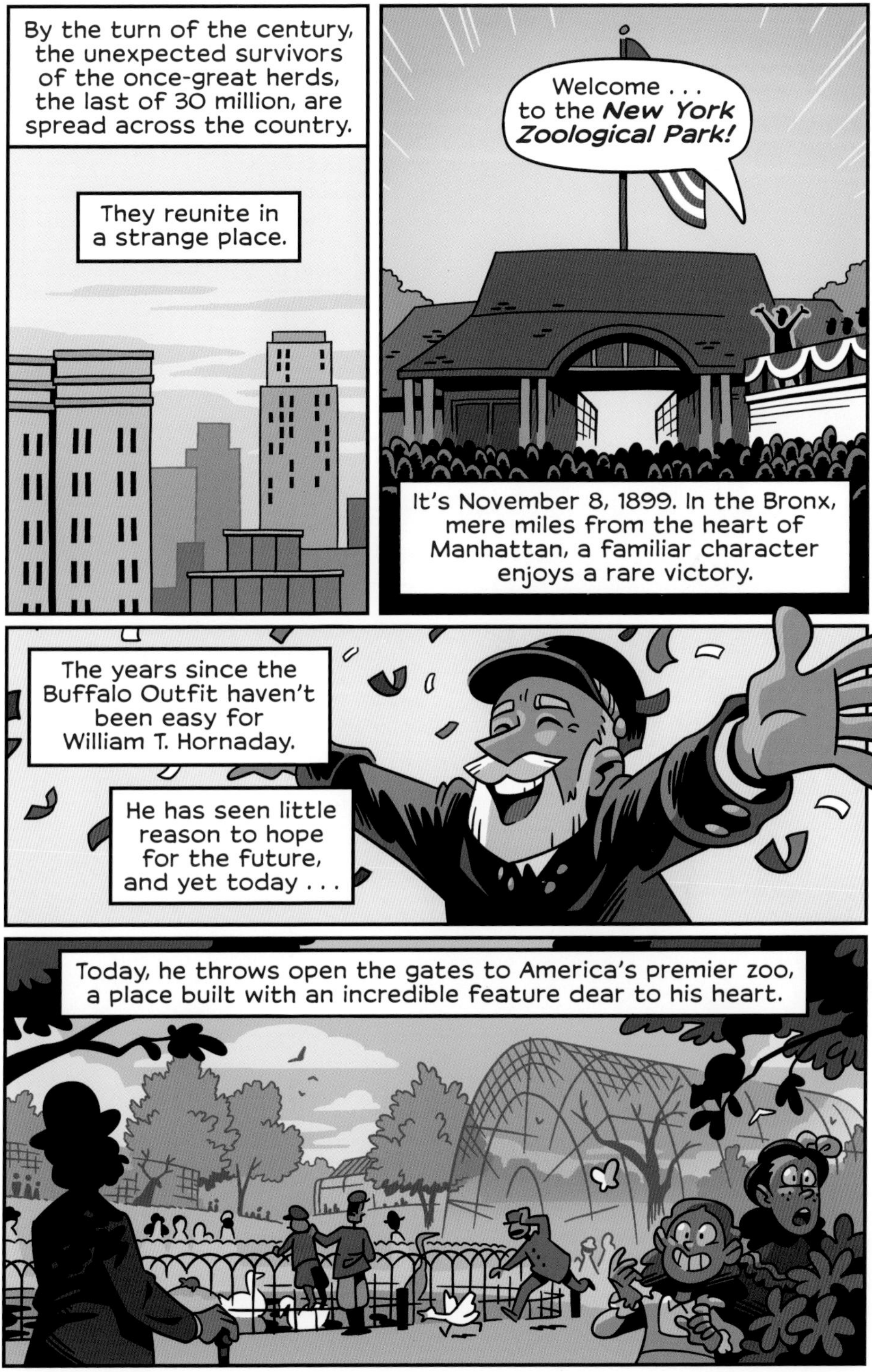
By the turn of the century, the unexpected survivors of the once-great herds, the last of 30 million, are spread across the country.
They reunite in a strange place.
Welcome . . . to the ***New York Zoological Park!***
It's November 8, 1899. In the Bronx, mere miles from the heart of Manhattan, a familiar character enjoys a rare victory.
The years since the Buffalo Outfit haven't been easy for William T. Hornaday.
He has seen little reason to hope for the future, and yet today . . .
Today, he throws open the gates to America's premier zoo, a place built with an incredible feature dear to his heart.

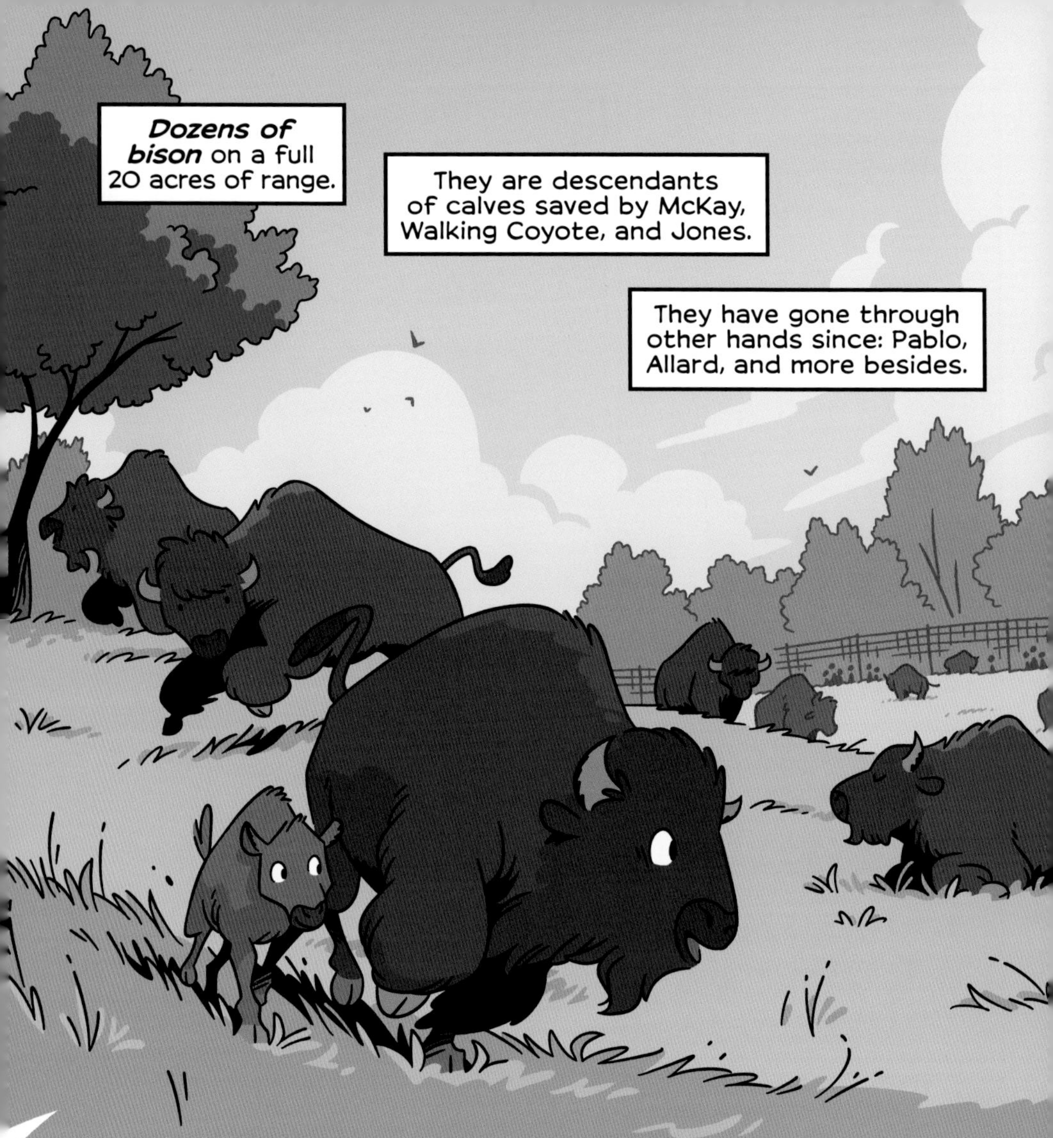
Dozens of bison on a full 20 acres of range.
They are descendants of calves saved by McKay, Walking Coyote, and Jones.
They have gone through other hands since: Pablo, Allard, and more besides.

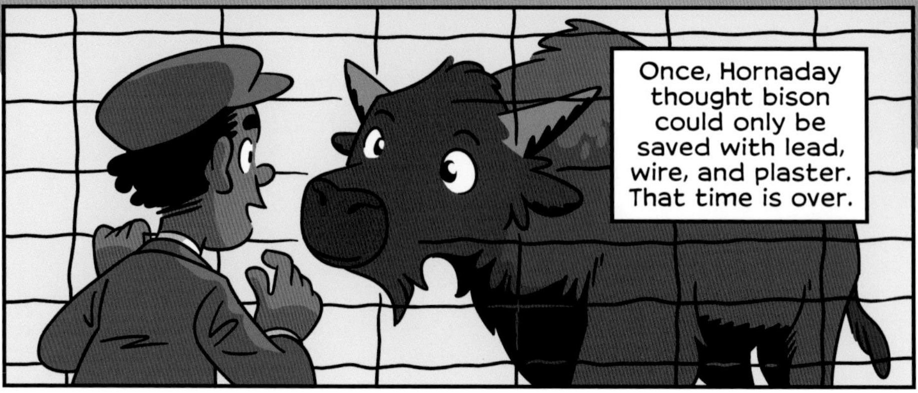
Once, Hornaday thought bison could only be saved with lead, wire, and plaster. That time is over.

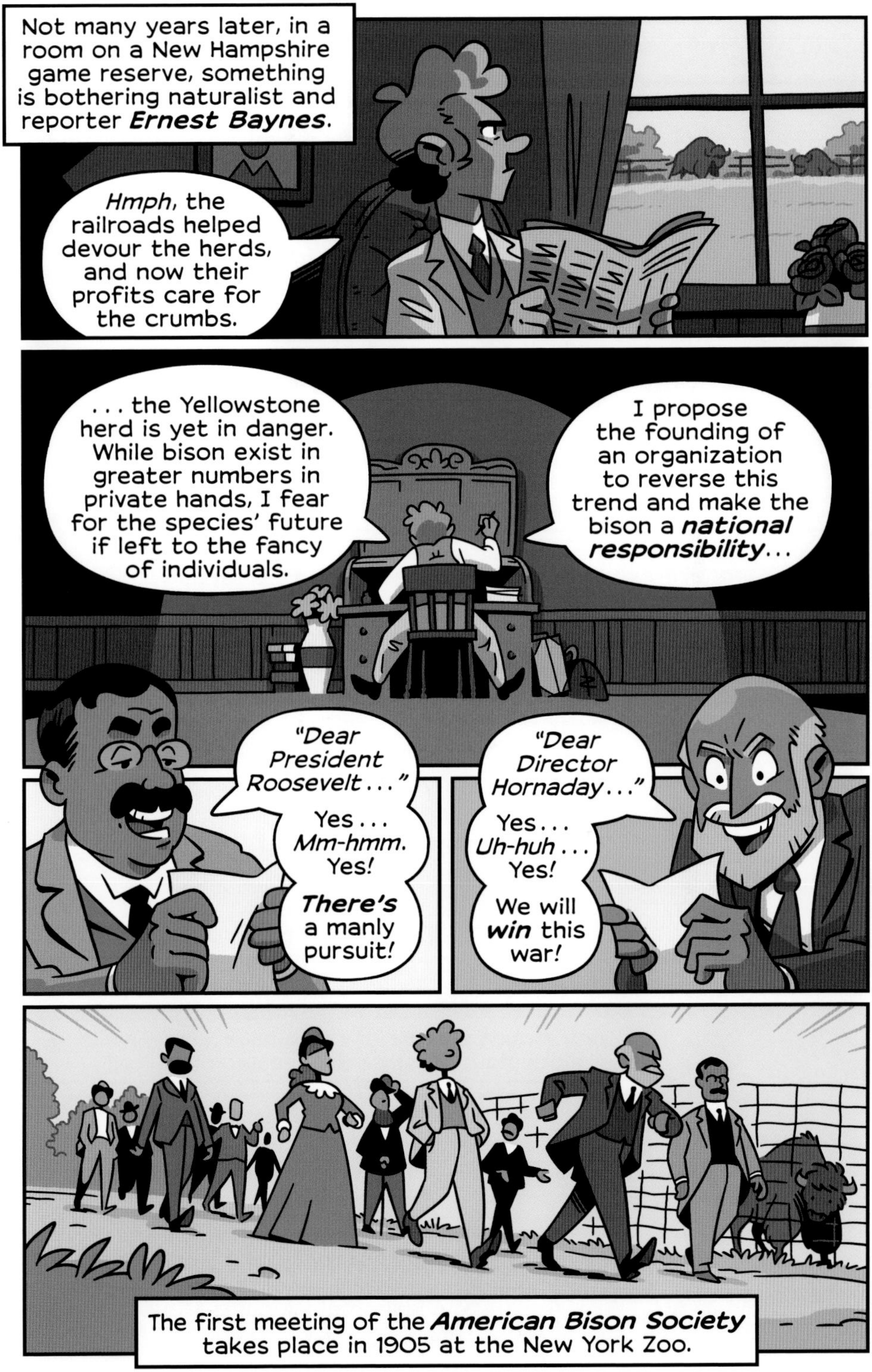
Not many years later, in a room on a New Hampshire game reserve, something is bothering naturalist and reporter ***Ernest Baynes***.
Hmph, the railroads helped devour the herds, and now their profits care for the crumbs.
. . . the Yellowstone herd is yet in danger. While bison exist in greater numbers in private hands, I fear for the species' future if left to the fancy of individuals.
I propose the founding of an organization to reverse this trend and make the bison a ***national responsibility***. . .
"Dear President Roosevelt . . ."
Yes . . . *Mm-hmm.* Yes!
There's a manly pursuit!
"Dear Director Hornaday . . ."
Yes . . . *Uh-huh* . . . Yes!
We will ***win*** this war!
The first meeting of the ***American Bison Society*** takes place in 1905 at the New York Zoo.

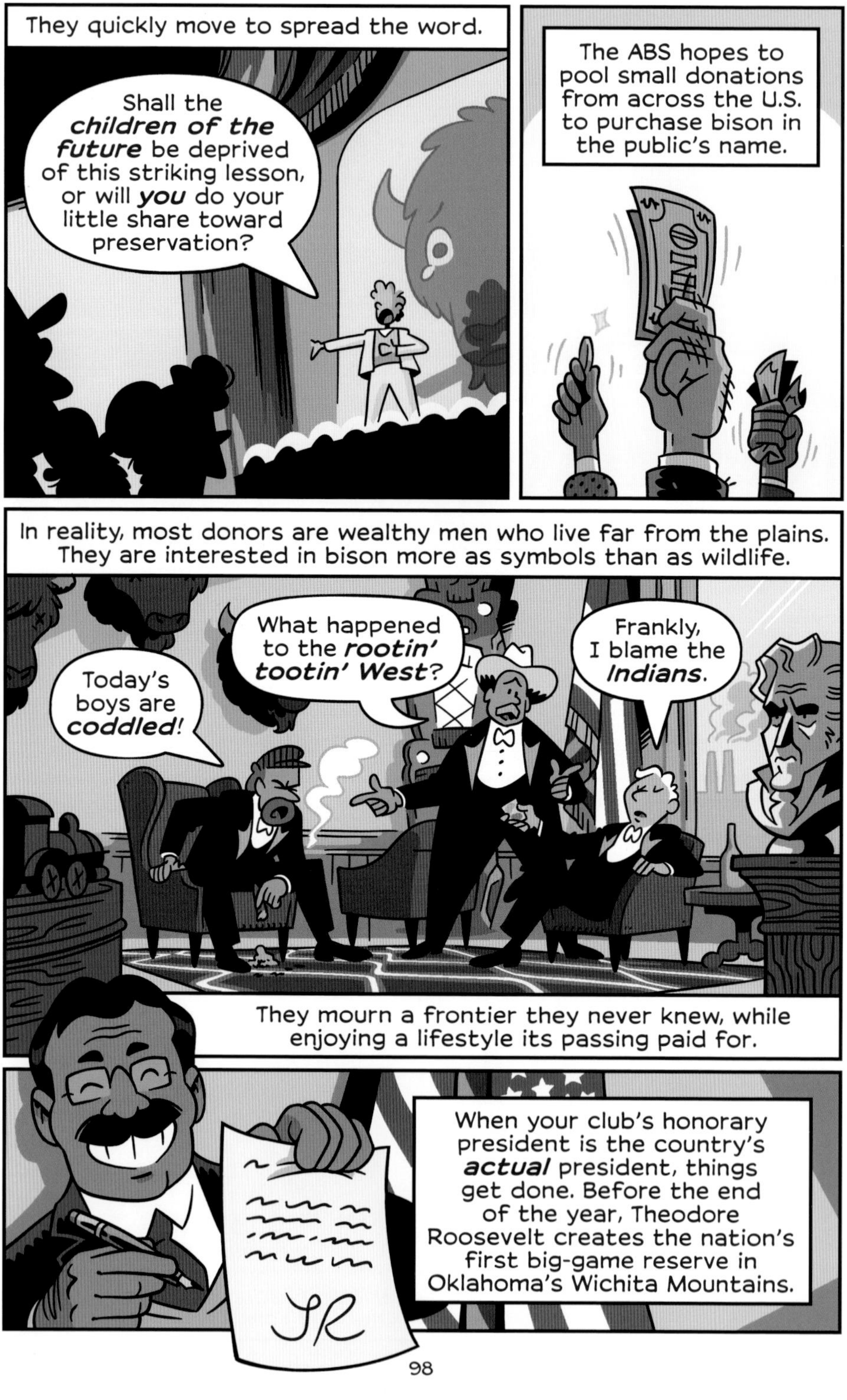
They quickly move to spread the word.
Shall the children of the future be deprived of this striking lesson, or will you do your little share toward preservation?
The ABS hopes to pool small donations from across the U.S. to purchase bison in the public's name.
In reality, most donors are wealthy men who live far from the plains. They are interested in bison more as symbols than as wildlife.
Today's boys are coddled!
What happened to the rootin' tootin' West?
Frankly, I blame the Indians.
They mourn a frontier they never knew, while enjoying a lifestyle its passing paid for.
When your club's honorary president is the country's actual president, things get done. Before the end of the year, Theodore Roosevelt creates the nation's first big-game reserve in Oklahoma's Wichita Mountains.

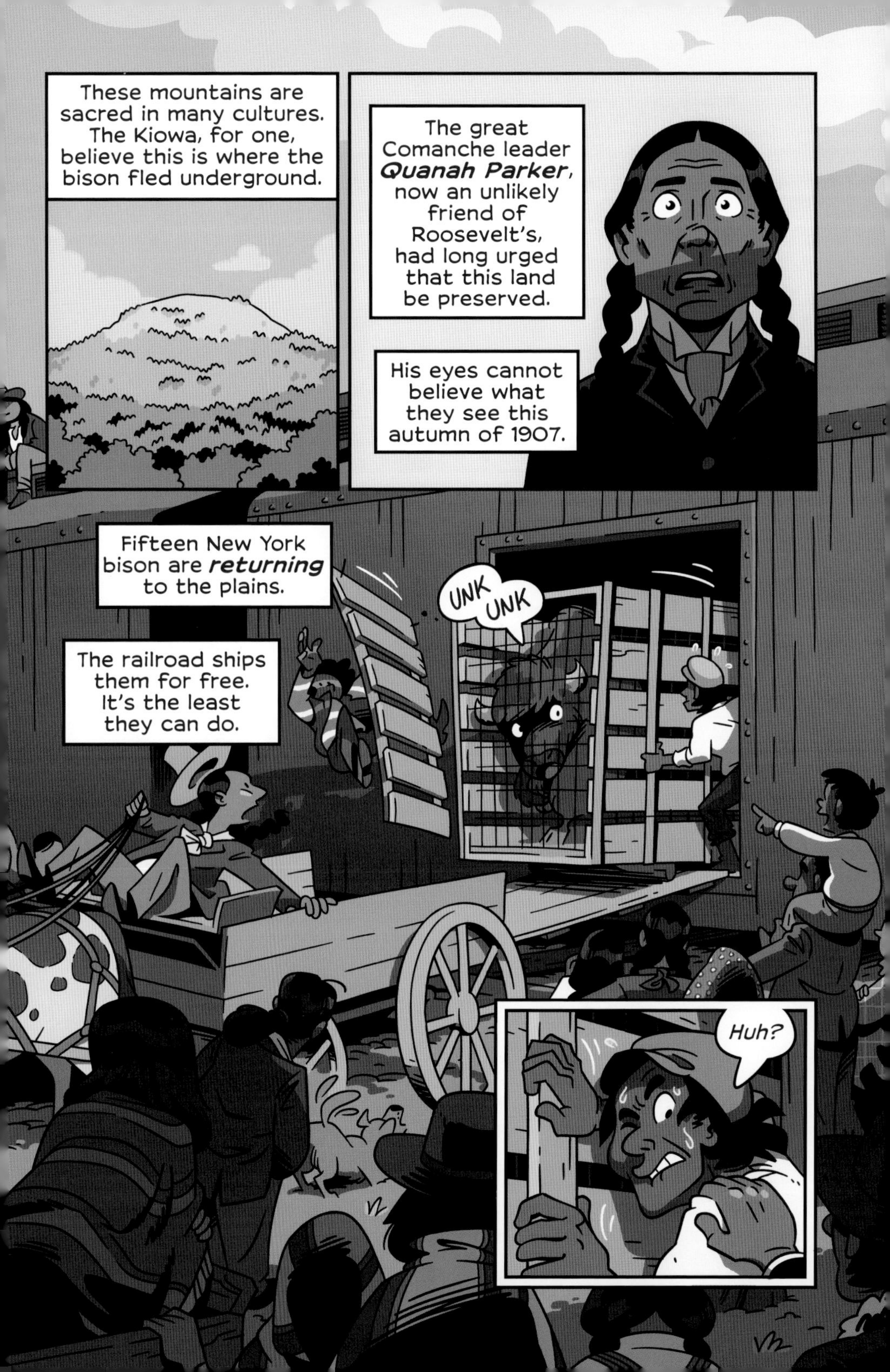
These mountains are sacred in many cultures. The Kiowa, for one, believe this is where the bison fled underground.
The great Comanche leader ***Quanah Parker***, now an unlikely friend of Roosevelt's, had long urged that this land be preserved.
His eyes cannot believe what they see this autumn of 1907.
Fifteen New York bison are ***returning*** to the plains.
The railroad ships them for free. It's the least they can do.
UNK UNK
Huh?

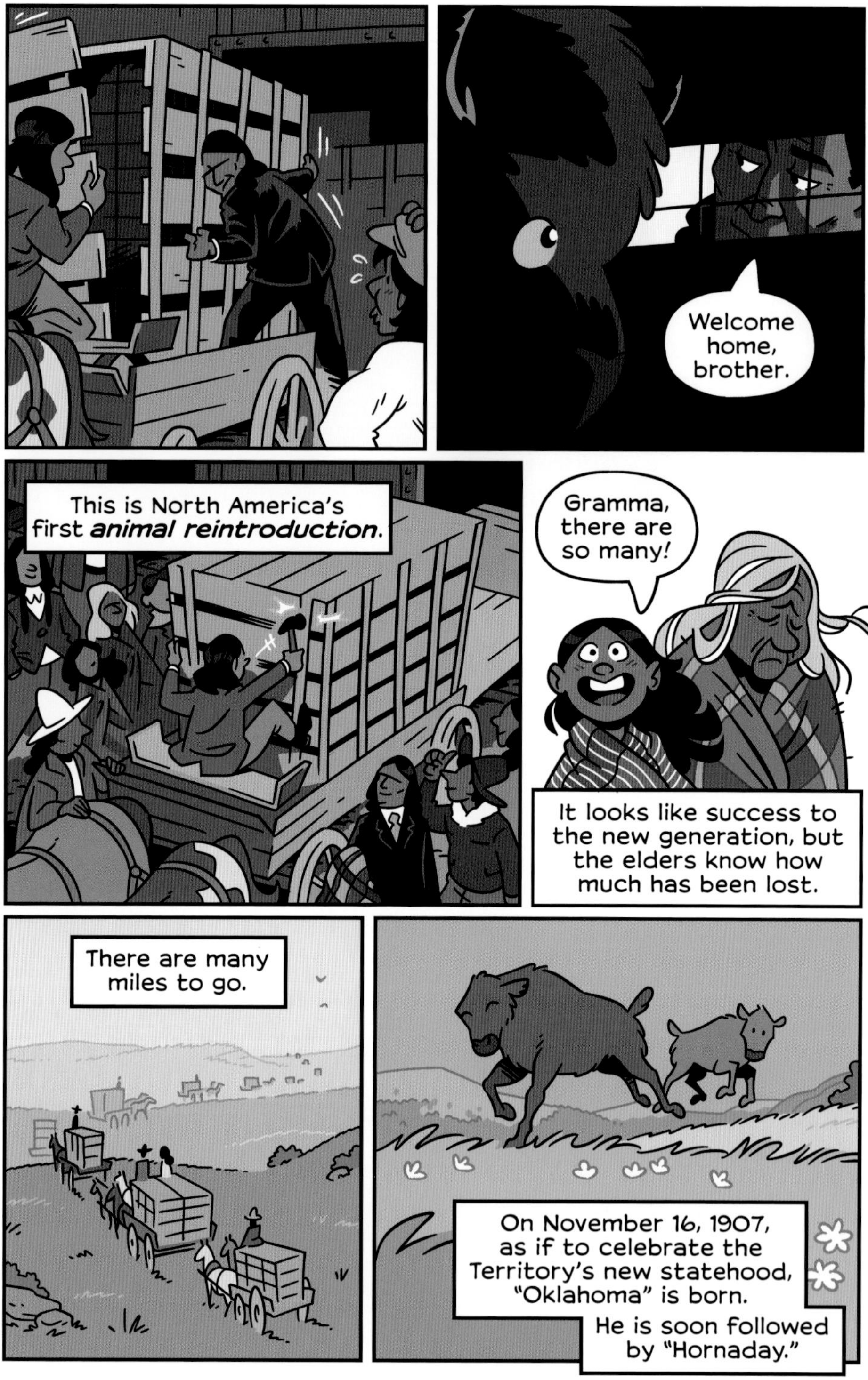

Welcome home, brother.
This is North America's first ***animal reintroduction***.
Gramma, there are so many!
It looks like success to the new generation, but the elders know how much has been lost.
There are many miles to go.
On November 16, 1907, as if to celebrate the Territory's new statehood, "Oklahoma" is born.
He is soon followed by "Hornaday."

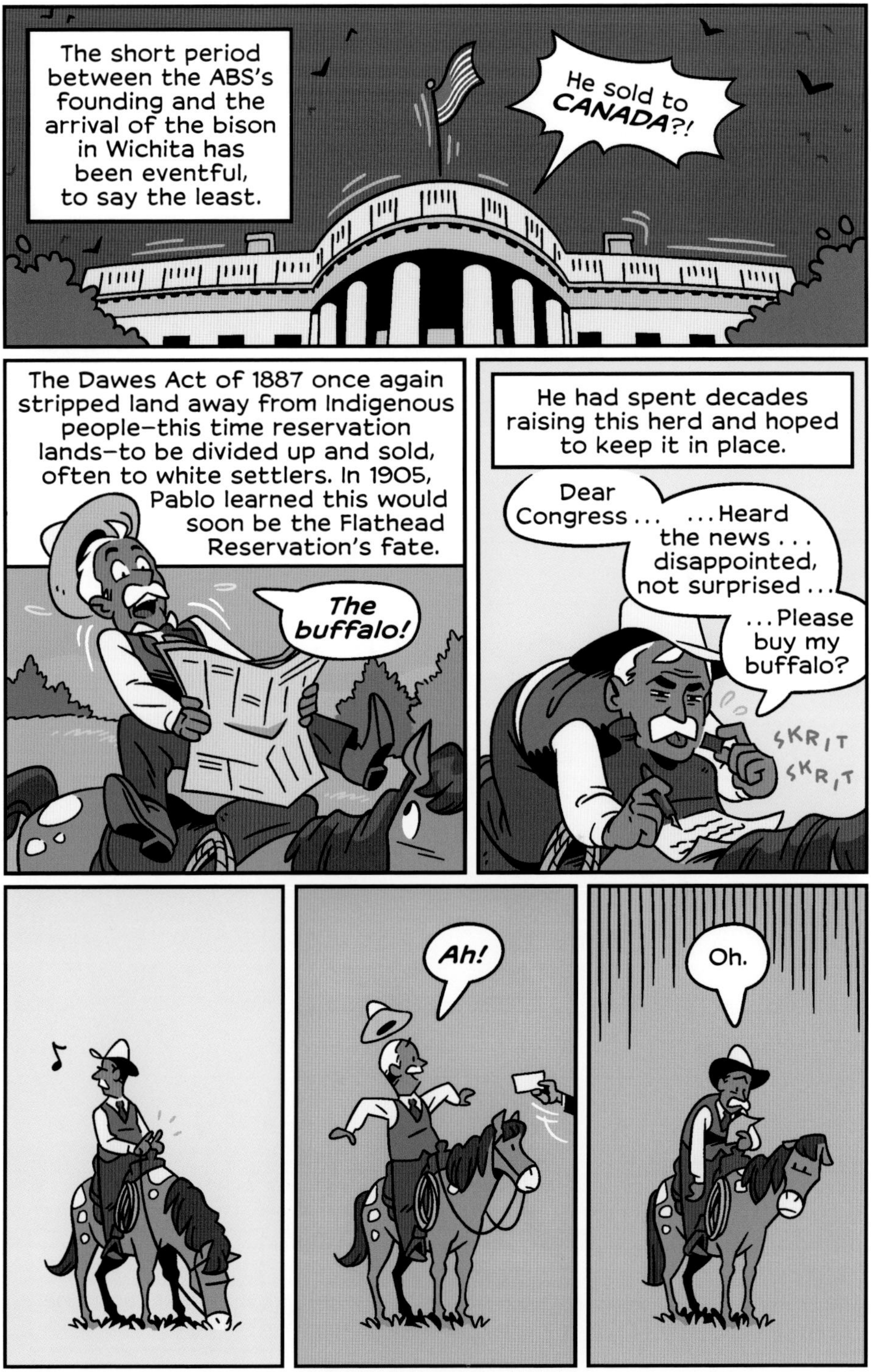
The short period between the ABS's founding and the arrival of the bison in Wichita has been eventful, to say the least.
He sold to CANADA?!
The Dawes Act of 1887 once again stripped land away from Indigenous people—this time reservation lands—to be divided up and sold, often to white settlers. In 1905, Pablo learned this would soon be the Flathead Reservation's fate.
The buffalo!
He had spent decades raising this herd and hoped to keep it in place.
Dear Congress . . .
. . . Heard the news . . . disappointed, not surprised . . .
. . . Please buy my buffalo?
SKRIT
SKRIT
Ah!
Oh.

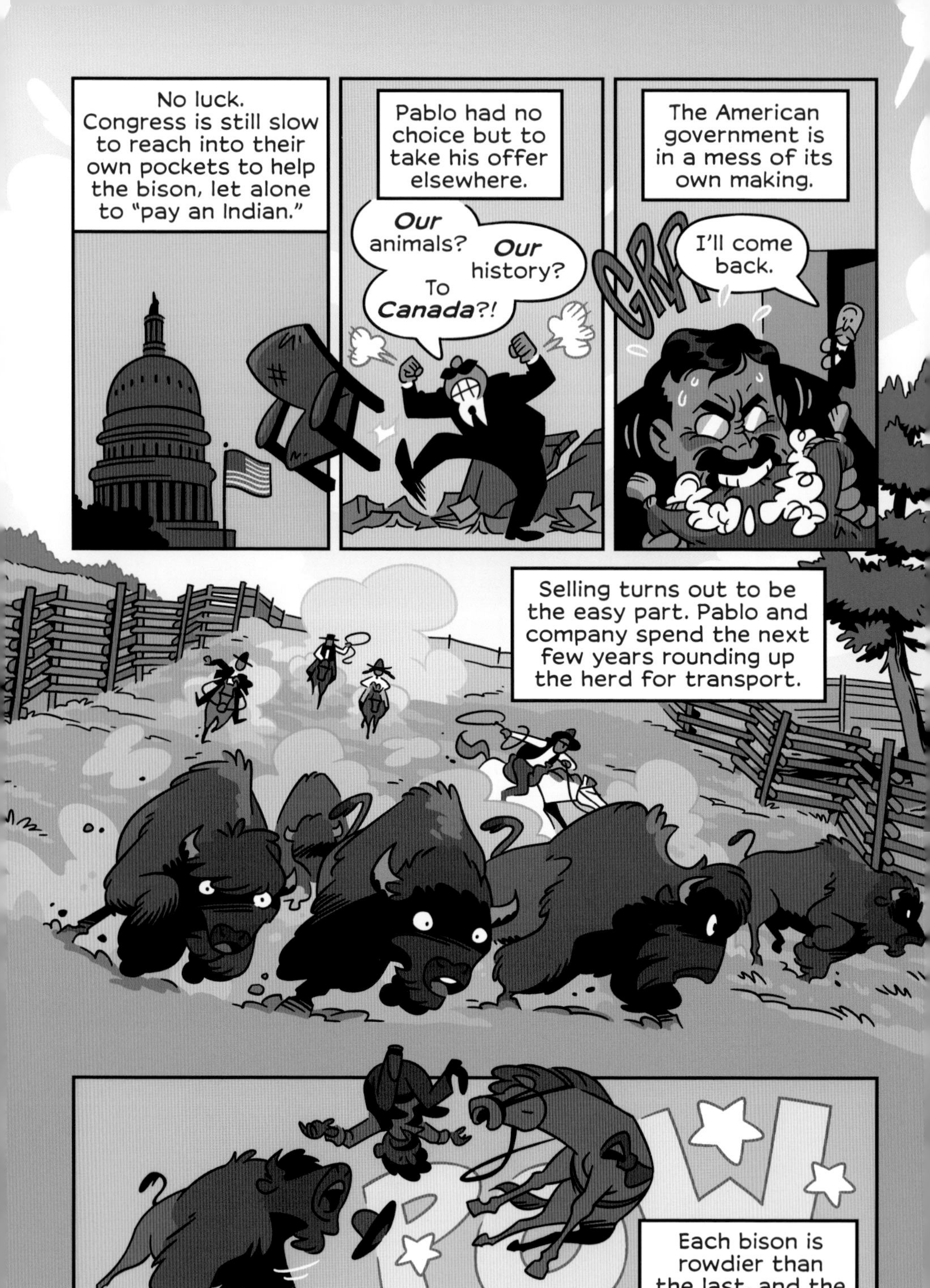
No luck. Congress is still slow to reach into their own pockets to help the bison, let alone to "pay an Indian."
Pablo had no choice but to take his offer elsewhere.
Our animals? Our history? To Canada?!
The American government is in a mess of its own making.
I'll come back.
Selling turns out to be the easy part. Pablo and company spend the next few years rounding up the herd for transport.
POW
Each bison is rowdier than the last, and the first is no picnic.

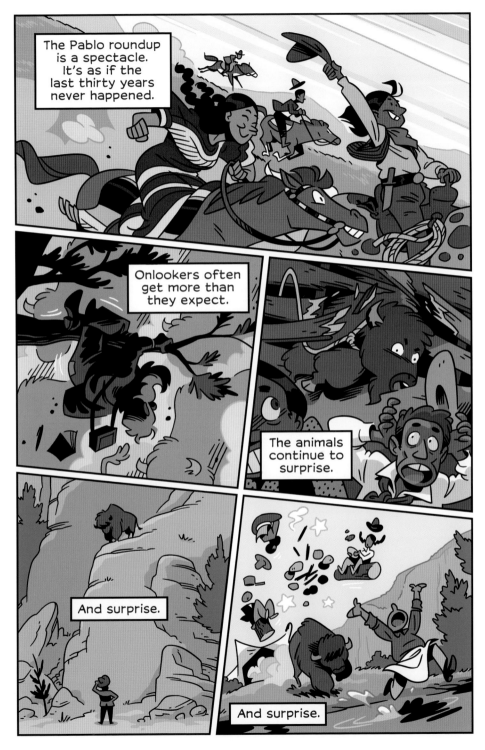

The Pablo roundup is a spectacle. It's as if the last thirty years never happened.

Onlookers often get more than they expect.

The animals continue to surprise.

And surprise.

And surprise.

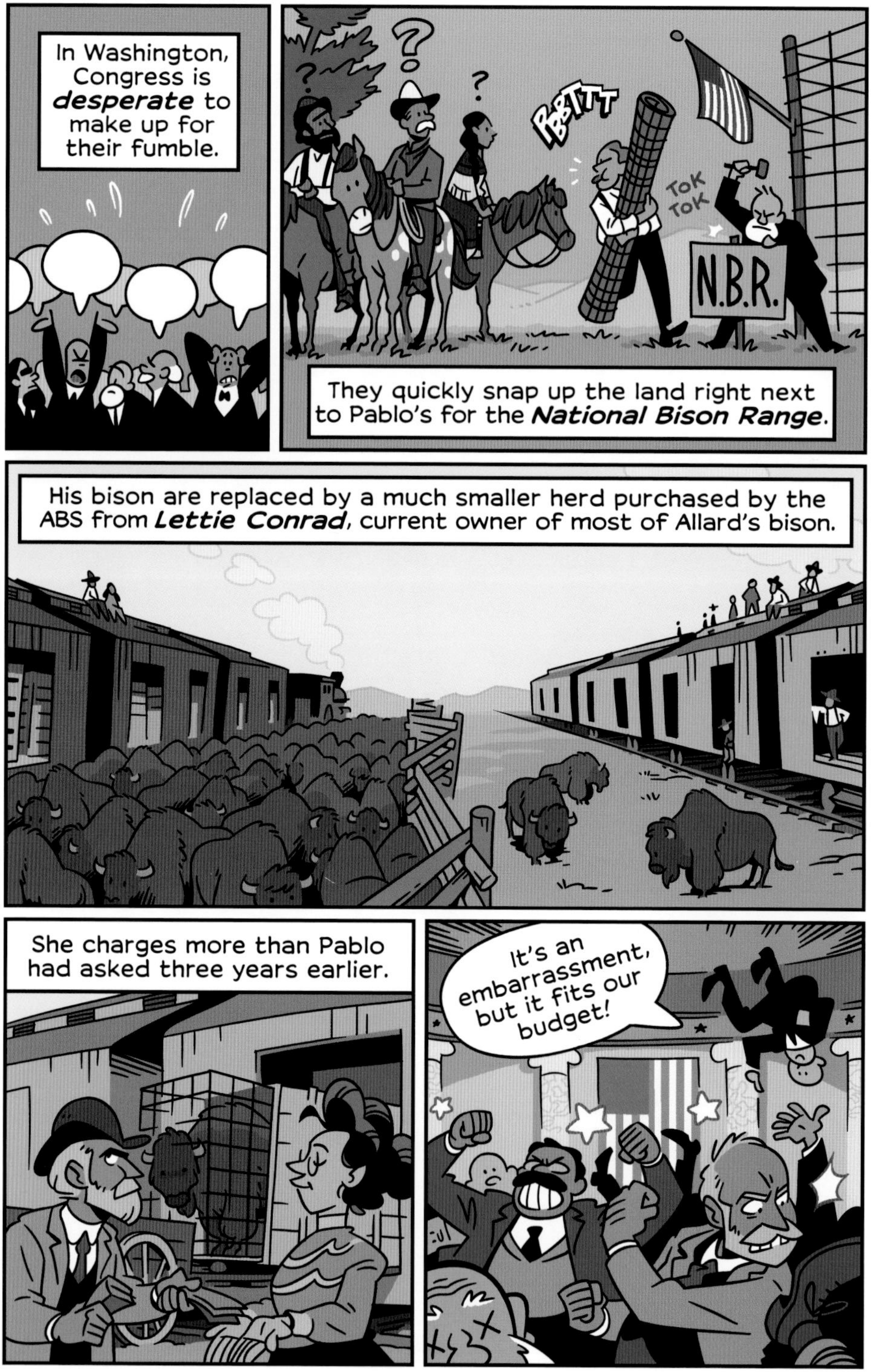
In Washington, Congress is *desperate* to make up for their fumble.
PBBTTT
TOK TOK
N.B.R.
They quickly snap up the land right next to Pablo's for the *National Bison Range*.
His bison are replaced by a much smaller herd purchased by the ABS from *Lettie Conrad*, current owner of most of Allard's bison.
She charges more than Pablo had asked three years earlier.
It's an embarrassment, but it fits our budget!

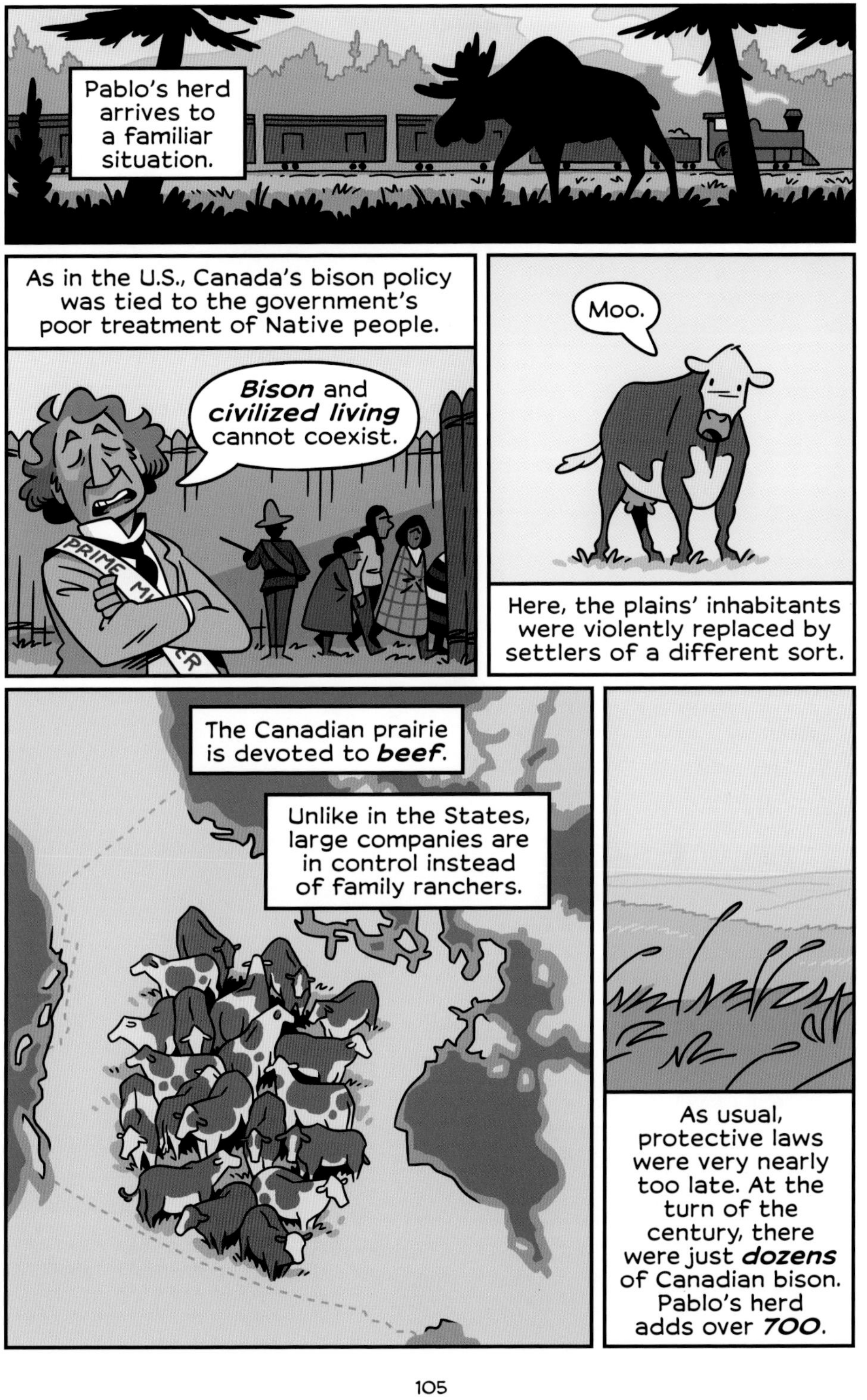
Pablo's herd arrives to a familiar situation.
As in the U.S., Canada's bison policy was tied to the government's poor treatment of Native people.
Bison and *civilized living* cannot coexist.
Moo.
Here, the plains' inhabitants were violently replaced by settlers of a different sort.
The Canadian prairie is devoted to *beef*.
Unlike in the States, large companies are in control instead of family ranchers.
As usual, protective laws were very nearly too late. At the turn of the century, there were just *dozens* of Canadian bison. Pablo's herd adds over *700*.

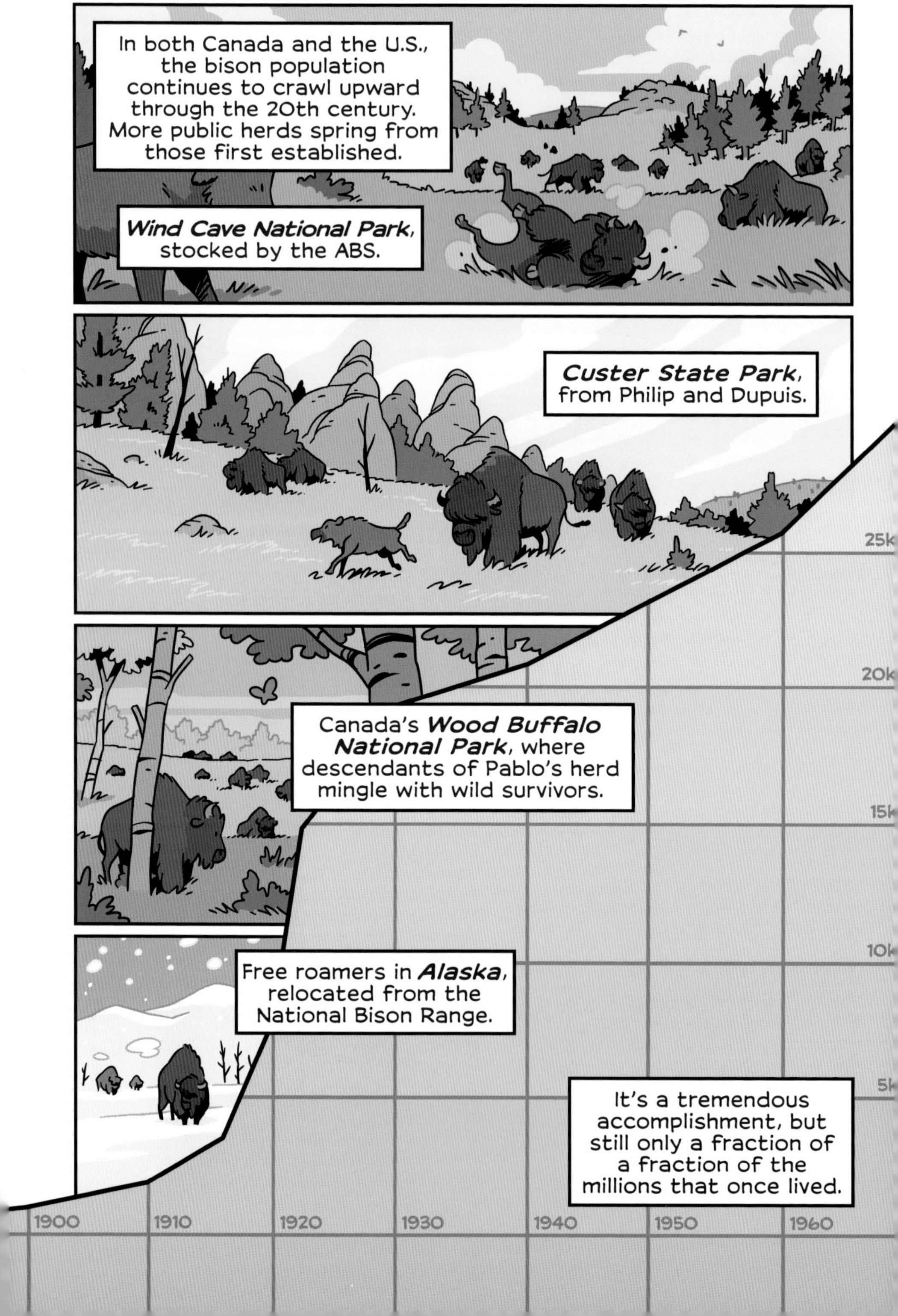

In both Canada and the U.S., the bison population continues to crawl upward through the 20th century. More public herds spring from those first established.
Wind Cave National Park, stocked by the ABS.
Custer State Park, from Philip and Dupuis.
Canada's *Wood Buffalo National Park*, where descendants of Pablo's herd mingle with wild survivors.
Free roamers in *Alaska*, relocated from the National Bison Range.
It's a tremendous accomplishment, but still only a fraction of a fraction of the millions that once lived.
25k
20k
15k
10k
5k
1900
1910
1920
1930
1940
1950
1960

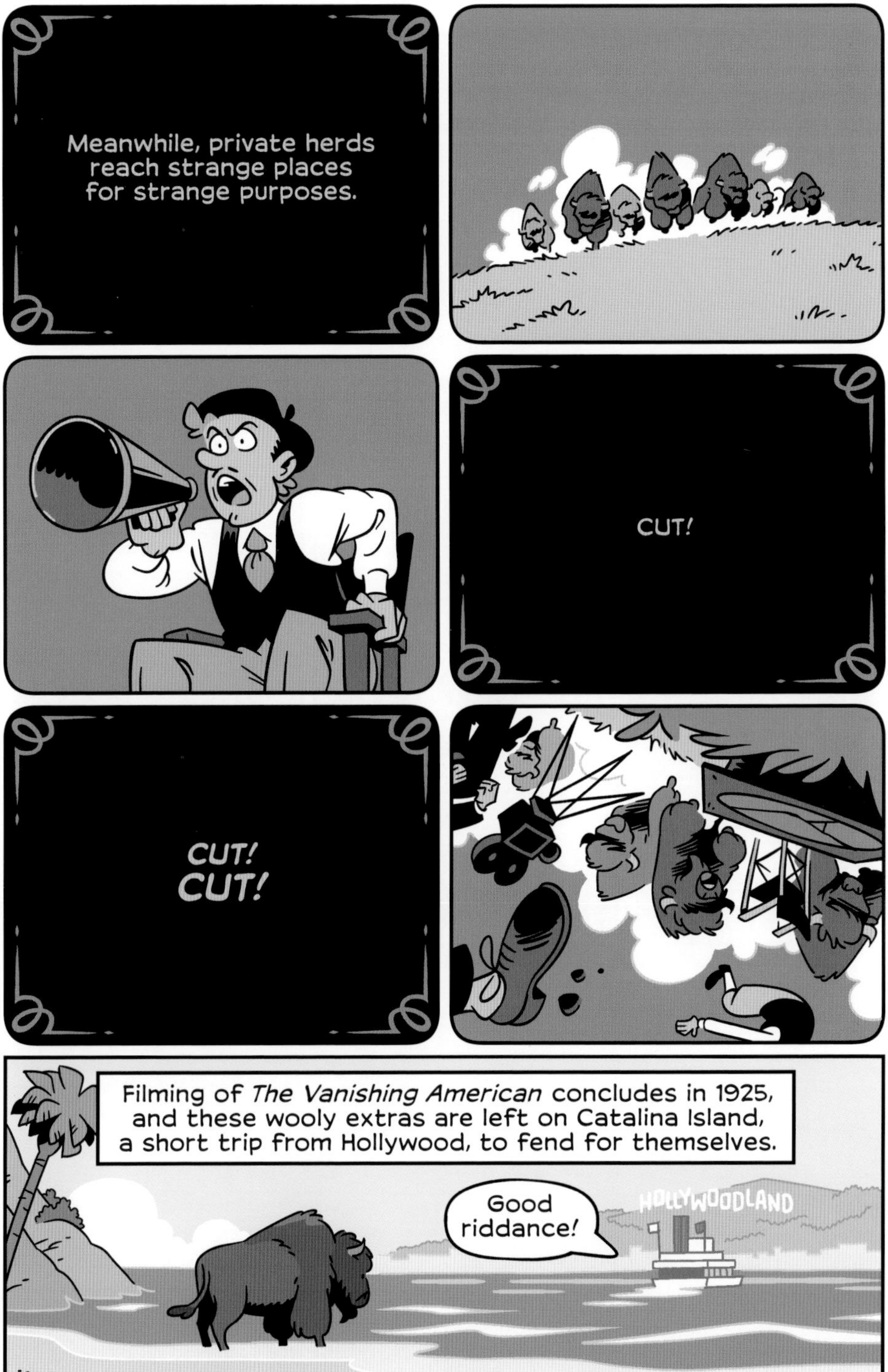
Meanwhile, private herds reach strange places for strange purposes.
CUT!
CUT! CUT!
Filming of *The Vanishing American* concludes in 1925, and these wooly extras are left on Catalina Island, a short trip from Hollywood, to fend for themselves.
Good riddance!
HOLLYWOODLAND

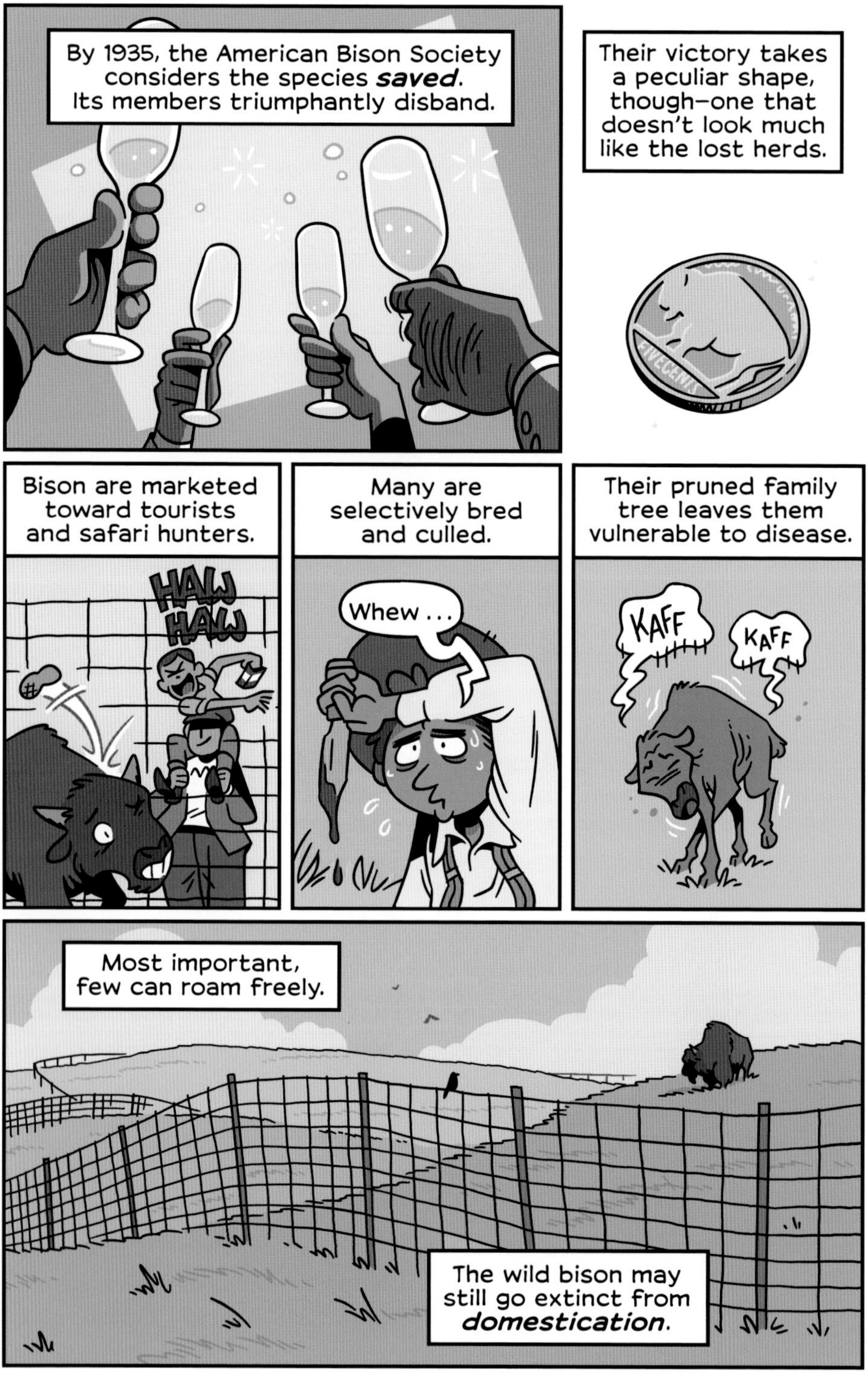
By 1935, the American Bison Society considers the species ***saved***. Its members triumphantly disband.
Their victory takes a peculiar shape, though—one that doesn't look much like the lost herds.
Bison are marketed toward tourists and safari hunters.
HAW HAW
Many are selectively bred and culled.
Whew . . .
Their pruned family tree leaves them vulnerable to disease.
KAFF
KAFF
Most important, few can roam freely.
The wild bison may still go extinct from ***domestication***.

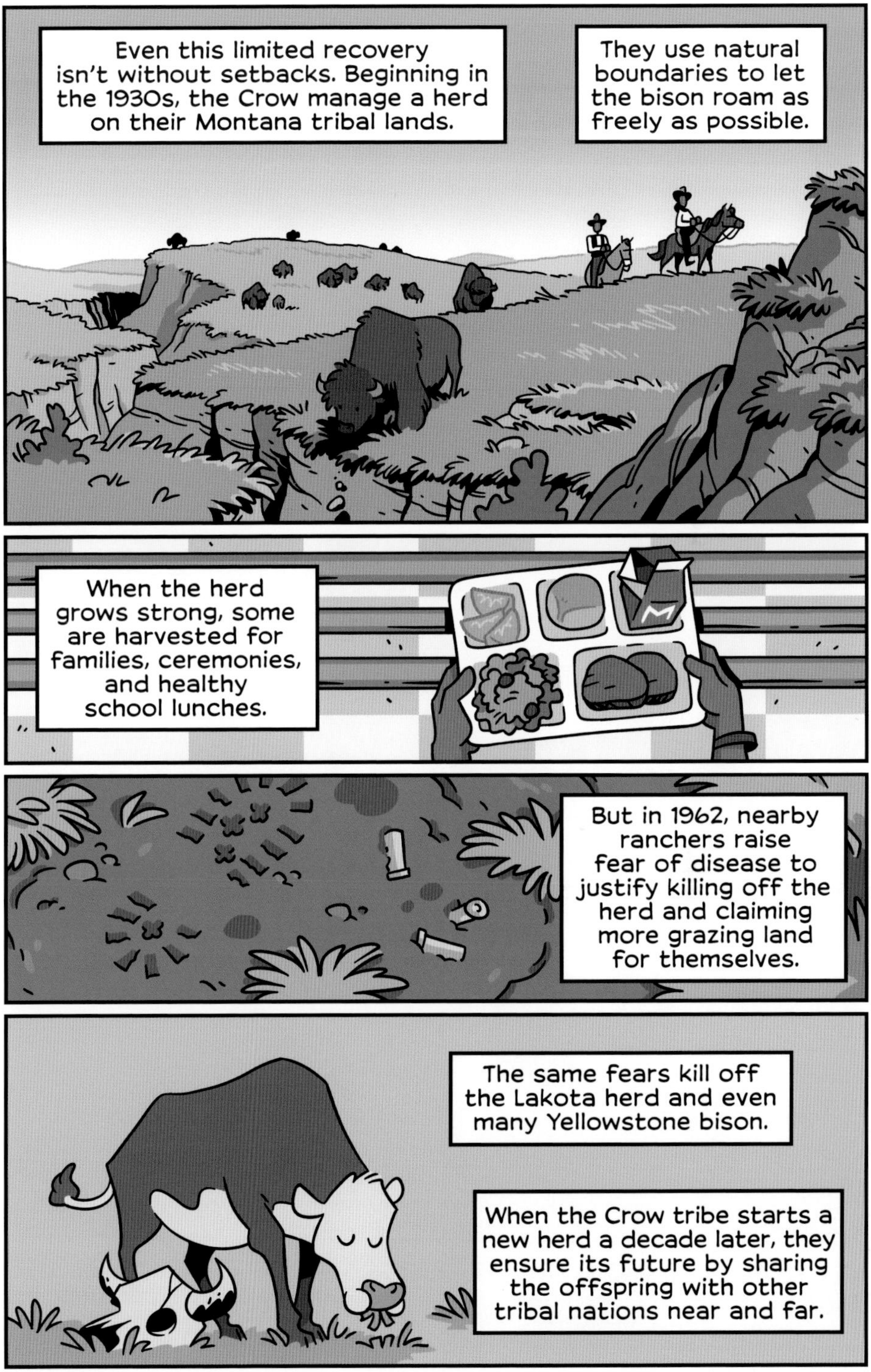
Even this limited recovery isn't without setbacks. Beginning in the 1930s, the Crow manage a herd on their Montana tribal lands.
They use natural boundaries to let the bison roam as freely as possible.
When the herd grows strong, some are harvested for families, ceremonies, and healthy school lunches.
M
But in 1962, nearby ranchers raise fear of disease to justify killing off the herd and claiming more grazing land for themselves.
The same fears kill off the Lakota herd and even many Yellowstone bison.
When the Crow tribe starts a new herd a decade later, they ensure its future by sharing the offspring with other tribal nations near and far.

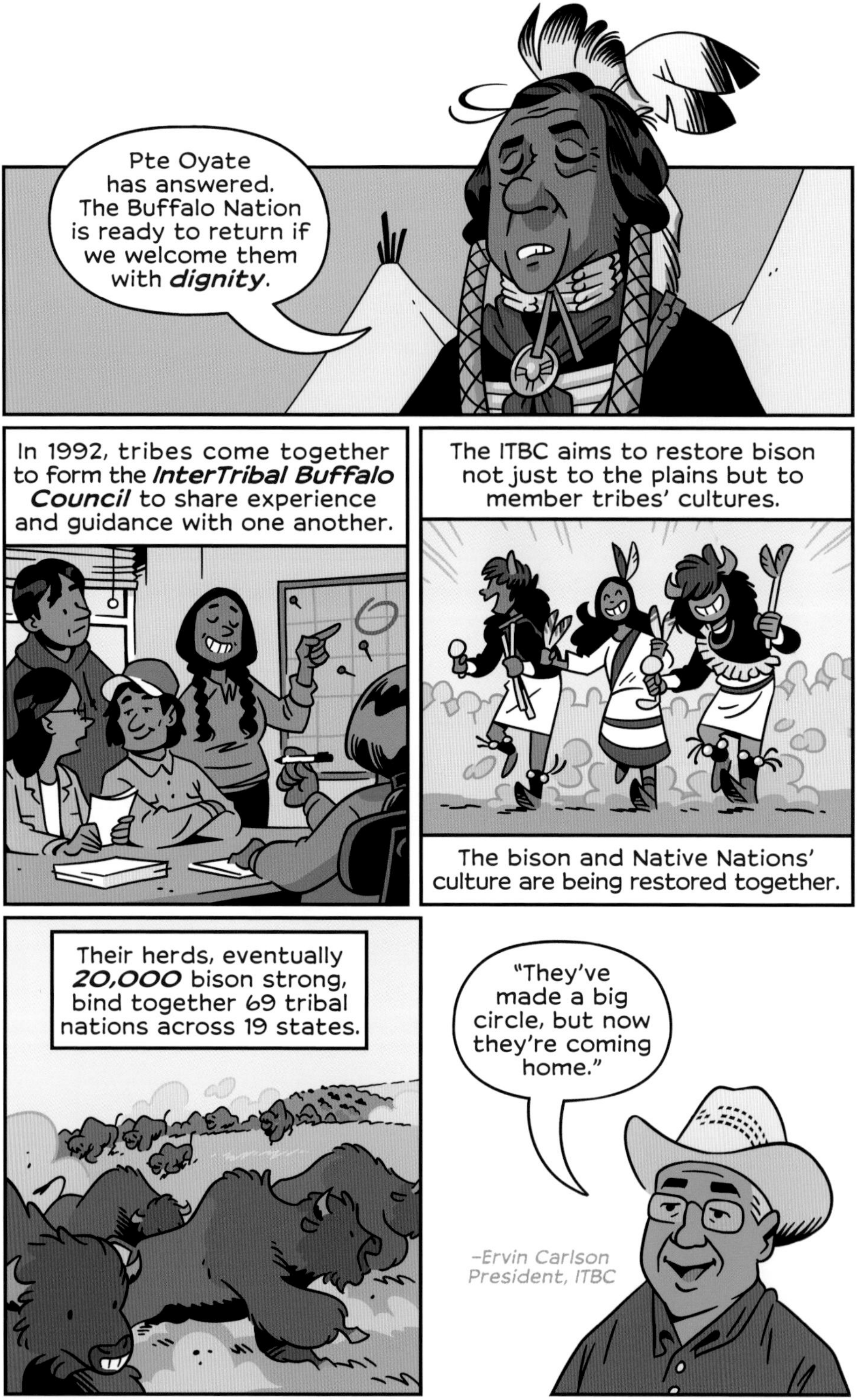
Pte Oyate has answered. The Buffalo Nation is ready to return if we welcome them with *dignity*.
In 1992, tribes come together to form the *InterTribal Buffalo Council* to share experience and guidance with one another.
The ITBC aims to restore bison not just to the plains but to member tribes' cultures.
The bison and Native Nations' culture are being restored together.
Their herds, eventually *20,000* bison strong, bind together 69 tribal nations across 19 states.
"They've made a big circle, but now they're coming home."
–Ervin Carlson President, ITBC

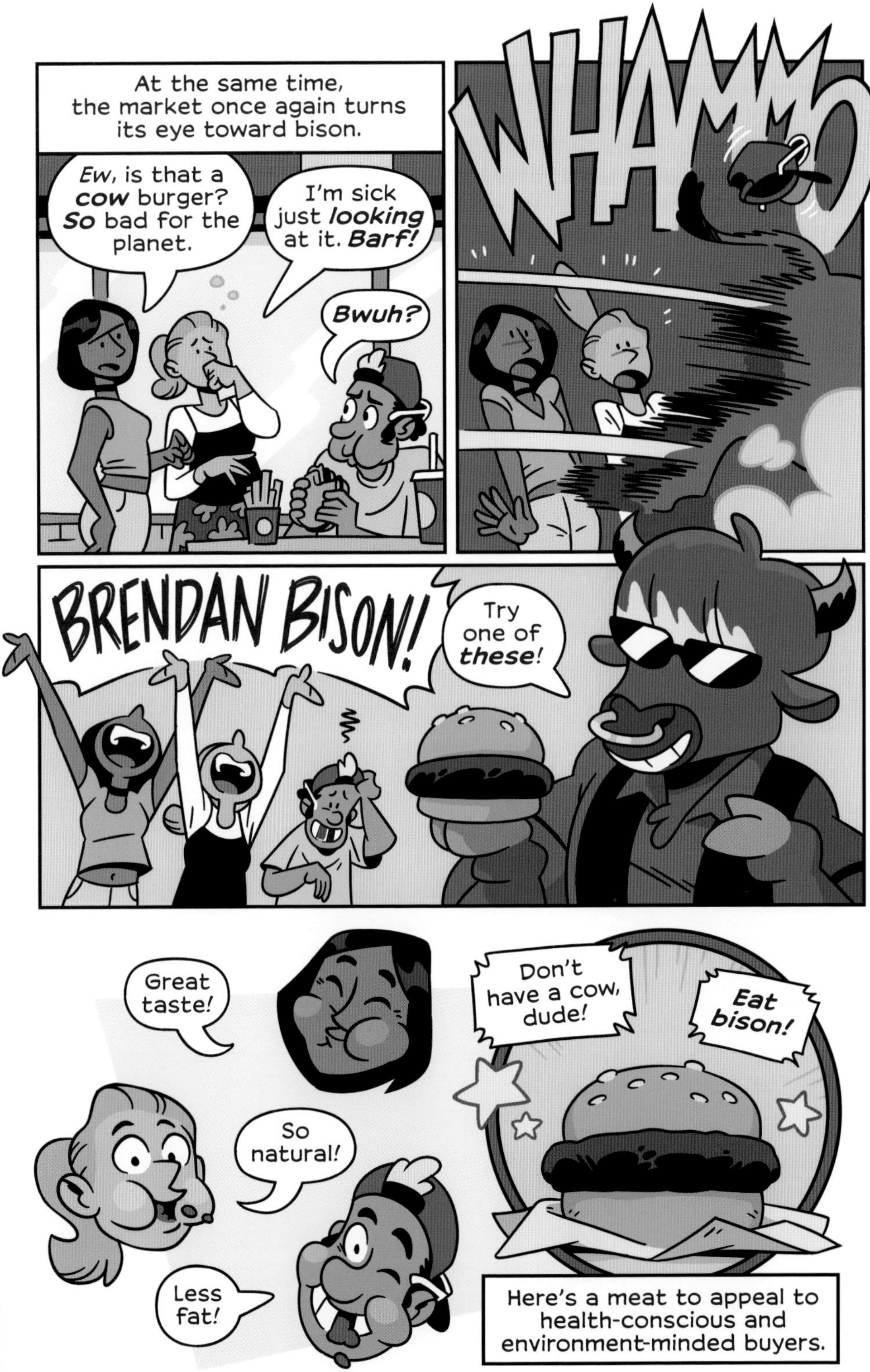
At the same time, the market once again turns its eye toward bison.
Ew, is that a **cow** burger? ***So*** bad for the planet.
I'm sick just ***looking*** at it. ***Barf!***
Bwuh?
WHAMMO
BRENDAN BISON!
Try one of ***these***!
Great taste!
So natural!
Less fat!
Don't have a cow, dude!
Eat bison!
Here's a meat to appeal to health-conscious and environment-minded buyers.

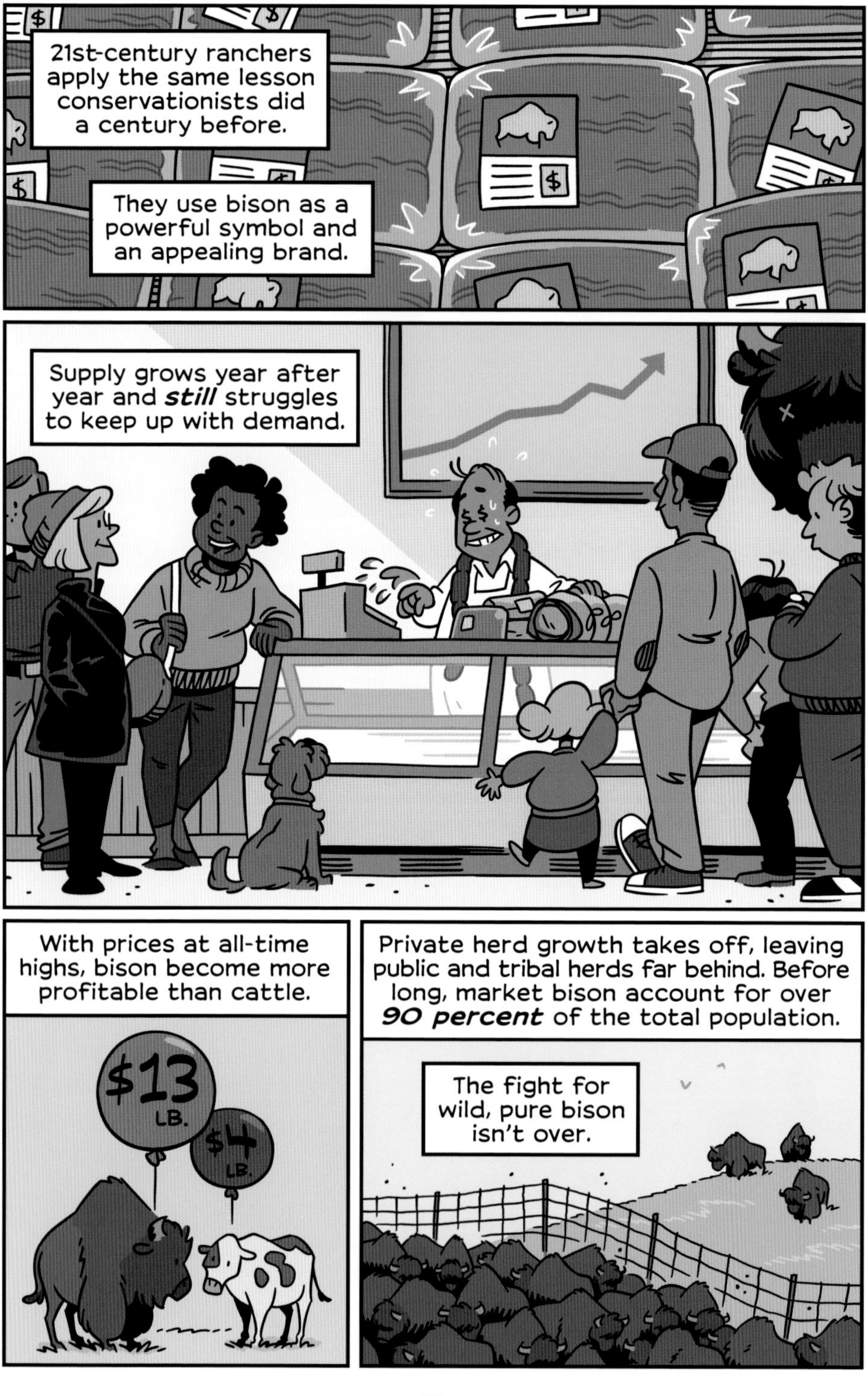
21st-century ranchers apply the same lesson conservationists did a century before.
They use bison as a powerful symbol and an appealing brand.
Supply grows year after year and *still* struggles to keep up with demand.
With prices at all-time highs, bison become more profitable than cattle.
$13 LB.
$4 LB.
Private herd growth takes off, leaving public and tribal herds far behind. Before long, market bison account for over ***90 percent*** of the total population.
The fight for wild, pure bison isn't over.

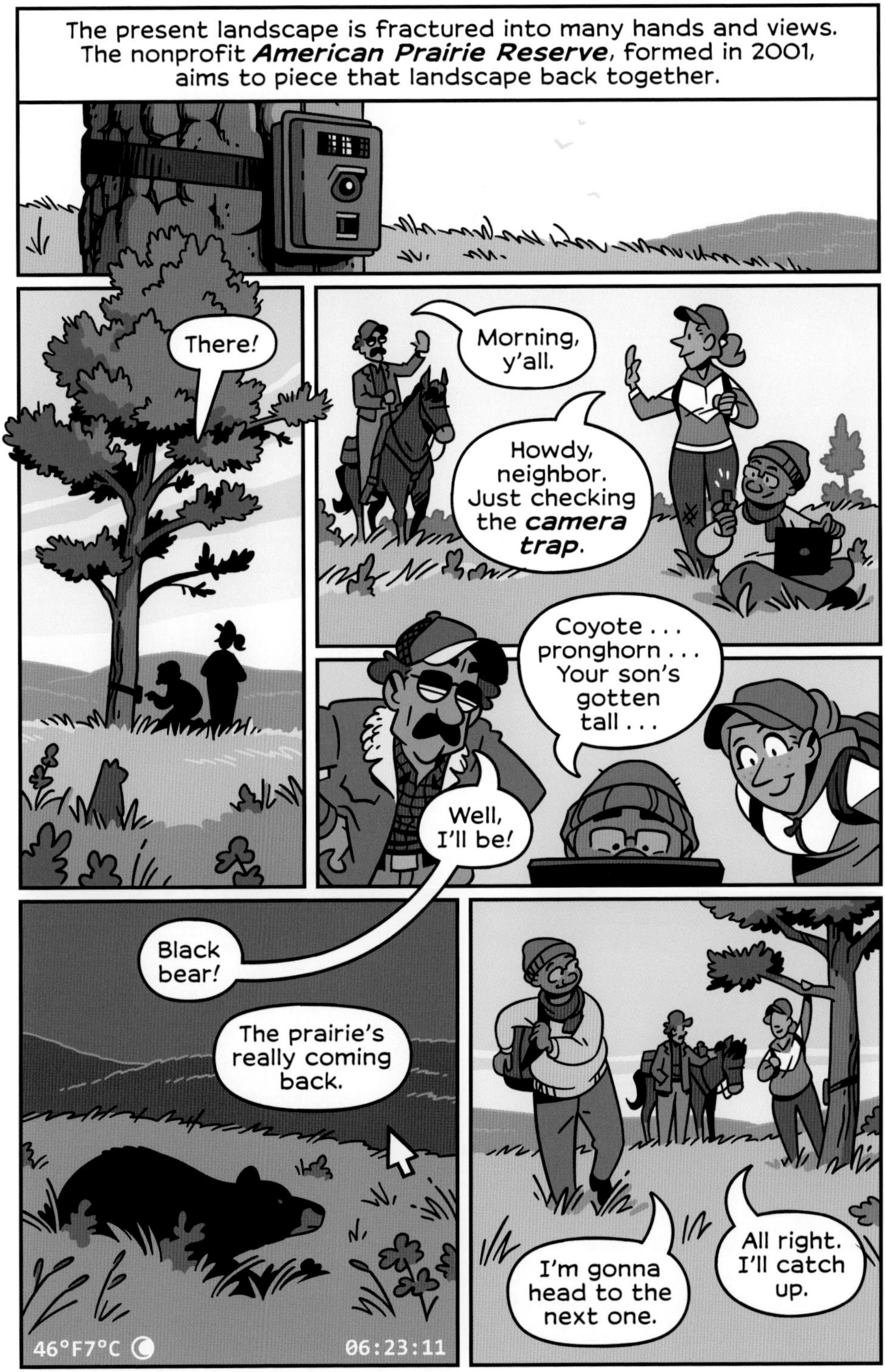
The present landscape is fractured into many hands and views. The nonprofit ***American Prairie Reserve***, formed in 2001, aims to piece that landscape back together.
There!
Morning, y'all.
Howdy, neighbor. Just checking the ***camera trap***.
Coyote . . . pronghorn . . . Your son's gotten tall . . .
Well, I'll be!
Black bear!
The prairie's really coming back.
46°F7°C
06:23:11
I'm gonna head to the next one.
All right. I'll catch up.

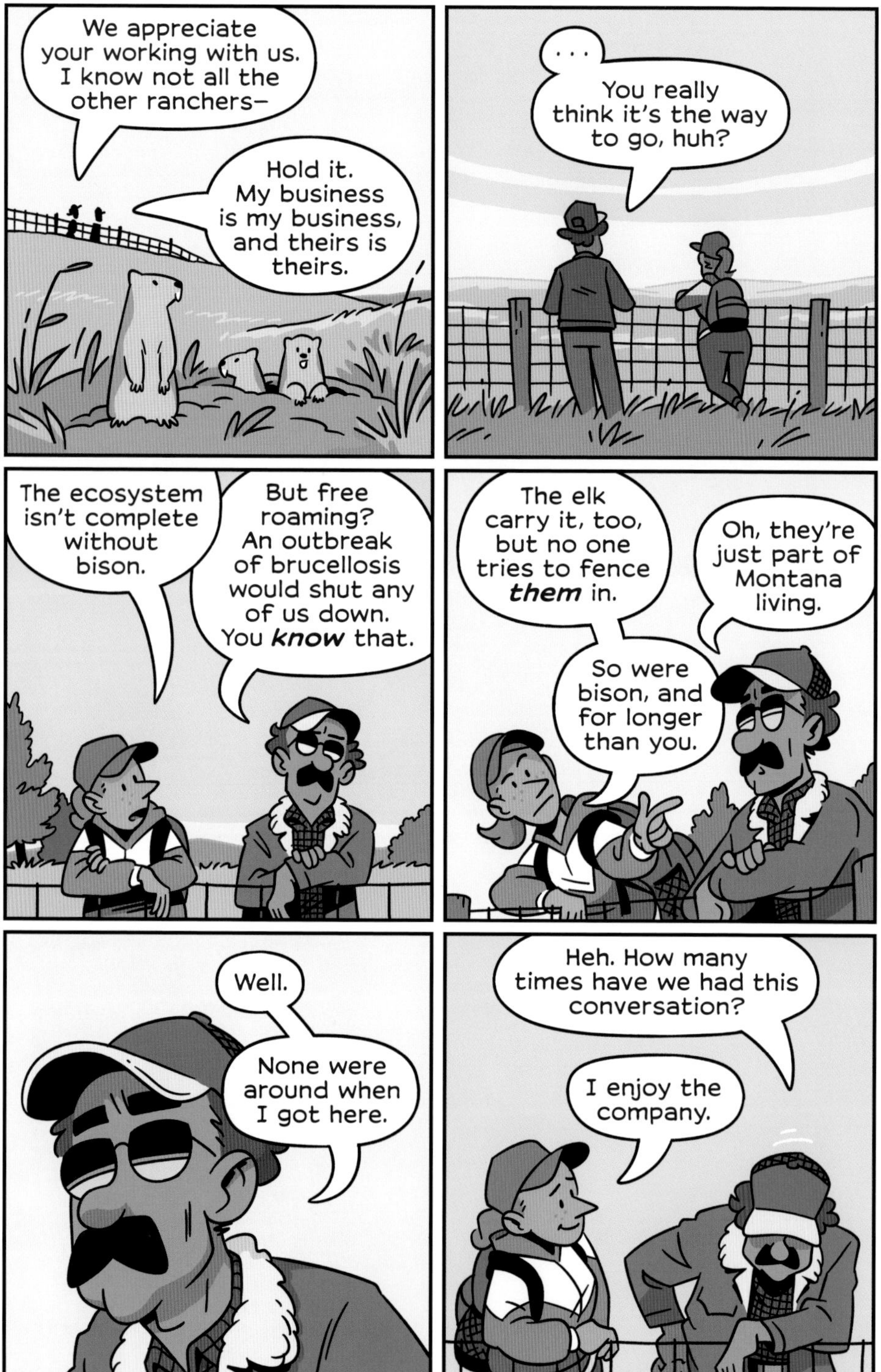
We appreciate your working with us. I know not all the other ranchers–
Hold it. My business is my business, and theirs is theirs.
. . .
You really think it's the way to go, huh?
The ecosystem isn't complete without bison.
But free roaming? An outbreak of brucellosis would shut any of us down. You ***know*** that.
The elk carry it, too, but no one tries to fence ***them*** in.
Oh, they're just part of Montana living.
So were bison, and for longer than you.
Well.
None were around when I got here.
Heh. How many times have we had this conversation?
I enjoy the company.

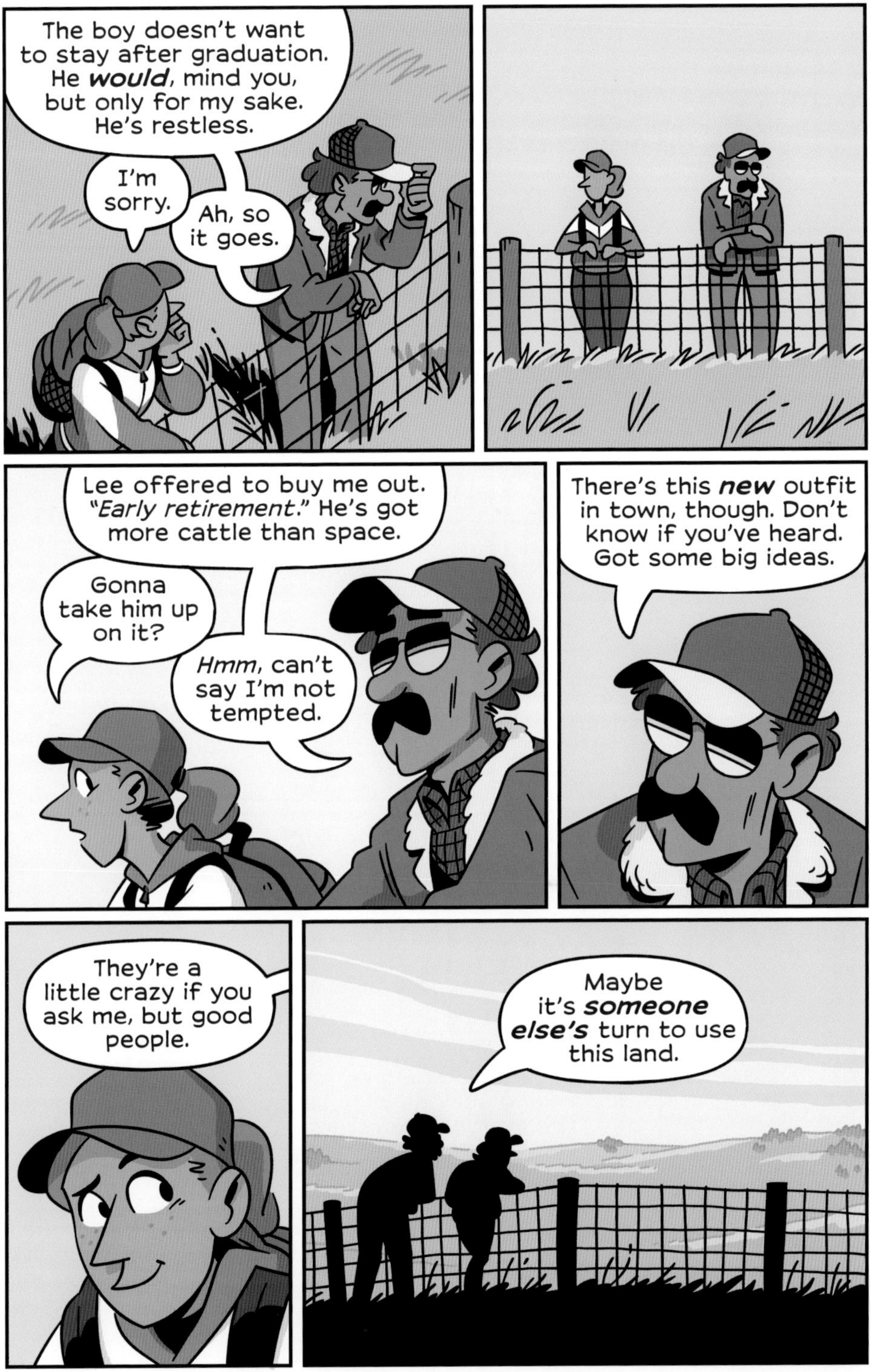
The boy doesn't want to stay after graduation. He *would*, mind you, but only for my sake. He's restless.
I'm sorry.
Ah, so it goes.
Lee offered to buy me out. "*Early retirement*." He's got more cattle than space.
Gonna take him up on it?
Hmm, can't say I'm not tempted.
There's this ***new*** outfit in town, though. Don't know if you've heard. Got some big ideas.
They're a little crazy if you ask me, but good people.
Maybe it's ***someone else's*** turn to use this land.

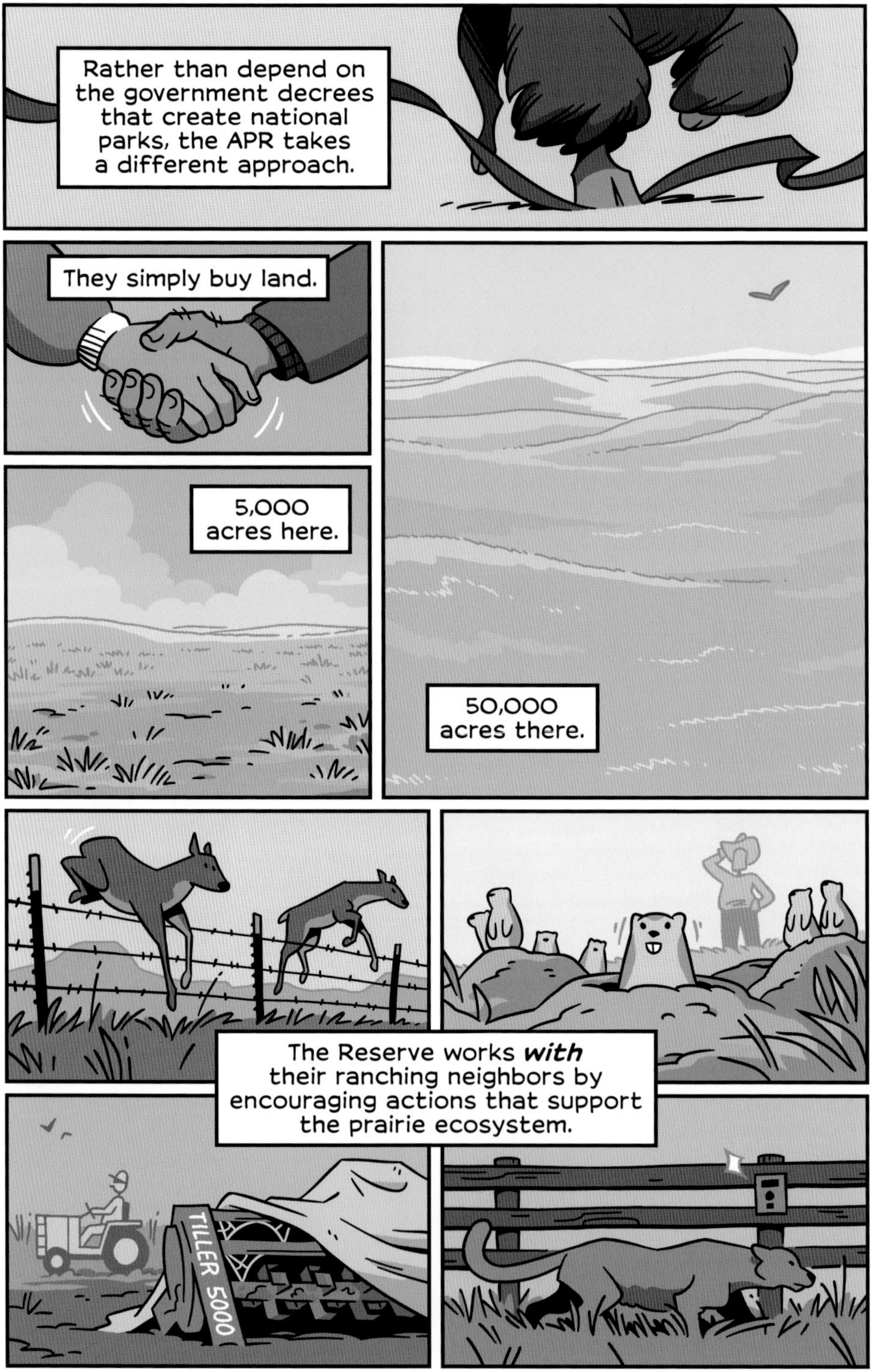

Rather than depend on the government decrees that create national parks, the APR takes a different approach.
They simply buy land.
5,000 acres here.
50,000 acres there.
The Reserve works ***with*** their ranching neighbors by encouraging actions that support the prairie ecosystem.
TILLER 5000

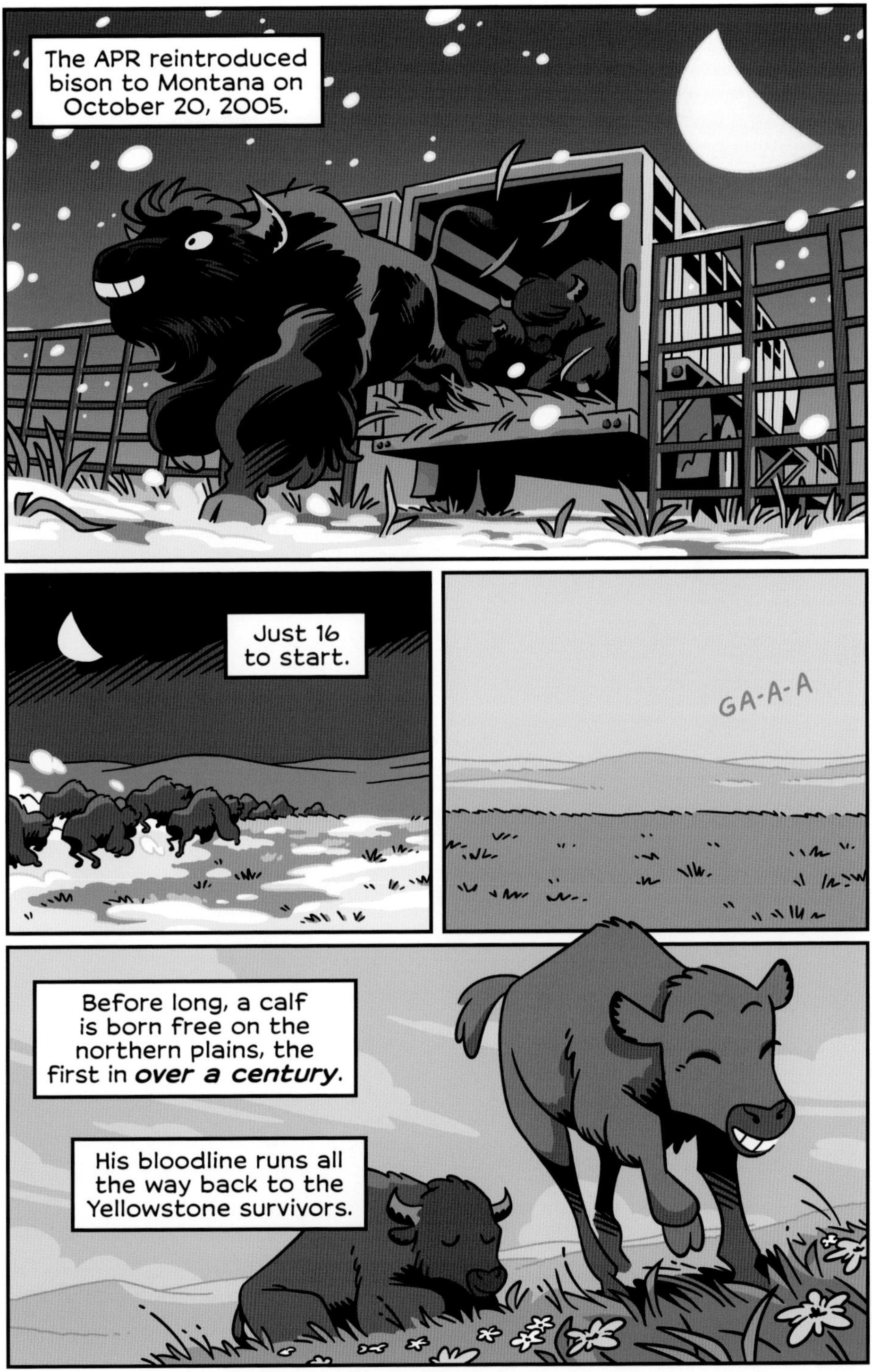

The APR reintroduced bison to Montana on October 20, 2005.
Just 16 to start.
GA-A-A
Before long, a calf is born free on the northern plains, the first in ***over a century***.
His bloodline runs all the way back to the Yellowstone survivors.

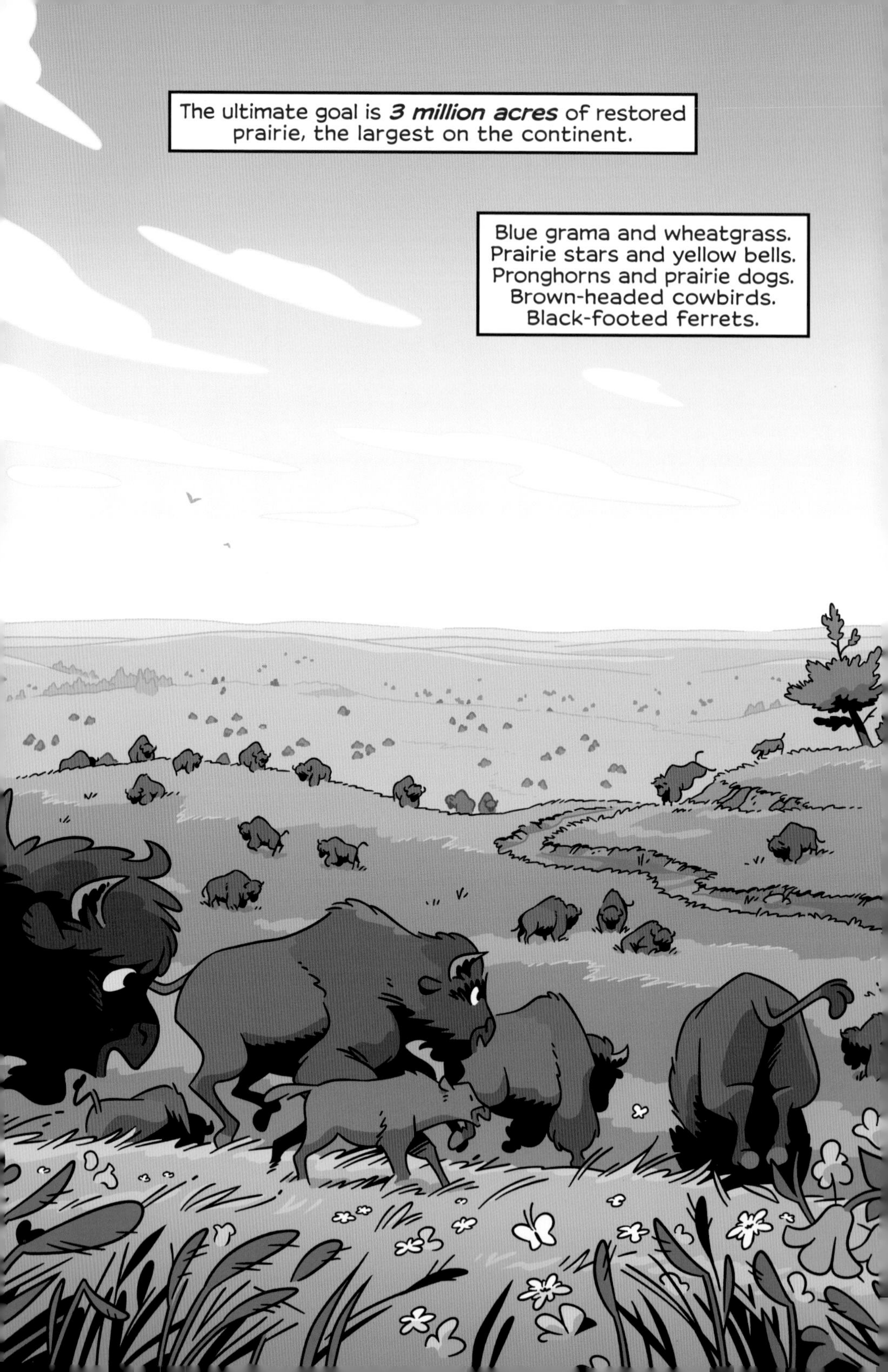
The ultimate goal is ***3 million acres*** of restored prairie, the largest on the continent.
Blue grama and wheatgrass. Prairie stars and yellow bells. Pronghorns and prairie dogs. Brown-headed cowbirds. Black-footed ferrets.

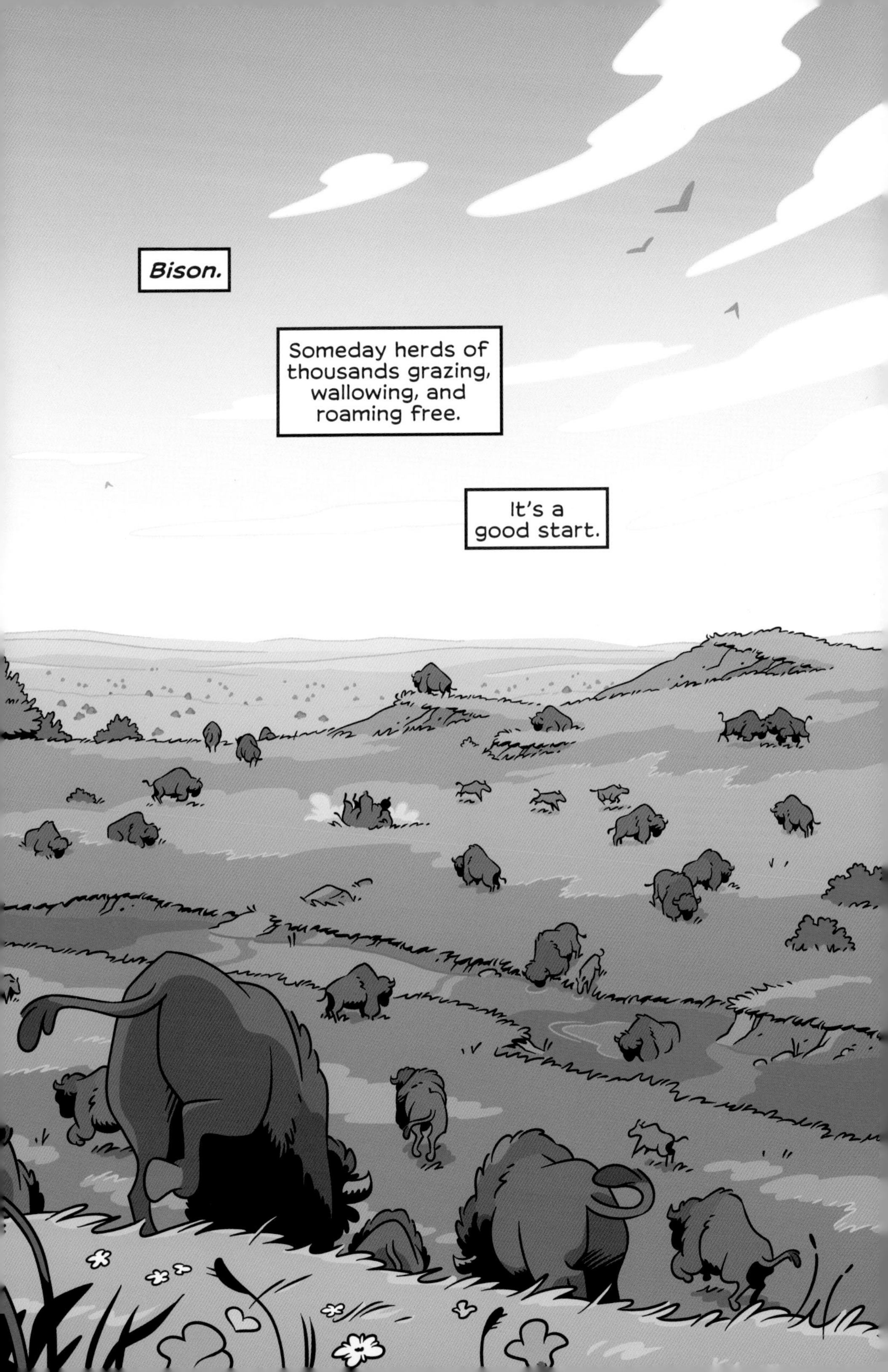
Bison.
Someday herds of thousands grazing, wallowing, and roaming free.
It's a good start.

1890 1880

1870

PEAK
BISON
RANGE

Author's Note

We study history hoping to see the next jump before we reach it. What moment was the cliff's edge? What paths joined there? What actions, what attitudes marked them? The bison's story is a tragedy, without a doubt, and many of its tellings leave it at that. But let's not forget those who bent history away from the worst. There are more bison on the prairie today than a decade ago, than a decade before that, than a decade before that. I hope you'll learn to look for the next jump, and I hope you'll bend history toward better.

—**Andy Hirsch**

SPECIAL NOTE:

About the use of bison vs. buffalo: Though the terms are often used interchangeably, **buffalo** and **bison** are distinct animals. Old World "true" **buffalo** (Cape **buffalo** and water **buffalo**) are native to Africa and Asia. **Bison** are found in North America and Europe. Both **bison** and **buffalo** are in the bovidae family, but the two are not closely related. Even today, different groups, like the InterTribal Buffalo Council prefer different terms.

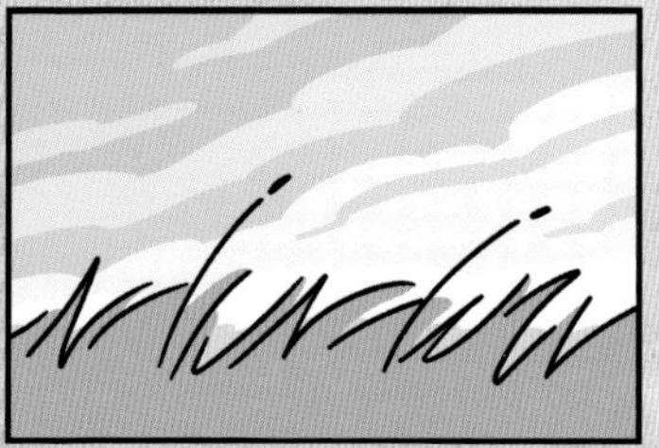

Select Sources

Many documents from the late 1800s and early 1900s not only survive but are more accessible than ever. The digital library Archive.org hosts a wealth of history written while it happened. Some sources for this book include:

American Bison Society. *Annual Report of the American Bison Society, 1905–1907*. American Bison Society, 1908. archive.org/details/annualreportofambs00amer/.

This volume describes the founding of the Wichita herd, the search for the future site of the National Bison Range, and a census of known survivors at the time.

Hornaday, William T. *Taxidermy and Zoological Collecting*. Charles Scribner's Sons, 1894. archive.org/details/taxidermyzoologi00horn/.

Hornaday is generous with his expertise, describing the latest materials and methods for preserving any type of creature, from bug to bison.

Hornaday, William T. *Popular Official Guide to the New York Zoological Park*. 10th ed., New York Zoological Society, 1909. archive.org/details/popularofficialg00horniala/.

This "Bison Edition" guidebook, published upon the zoo's completion, includes a wealth of photos of the grounds and its many inhabitants.

Hough, Emerson. "The Account of Howell's Capture." *Forest and Stream,* vol. 42, no. 18, May 5, 1894, p. 372. archive.org/details /Foreststream42/page/372/.

The first article in the thirteen-part series *Forest and Stream*'s Yellowstone Park Game Exploration" includes Felix Burgess's humble account of the poacher's capture.

Separately, the Library of Congress's collection "A Century of Lawmaking for a New Nation" at Memory.LOC.gov preserves the debate over Congressman Fort's bill in lawmakers' own words.

"Protection of Buffalo." **Congressional Record, House of Representatives, 43rd Congress, 1st Session, March 10, 1874, pp. 2105–2109.**